The United States and the Americas

Lester D. Langley, General Editor

This series is dedicated to a broader understanding of the political, economic, and especially cultural forces and issues that have shaped the Western hemispheric experience— its governments and its peoples. Individual volumes assess relations between the United States and its neighbors to the south and north: Mexico, Central America, Cuba, the Dominican Republic, Haiti, Panama, Colombia, Venezuela, the Andean Republics (Peru, Ecuador, and Bolivia), Brazil, Uruguay and Paraguay, Argentina, Chile, and Canada.

The United States and the Americas

Central America and the United States

Thomas M. Leonard

Central America and the United States: The Search for Stability

The University of Georgia Press
Athens and London

© 1991 by the University of Georgia Press
Athens, Georgia 30602
All rights reserved

Set in 10 on 14 Palatino
The paper in this book meets the guidelines
for permanence and durability of the Committee on
Production Guidelines for Book Longevity of the
Council on Library Resources.

Printed in the United States of America

95 94 93 92 91 C 5 4 3 2 1

95 94 93 92 91 P 5 4 3 2 1

Library of Congress Cataloging in Publication Data

Leonard, Thomas M., 1937–
     Central America and the United States: the search
for stability / Thomas M. Leonard.
          p.   cm. — (The United States and the Americas)
     Includes bibliographical references and index.
     ISBN 0-8203-1320-3 (alk. paper). — ISBN 0-8203-1321-1
     (pbk.: alk. paper)
          1. Central America—Foreign relations—United States.
     2. United States—Foreign relations—Central America.
     I. Title.   II. Series.   F1436.8.U6L45   1991
     327.728073—dc20   90-24818
                                                             CIP

British Library Cataloging in Publication Data available

For My Parents
Amelia T. and Edward C. Leonard

Contents

Acknowledgments   xi

Introduction   xiii

1. A Hesitant Beginning   1

2. The Outside World Comes to Central America,
   1845–1865   15

3. Relationships Established, 1865–1903   35

4. The Search for Stability, 1903–1920   55

5. Abandoning Intervention, 1920–1940   79

6. Incorporating Central America into Global Strategies,
   1933–1948   102

7. Nationalism or Communism: Costa Rica and
   Guatemala   124

8. From False Hope to Entrenchment of the Old Order,
   1960–1976   146

9. Crisis of the Old Order: Carter, Reagan, and Central
   America   167

Epilogue   192

Notes   199

Bibliographical Essay   223

Index   237

Acknowledgments

I want to thank several persons and institutions for their support of this project. Lester D. Langley, the editor of the series in which this book appears, and Karen Orchard of the University of Georgia Press and her staff provided both the opportunity for its publication and immeasurable guidance. Ralph Lee Woodward's 1986 summer seminar on Central America, sponsored by the National Endowment for the Humanities, allowed me to avail myself of not only his expertise and the Central American collection at Tulane University but also the valuable comments from seminar colleagues such as Hugh Miller (Pan American University), Tom Schoonover (University of Southwestern Louisiana), and Larry Yates (U.S. Army General Command and General Staff College).

Research support came from the Division of Sponsored Research and Training of the University of North Florida, the Travel to Collections program of the National Endowment for the Humanities, and the Albert C. Beveridge program of the American Historical Association. The continued friendship of Marty and Terry Galvin in Chevy Chase, Maryland, facilitated research in the vast resources available in the Washington, D.C., area.

Numerous librarians and others gave generously of their time, but space permits me to name only a few. Important assistance was provided by Kathy Cohen, Bruce Latimer, and Peggy Pruitt of the University of North Florida, Tom Niehaus of Tulane University, and Kathy NiCastro and Sally Marks of the National Archives. Equally important was the assistance rendered by the library staffs at Columbia University, University of Florida, Princeton University, and the Library of Congress. Deborah Martin and Donna Pelt Leonard assisted with typing various drafts of the manuscript.

Finally, I want to thank my wife, Yvonne, who has not read this manuscript but whose support for over a generation has made research and writing possible.

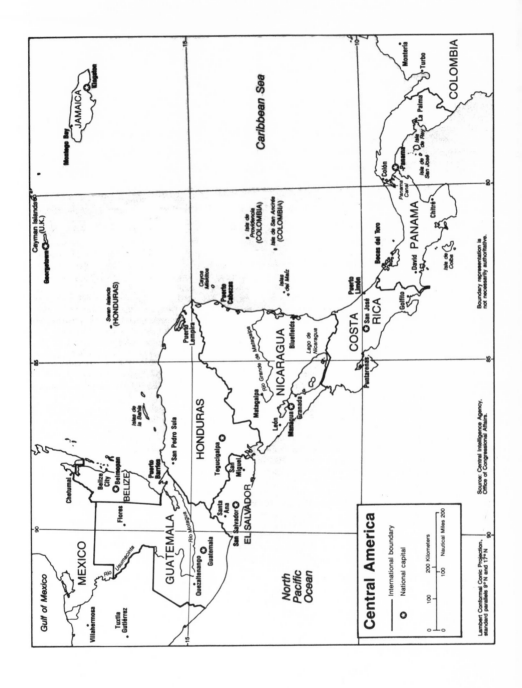

Central America

Introduction

The contemporary crisis in Central America since the downfall of Nicaraguan strongman Anastasio Somoza in July 1979 has yielded an abundance of literature, most of it dealing with recent events in Central America and especially U.S. policy toward the region. Two studies, however, provide historical perspectives on U.S. relations with Central America: Walter LaFeber's *Inevitable Revolutions: The United States in Central America* (New York, 1983), and John Findling's *Close Neighbors, Distant Friends: United States–Central American Relations* (Westport, Conn., 1987). LaFeber's revisionist argument charges that the imperialistic pursuits of U.S. private business interests, encouraged and defended by Washington, produced conditions that made the turmoil of the 1980s inevitable. Findling's straightforward account is less provocative. He outlines the course of U.S. relations with Central America and argues that an isthmian canal and the need to secure it was the centerpiece of U.S. policy. Like LaFeber, Findling concludes that Washington's policymakers ignored the economic and social needs of the Central American masses. The relationship between the United States and Central America is much more complex.

Since the beginning of their relationship in the 1820s, both the United States and Central America pursued different foreign policy objectives with the other, but it is not surprising, given the strength and position of the United States, that U.S. interests dominated the relationship. For the United States, Central America was but part of its larger circum-Caribbean policy, which since the 1820s consistently sought to secure the region from various forms of foreign intrusion. It used a variety of methods to meet the challenge. At times the United States tried to impose its political culture, social institutions, or economic structure upon the region, but it did so without understanding the consequences of its actions. Central Americans lacked such a consistency of purpose. At times they sought U.S. protection against powers foreign to the region; at other times they resisted Washington's advances; but Central American governments, individually or collectively, generally tried to direct the U.S. presence to their own purpose, which was usually the maintenance of the status quo.

Three distinct time periods can be observed in the history of U.S.– Central American relations: 1820–1903, 1903–48, and 1948–present. During the first period, the United States gave little attention to Central America until European powers expressed interest in a transisthmian canal, expanded commercial relations, or sought to influence isthmian political affairs. For the most part, the British were the culprits, but after 1865 French canal interests and German economic expansion heightened Washington's concern. Concurrently, the Central Americans were divided in their opinion of the U.S. presence in the region. One political faction, usually the Conservatives, wanted to avoid close ties to the United States, fearing that the relationship would disrupt their privileged position in the established economic, social, and political order. The other political faction, usually the Liberals, generally favored close ties to the United States, anticipating that its advanced society would help modernize Central America. Occasionally, Central Americans united against U.S. influence in the region, especially during the William Walker era of the 1850s and when Abraham Lincoln suggested relocating freed slaves in Central America in the early 1860s. Late in the nineteenth century, when the Liberals occupied presidential palaces across the isthmus, private U.S. business interests took advantage of Liberal concessions, but the U.S. government was interested more in a transisthmian canal and less in the commercial opportunities for American entrepreneurs.

The decision to build the interoceanic canal at Panama in 1903 assured the primacy of strategic considerations in U.S. policy. From then until 1948, virtually any form of threat, direct or indirect, to the Panama Canal prompted Washington to respond instinctively to Central America's domestic political discord in order to forestall foreign interference. The means varied from efforts to impose constitutional government by a treaty system, to ensure financial order by "dollar diplomacy," and, when these failed, to encourage political order by the presence of the marines. In dealing with the regional leadership, Washington incorrectly concluded that if the American political culture were imprinted upon Central America, stability and progress would follow. Central Americans reacted ambivalently to these intrusions. Those who owed their political positions to U.S. policy favored the interventionist policies, while those out of political power opposed them. The political rivalries, which often became violent, were complicated by the presence of American entrepreneurs, who found themselves choosing sides and seeking Washington's interference in order to protect their own investments. Central American dictators who came to power during this era willingly cooperated with the United States, believing cooperation assured their perpetuation, despite the Department of State's criticism of cozy alliance with isthmian dictators. At the same time, Central America's economic dependency upon the United States deepened. The leadership in Washington and Central America shunted the desire of the middle sector to enter the political process and ignored the dire poverty of the urban and rural poor.

After World War II, the overriding consideration of U.S. foreign policy was the threat of international communism, fostered by and spreading in all directions from Moscow. In the forty years after World War II, the United States became increasingly alert to communist efforts to capitalize on Central America's restricted political systems and economic and social adversities in order to establish leftist governments, which were threatening U.S. private business interests in the region. Central America's ruling elite utilized the policy shift for their own advantage and often found kindred spirits in the North American business community. Both groups charged that critics of the established order received their directions from Moscow. Unwilling to risk U.S. security interests by differentiating between legitimate indigenous movements and international communism, the United States supported the old order.

Throughout the 1980s, American leaders and the isthmian elite clung to policies rooted in the past. From 1980, the Reagan administration perceived in Central America a communist threat that needed to be excised, a view generally shared by Central American elites because it justified their clinging to power. Throughout the 1980s, deterioration in the quality of life for Central America's lowest socio-economic groups provided a powerful incentive in the United States and Central America for establishing governments that were more responsive to their needs. This book discusses how we got to that crossroad.

The United States and the Americas

Central America and the United States

1   A Hesitant Beginning

Writing in 1930, in an era when the United States was mired in a jungle war in Nicaragua, historian Joseph B. Lockey examined the state of U.S. relations with the United Provinces of Central America—the federation of Guatemala, El Salvador, Honduras, Nicaragua, and Costa Rica—of a century before, and he described it as one of "diplomatic futility." From 1824 to 1839, only five of the twelve U.S. representatives commissioned to Central America actually reached the capital of Guatemala City.[1] Lockey's observation of diplomatic futility might equally apply to Central American efforts, for during the same period the United Provinces had only sporadic representation in Washington. Two missions to the United States—those of Manuel José Arce and Juan Manuel Rodríguez in 1822 and Juan Galindo in 1835—were largely ineffective.

Yet during these years of limited diplomatic contacts, the character of U.S. policy toward Central America took shape. As it changed, so did isthmian perceptions of the United States and its place in Central America's future. From the outset, the United States had a more clearly defined foreign policy because of its greater experience in world affairs. As an outpost of the Spanish colonial empire for three hundred years, Central America lacked this experience. At the same time, a parallel colonial heritage had bequeathed to each a hostility to European imperialism and, presumably, a commitment to certain foreign policy objectives—a transisthmian canal, increased commerce, and an unfriendly stance toward foreign intervention in a region already characterized as the crossroads of the Western Hemisphere.

Basis for Dominance: Foreign Policy Foundations

In 1824, Secretary of State John Quincy Adams informed the nation's first agent to Central America, Thomas N. Mann, that the first objective of his mission was to gather all the information possible about this "new central South American country . . . situated at and including the Isthmus of Panama, a position of highest geographical importance— important also by the commercial connections, and lodgements on the soil by the British, with the neighboring Bay of Honduras and Mosquito Shore."[2] As were his countrymen, Adams was largely ignorant about Central America, but he was alert to its strategic importance to U.S. foreign policy.

In the colonial era, Spain had closed Central America to foreigners, but a few outsiders—among them Thomas Gage, Raveneau de Lussan, John Cockburn, John Roach, and one North American, John Rhodes—recorded the experiences of their travels inside this backwater of the Spanish empire. No North American library contained their works. Thomas Jefferson read Alexander von Humboldt's 1808 classic, *Political Essay on the Kingdom of New Spain*, about the illustrious sojourner's travels to Venezuela, Peru, Mexico, and Cuba, but not to Central America.[3]

As Latin American independence movements gained momentum after 1810, Americans gained a fleeting impression of Central America. Infrequent statements by government officials and newspaper reports applauded the hemispheric revolution, as Americans obviously anticipated commercial opportunities in the independent republics that followed. But the absence of a genuine war across the isthmus and U.S. preoccupation with revolutionary struggles in South America and nearby Mexico distracted them from the isthmus and its less violent revolutionary struggle.[4]

Thus few Americans in 1824 understood the conflicts within Central America's political, economic, and social structures. The centralized Spanish colonial system placed all decision making in the Old World. Within this structure, Central America was part of the Mexican viceroyalty; its regional government (*captaincy general*) had its headquarters in Antigua and, later, Guatemala City. From there, the Spanish ruled the provinces: Comayagua, San Salvador, León, San José, and Ciudad Real (Chiapas). Throughout, local town councils (*cabildos*) provided local elites with the opportunity to participate in politics and,

in effect, to subvert Spanish authority. Rivalries between these isolated political units further diminished royal authority. In mountainous Central America, the king's emissary learned early the futility of
trying to carry out policies that could not be enforced or issuing orders
that would not be obeyed.

Central America cast off Spanish rule but retained the colonial economic monoculture. Local haciendas produced staple crops (indigo,
cochineal, and cocoa) for export, while Nicaraguan and Honduran
ranches raised cattle and foodstuffs for local consumption. The limited export market for these products sustained a small but important
group of merchants and landowners, with Guatemala as the central
point for shipping the staple products abroad and selling the imports
to the interior markets. Fluctuations in the world market prices and
competition from other supply sources contributed to the emergence
of a debtor-creditor relationship between merchants and landowners
and to an economic rivalry between Guatemala and the outlying provinces.

With the preserved colonial economy, Central America retained its
rigid social structure. Of the region's estimated 1.5 million inhabitants on the eve of independence, an estimated 100,000 were pure
white, about 900,000 pure Indian, about 450,000 mestizos (Spanish
and Indian mixed bloods), and another 20,000 blacks and mulattoes.
Spanish administrators (*peninsulares*) dominated the imperial bureau-
cracy, but many of their rivals, criollos (Spanish descendants born in
the New World and thus denied political office), had become large
landowners and successful merchants, gaining social and economic
privileges but not political participation. Criollos ignored the mixed-
blood mestizos beneath them and reduced Indians, blacks, and mulattoes to forced labor, debt peonage, and slavery. The Roman Catholic
church, entrenched in Central America as elsewhere in Latin America,
gave its tacit, if not enthusiastic, support to this rigid structure.[5]

Central America's colonial experience and isolation severely restricted its understanding of the outside world, especially the United
States. A small number of Central Americans may have read the
works of Antonio de Alcedo Bexarano, Abbé Reynal, and Abbé de

Pradt, who provided descriptions of the U.S. economy and geography and some discussion of the country's revolution, constitutional government, and religious toleration. Certainly, most of the early Latin American patriots had read the Declaration of Independence, the U.S. Constitution, and some of Tom Paine's writings. But personal contacts between Central Americans and U.S. citizens after the American Revolution were negligible. Most who came north were on official business seeking to enlist U.S. support for the fledgling independence movements. A few, such as the Guatemalan scientist José Felipe Flores, returned home to spread their favorable impressions of the United States, but perceptions were generally varied. Spanish American Liberals applauded the great extent of civil and political freedom, religious toleration, social equality, and literacy and the lack of pomp and ceremony. Others understood that the societies of both hemispheres differed greatly and suggested that the federal form of government might not apply to Spanish America. Conservatives, who feared that any changes in the existing institutions would destroy their orderly world and privileged position, remained largely pessimistic about using the United States as a political or social model.[6]

Despite their mutual isolation and ignorance, the United States and the United Provinces of Central America shared three foreign policy objectives—a transisthmian canal, new markets, and opposition to the intervention of a European power in Central America.

The dream of a transisthmian canal was as old as Balboa, conqueror of Panama, but early Spanish interests in a passageway across Darien or Tehuantepec or the dredging of the San Juan River collapsed with the wars of independence.[7] Independent Central America revived the dream just as American political leaders and merchants awakened to the canal's significance for the evolution of the nation's worldwide commercial contacts. Central Americans looked to a canal as vital to their own economic development.

Transatlantic imperial rivalries frustrated U.S. trade in the Caribbean for thirty years after independence. Similarly, independent Central America was unable to chart its own foreign economic policy. From the start, U.S. vessels and their crews had fallen prey to British, French, and Spanish gunboats while seeking trade in the Caribbean, which centered on Cuba, then on Puerto Rico and Venezuela, and by 1807 on Veracruz, Mexico. Through these Caribbean ports American merchants had limited contact with Central America.[8] Yet they anticipated a Central American market for American wares, a notion reinforced in 1825 by Englishman John Hale, who wrote that Central Americans "look upon foreign products as miraculous articles." This was especially the case in Costa Rica, where farmers used wooden tools and agricultural development was "more than a century behind that of Europe and the United States." Hale foresaw a limitless market for iron shovels and hoes, garden rakes, paint, turpentine, machines for planting cotton, and sawmills.[9] Given the collapse of formerly guaranteed Spanish markets, the limited domestic demand for staples, and the lack of a merchant fleet, Central America's exporters found themselves at the mercy of international markets and rivalries.

An immediate issue, as it had been for three decades after the American Revolution, was the concern with foreign intervention. Since its independence in 1783, the United States constantly sought to remove the dangers posed by Britain, Spain, and France in the Western Hemisphere, first from its border areas and then from the high seas. In 1803, President Thomas Jefferson, determined "to exclude all European influence from the hemisphere,"[10] persuaded a reluctant Congress to purchase Louisiana in order to secure the American West, the Mississippi River, and New Orleans against further European intrigue. An 1811 congressional resolution railed against the transfer of the Floridas and Cuba to another European power. A year later, the United States went to war to reaffirm its independence and, more precisely, to rid its southern flank of menacing European influence. By 1819, it absorbed the Floridas, forcing the Spanish to retrench and the British to reassess their imperial strategy in Spanish America.[11]

Thus, when President James Monroe asserted before Congress in December 1823 that the Western Hemisphere was off-limits to further European colonization and political ideologies, he was reaffirming the fundamental tenets of U.S. foreign policy, based upon its forty years of international experience since independence.[12] The United States had fashioned a coherent foreign policy.

Central America's foreign policy, by contrast, was not as clearly articulated as that of the United States. Certainly, Central Americans were alert to the foreign presence, especially the British, whose logging establishments on the Caribbean coast, which dated to the early seventeenth century, intruded upon Honduran, Guatemalan, and Nicaraguan territory. With a base at Belize, the British built a string of forts stretching south to Panama. By 1741, British officials in Jamaica regularly appointed a superintendent to Belize and established a virtual protectorate over the Mosquito Indians. From the Mosquito territory, the British carried on illicit trade with Nicaragua and Costa Rica and attacked Spanish positions and shipping in the region. During the American Revolution, the British plan to seize the San Juan River in Nicaragua, which was prefatory to their plan to construct an interoceanic transit route, fell victim to the weakness of their own forces in the region, the course of the American Revolution, and the strength of the Spanish response, which included the recruitment of a Central American army. Although the 1783 and 1786 Treaties of Paris failed to dislodge the British, their interest in the Caribbean coast waned by the eve of Central America's independence.[13]

In addition to the British presence at Belize, the Napoleonic Wars, which began in 1803, raised across the isthmus the fear of a possible French invasion and disrupted isthmian trade with Spain. The trade problem ignited a debate that split the landholding aristocracy and local merchants. Landholders favored expanded foreign commerce so that the expected profits and taxes could be used to protect the region against foreign attack. Merchants, who wanted to maintain their relationship with Spain, looked instead to church properties as the source of income for the common defense. The conflicts over foreign commerce and the conflicts over taxation were but two of the issues that carried over into the postindependence period.[14]

Despite the isthmian vulnerability to foreign intrusion, the United Provinces lacked a unifying statement like Monroe's. There was no "second war for independence," as the United States had fought in the War of 1812. The pursuit of markets and quest for security provided no common agenda in the political wars of Central America's first generation of rulers. Unlike the United States, Central America began its independence without a consensus about its posture toward the outside world, and, unlike the hemisphere's first republic, it was unable to fashion one.

Initial Encounters: To the 1840s

The first American emissaries to reach Central America—Charles Savage, his nephew Henry, and John Williams[15]—arrived on an isthmus racked by a political struggle between Liberals and Conservatives that soon erupted into a civil war. The roots of that struggle dated to Spain's introduction of the intendancy system in 1786, which increased provincial autonomy and separatist feelings. After 1811, as liberalism flourished in Spain, isthmian Liberals called for elective offices, removal of commercial restrictions, a freer press, and, ultimately, independence. Local Conservatives, fearful of revolution in the social order, denounced them, and in 1820, when Spanish Liberals compelled the crown to restore the 1812 Spanish constitution, isthmian Conservatives remained loyal.

But as so often happens in Central America, international politics denied Central American self-determination. In Mexico, Agustín de Iturbide's Plan of Iguala, which proclaimed the region's independence but safeguarded the social order, provided Central American Conservatives with an opportunity to declare the Guatemalan captaincy a general part of the new Mexican empire in January 1822. The union was short-lived, but it served as a harbinger of things to come for Central Americans who looked to an external power to maintain their local influence. When Liberal Salvadorans declared independence (and proposed that the province be annexed by the United States), Iturbide's authority disintegrated. In its collapse, triumphant Liberals seized the opportunity and declared Central America's independence on 1 July 1823.

Over the next sixteen months the Liberals modeled the United Provinces as a modern progressive state. Their implacable Conservative enemies sought moderation and stability through the preservation of traditional institutions. The 1824 constitution, essentially a Liberal document, drew upon the 1812 Cádiz constitution, the U.S. federal constitution, the French codes, and Colombian and Portuguese documents. It created a federal structure that reserved considerable autonomy for the states but failed to reconcile the powerful social antagonisms and state rivalries that characterized their mutual relations. War erupted in 1826 when a former Liberal, the Salvadoran Manuel José Arce, joined forces with Conservative Guatemalans. In the struggle, the Liberals found a heroic symbol and leader in the Honduran Francisco Morazán, who crushed his enemies on the battlefield, exiled leading Conservatives, and confiscated church property. From 1829 to 1831, infuriated Conservatives launched two unsuccessful invasions from Mexico and Caribbean bases. Again, Morazán was victorious, but five years of civil war ruined the local economy and drove the federal deficit to nearly five million pesos. Ominously, the federal government could not meet its normal administrative expenses or pay off its foreign bondholders.[16]

Understandably, the first U.S. agents to Central America were uniformly pessimistic about its future and often quickly departed from the region. They also laced their reports with sarcastic references to the region's Hispanic past. One observed that, if Central America cast off the shackles of "ignorance, superstition and oppression . . . engrafted on all their social institutions" by Spaniards, democratic government might work in the future.[17] Another, Charles DeWitt, who arrived in Guatemala City in 1833 and refused to venture outside the capital during his five-year tenure, dispatched gloomy reports about the union, which he predicted would "melt away like a piece of ice in the bright sun" before Guatemalan dominance.[18]

But Central America's Liberals, creators of this ill-fated union, though denigrated by American agents, considered the institutions of the United States as models for emulation. In 1823, Manuel José Arce and Juan Manuel Rodríguez told Secretary of State John Quincy Adams that they believed El Salvador's progress was linked to U.S. laws and institutions and not the centralized authority of Iturbide's Mexico. Later, Morazán and his close advisor, José Francisco Barrundia, unsuccessfully tried, through constitutional amendment, to implement a federal system of government akin to that of the United States. Liberals unsuccessfully encouraged U.S. private investment in enterprises not then present in Central America. A few features of the Anglo-American legal tradition took root, and the Liberal regime in Guatemala, which adopted Edward Livingston's penal codes, served as a model of educational, economic, and legal reform. Yet in triumph, as one admirer of the Liberal cause bemoaned, the Liberals were capable of "destroying everything without constructing anything." [19] Challenged by the Conservative opposition from within, the Liberals looked north for inspiration.

They found kindred spirits among U.S. proponents of an isthmian canal. In 1824, Juan José Cañas, the United Provinces' first minister to Washington, confident that U.S. businessmen would undertake the project, suggested construction of a canal through Nicaragua. His contemporary, José Aycinena (who resided in the United States during the height of its own canal construction) visualized a transisthmian canal that would draw world shipping to Central America, spur local agriculture and industry, and make the region a maritime power. A canal would foster across the region the extensive building of roads, which would bring local wares to market and attract Europeans, who, through marriage with its indigenous people, would procreate a more ambitious and educated people. Such was the vision of a "new Central America" that persisted throughout the nineteenth century.

In 1835, when Juan Galindo arrived in Washington with Central American canal proposals, British, Dutch, and French commercial groups were already showing varying degrees of interest. At the same time American canal promoters found in the U.S. Senate political allies who championed the construction of a transisthmian canal open to all nations and paid for with levied tolls, which would reimburse the capitalists who built it. President Andrew Jackson, whose diplomats were aggressively promoting U.S. markets in Latin America, commissioned Charles Biddle to Guatemala City, Nicaragua, Panama (a province of Colombia), and Bogotá to determine the status of various canal projects. Biddle first visited Panama, where he determined that anticipated costs prohibited the construction of a canal there for several generations. In Bogotá, Biddle negotiated a private contract for interoceanic transport by ship and road across Colombia. He then returned to the United States without visiting Central America, offering the lame excuse that authorities in Cuba, Jamaica, and Colombia had indicated that a canal through Nicaragua was impossible. The results of Biddle's mission disappointed Jackson. He told the Senate in January 1837 that he did not have sufficient information to conduct with any government negotiations regarding the construction of a transisthmian canal. The issue remained dormant for nearly a decade.[20]

The aim of improved commercial relations was also frustrated. When Cañas arrived in Washington, he hoped to find new markets for the region's wares and a source for goods previously imported from Spain. His arrival occurred at a time when western spokesmen, such as Henry Clay, looked to the Caribbean as an outlet for goods from the Old Northwest. The mutual interests culminated in the 1825 Treaty of Amity and Commerce, which provided for complete reciprocity. Unfortunately, little materialized. Until 1839, both imports from and exports to Central America remained a minuscule part of U.S. trade, and Britain (followed by France, Germany, and Holland) continued to dominate Central American shipping and markets.[21]

Galindo's mission in 1835 signaled the first test of U.S. intentions to invoke the Monroe Doctrine and shield Central America from European, and especially British, expansion. After 1824, as the threat of Mexican and Spanish intervention in Central America abated, British interests dramatically increased. The United Provinces negotiated its first foreign loan with London bankers. When Frederick Chatfield became minister to Central America in 1834, he quickly negotiated a commercial treaty with the United Provinces and traveled along the Mosquito coast and to Belize, where English settlers, who had first arrived in the seventeenth century, had bequeathed to the king's government a de facto protectorate. When Chatfield refused to discuss Guatemala's claims to Belize, Galindo (who had a large tract of land there) headed for the United States in hopes of persuading Jackson to invoke the Monroe Doctrine. In his appeal, Galindo said, "It has always been the policy of the United States that there should be no European settlement upon the American continent." He added that the British encroachment at Belize was a "dangerous and alarming violation of that principle." But for Jackson, who had already acquiesced in Britain's reoccupation of the Falkland Islands, the British presence in Central America did not jeopardize U.S. interests.[22] Denied Washington's protection, Galindo sailed to London, where he predictably failed in pleading his case.

Drifting Apart: The 1840s

Juan Galindo had encountered a political stumbling block that continued to impede Central America's international goals: lacking an internal unity among its governments, the isthmus easily fell prey to the apparently rivalrous desires of the larger and more ambitious powers. In 1835, Charles DeWitt warned that "a storm is brewing . . . and bye and bye . . . will burst upon us with a tremendous fury that would end the republic and replace it with something more simple."[23] DeWitt's fear of a racially motivated conflict proved well founded.

An early sign of the union's fragility was the provinces' refusal to meet their financial obligations to the central government. The debate over the Livingston Codes and their appropriateness to Central America was yet another sign of Liberal naïveté. Liberals such as Francisco Morazán and Mariano Gálvez concluded that progressive legislation would vault Central America into the age of modernity. Their programs appeared to gain slow acceptance among the elite but not the underprivileged. Each of the five states experienced Liberal change, but change was most evident in Guatemala. There, protective tariffs on cotton and textiles came only after foreign imports adversely affected the indigenous weavers and workers. A head tax and the requirement that all men labor on state-sponsored roads served as reminders of the Spanish past. At the same time, land development programs resulted in a *latifundia* system, which relegated Indians to a life of sharecropping and debt peonage. Stripping the clergy and the church of the Hispanic privileges deprived the rural communities of their confidant, banker, and spiritual leader. The clergy were further infuriated by colonization schemes that sought the introduction of Protestant northern Europeans.

Although sporadic violence against the Liberals surfaced across the isthmus, its eruption in Guatemala led to the demise of the United Provinces. A cholera epidemic in 1837 frightened the Indians and provided the church with an opportunity to play on their ignorance. At this juncture, the caudillo Rafael Carrera, a mestizo, emerged as the leader of a rebellion in eastern Guatemala against Gálvez, who had grafted enlightened liberal political and economic policies onto a profoundly conservative social order. Anxious to oust Gálvez in order to secure their own position, the Conservatives sustained the rebellion, which unleashed the conflicting social elements across the isthmus. With Gálvez's defeat in 1838, the federal government began to disintegrate. By the end of the year, Costa Rica, Honduras, and Nicaragua had seceded from the union. A year later, Rafael Carrera proclaimed Guatemalan independence. Morazán resigned as president of the federal government, and in February 1839 the United Provinces of Central America disappeared into history.[24] Morazán, its champion, began another military campaign to restore it a few years later, but the cause abruptly perished when he fell prisoner to the defiant Costa Ricans, who executed him in San José.

Triumphant, the Conservatives struck at the Liberal reforms of the 1830s, reestablishing much of the institutional structure from the colonial period: government was centralized; religious orders were restored and given control over education. Indian codes, while couched in paternalistic terms, placed the Indians in secondary status and forced them to provide public services. An elite group of educated landowners governed the state, ran the economy, and subjugated the Indian masses. But even with the restoration of Spanish heritage, Central Americans hesitantly sought contact with Europe's social elite by inviting British and Belgian colonists in the 1840s, in hopes of bringing finer European values to Central America. With the rejection of the foreign political and economic models the Liberals had imported,

Central America's international status rapidly diminished. To the intruding powers, as José Aycinena bitterly wrote, the provinces had shown themselves "unable to lay the foundation of their prosperity, or take their place among enlightened nations."[25] But a more telling self-assessment came from Guatemala's *Gaceta*, which observed that Central America had not developed institutions conforming to its own customs and history. Liberal ideas therefore "had disastrous consequences and retarded economic development." The "obligation of respecting the opinion of others . . . [is] the surest means, although slow, of uplifting the ignorant masses." To preach such ideas as liberty and equality "is to lead them to insurrection."[26]

Until the late 1840s, U.S. interest in the region dwindled following the fall of the United Provinces in 1839. When John L. Stephens arrived as minister in Guatemala City in 1839, he found no functioning government. The lack of official duties enabled him to close the legation and pursue his personal avocation, the exploration of the region's archaeological wonders, and ultimately to write a classic account of Mayan ruins. His *Incidents of Travel in Central America, Chiapas, and Yucatán* provided Americans with their first account of the geography, the people, and the Indian ruins that graced the isthmus. When first published in 1841, Stephens's volume contributed to a temporary increase in American interest in the region.[27] But for most Americans, Central America remained a distant land racked by political turmoil and plagued by cultural backwardness.

While Stephens roamed the Guatemalan interior, his British counterpart, Frederick Chatfield, aggressively promoted British interests. In 1839, he persuaded the Royal Navy to secure British control over the Bay Islands on the north Honduran coast. Two years later, the British superintendent at Belize, Alexander MacDonald, extended his administration to include the Bay Islands. Honduras alone could not dislodge the British.[28]

Prompted by the expansion of the mahogany trade conducted by Belizean settlers seeking new riches in more accessible woods and by the recognition that the port of San Juan del Norte was the most likely Caribbean terminus for an interoceanic canal, the British had already extended their influence on the Mosquito coast. In June 1837, London directed that the Mosquito Indians be protected from Central American encroachments. Three years later, determined to prevent Central America from controlling the mouth of the San Juan River, the superintendent of Belize raised the Mosquito flag over San Juan, then a small town on the river's mouth, and proclaimed a British protectorate over the Mosquito kingdom.[29]

The U.S. agents that followed Stephens—William S. Murphy and Henry Savage—warned Washington about British expansion and even suggested that commercial treaties with the five republics be forged as a counterweight to the British. But to no avail. During the 1840s, the State Department was oblivious to Central America. This situation only fueled the Central American Conservatives' distrust of the United States. Having rejected the American political model, Conservatives were now convinced that U.S. foreign policy was all too self-serving. The low point of Washington's status in Central America came in 1847, when Guatemala refused to invite Henry Savage to its independence day celebrations. Washington ended its silence in June 1848, two months after the Treaty of Guadalupe Hidalgo brought the Mexican War to its official conclusion. Secretary of State James Buchanan thanked Savage for sending "most acceptable information" during the previous six years.[30] His letter made it apparent that the United States was poised for a more aggressive policy in Central America.

2   The Outside World Comes to Central America, 1845–1865

Until the late 1840s, the United States looked west, not south, in its territorial expansion. When the Mexican War erupted in 1846, North Americans were enjoying a prosperity buoyed by their economy's growth, their society's reforms, and the vitality of their democratic institutions, and their self-confidence led them to envision their spreading the American way of life to all within reach. "Away, away with all those cobweb issues of rights of discovery, exploration, settlement, continuity etc.," proclaimed New York writer John O'Sullivan, who declared that it was the "right of our manifest destiny to overspread and to possess the whole of the continent which Providence has given us for the development of the great experiment of liberty and federative self government entrusted to us."[1] The entire Western Hemisphere, O'Sullivan prophesied, would benefit from the U.S. experience. The Mexican War reinforced the sentiments of those in favor of the annexation of all of Mexico; some favored annexation of all lands south to Panama, so that the culturally alien and downtrodden populations there could receive the amenities of U.S. democracy and social order. The more pragmatic of the expansionists were mainly interested in seeing that markets and minerals were exploited and that a canal was constructed across the Isthmus of Tehuantepec.

The expansionist euphoria subsided with the war's end, but what did not abate was the enthusiasm for a transisthmian canal, an interest heightened by the United States' transcontinental expansion. A canal was considered to be the fastest and most secure pathway to the Pacific Coast and beyond. The first step toward a canal project came in 1846, when Benjamin Bidlack concluded a general Treaty of Amity, Commerce, and Friendship with New Granada (Colombia). Article 35 of that agreement granted the U.S. government and its citizens the

15

right to construct a canal across the Isthmus of Panama, provided that the United States guarantee the territory's neutrality and New Granada's sovereignty over it. At first, President James K. Polk delayed submitting the Bidlack Treaty to the Senate, but then he learned that the treaty ending the Mexican War omitted provisions for a canal across the Isthmus of Tehuantepec. When he learned that the United States was thus deprived of a Mexican route, the president quickly submitted, and the Senate quickly reviewed and ratified, the Bidlack Treaty.[2]

The British Challenge and the Clayton-Bulwer Treaty

At about the same time that the Bidlack Treaty was ratified, the British concluded that the next arena for U.S. expansion would be Central America. Anticipating a southward thrust by the United States, British authorities in the New World set the southern boundary of the Mosquito kingdom at the mouth of the San Juan River. There, on 1 June 1848, they hoisted the Mosquito flag over the enclave and renamed it Greytown, in honor of the British governor at Jamaica. The seizure of the port effectively prevented Nicaragua from using the San Juan River to grant canal rights to a third party.[3]

Alert to the British expansion and, more important, the British threat to U.S. strategic and commercial interests in Central America, Polk dispatched Elijah Hise as chargé d'affaires to Guatemala City in 1848, instructing him to determine what the United States could do to resist European interference in the region. Charged to encourage the reunion of the five states and to revive commercial treaties with Guatemala and El Salvador, Hise took up the British challenge by negotiating a far-reaching commercial treaty with Nicaragua. At the suggestion of Nicaragua's foreign minister, Buenaventura Selva, Hise signed a treaty that granted the United States exclusive privilege in opening an interoceanic canal through Nicaragua and that obligated the United States to fortify the route and to protect the neutrality and sovereignty of Nicaragua in all territory "rightfully theirs," that is, the Mosquito coast. Hise returned to Washington and delivered the treaties to the new secretary of state, John M. Clayton, in September 1849.[4]

Clayton was no less anxious than Polk to deter British expansion, and he dispatched Ephraim George Squier, as the new U.S. representative to Central America, with a directive pledging the full force of U.S. moral pressure for "the purpose of frustrating the apparent designs of Great Britain in countenancing the claims to sovereignty over the Mosquito Coast and the Port of San Juan."[5] Though Squier was empowered to assist American capitalists in obtaining a canal right-of-way, he was not to obligate the United States to guarantee regional neutrality, a position consistent with Henry Clay's instructions to the American representatives to the Panama Congress in 1826, the 1835 Senate resolution, and the 1839 House resolution, all of which disavowed a U.S. monopoly over a transisthmian canal. "If we held and enjoyed such a monopoly," Clayton wrote, "it would entail upon us more bloody and expensive wars than the struggles for Gibraltar has caused to England and to Spain."[6] Rather, the United States sought a canal impartially open to the world's commerce, an admirable principle but, given the vigor of U.S. intrusion, an impolitic one.

Squier alertly noted Nicaragua's general political weakness and the fractured character of Central American unity, both of which he attributed to British intrigue. To offset it, Squier called for a U.S. naval squadron to patrol Central America's Pacific coast and recommended a Central American union headquartered in El Salvador. His request denied, the indomitable Squier (assisted by David L. White of the American Atlantic and Pacific Ship and Canal Company) nonetheless plunged ahead. He negotiated with Nicaragua a contract granting the company the exclusive right to construct a canal across the republic, and he reinforced the contract with a standard treaty of amity and commerce, which granted U.S. citizens the right of free transit across the country by whatever facility might be constructed. Squier offered U.S. protection for the proposed canal and a guarantee of its neutrality. This was, of course, a violation of his instructions, but with the treaty he placated the Nicaraguans who had pledged to contest the British challenge to Nicaraguan sovereignty in the Mosquitia.

Satisfied with his efforts in Nicaragua, Squier descended on Honduras, where he arranged that Tigre Island in the Gulf of Fonseca— long considered the western terminus for a Nicaraguan canal—be ceded to the United States. The British, Squier believed, would not deter his efforts, because England's minister to Central America, Frederick Chatfield, was "a man of small calibre, easily excited, and more by little things, than great things," and therefore could be easily managed.[7] Squier misjudged, however, and Chatfield reacted with a vengeance. Believing that the cession of Tigre Island was a prelude to the establishment of a U.S. protectorate, Chatfield boarded the HMS *Gorgon* and directed it to the Gulf of Fonseca, where British troops seized the island for Honduras's failure to pay unsettled debts. Chatfield's superiors soon revoked the order; British troops departed; and the U.S. flag soon flew over the island. However, the incident was yet another example of the international rivalry over Central America and the determination of British agents to advance national interests.[8]

Even so, neither Washington nor London wanted a war over Central America. Clayton reasoned that the best way to limit British influence in the isthmus was to deal directly with British diplomats in Washington, not with hothead surrogates in Central America. Accordingly, he proposed to the British a treaty jointly guaranteeing Costa Rican, Honduran, and Nicaraguan neutrality; reaffirming British privileges derived from Anglo-Spanish treaties; recognizing Indian rights in Mosquitia; and providing for joint protection of transportation routes throughout the isthmus. It was a daring offer, but it was consistent with previous U.S. policy. By limiting the British in Central America, it upheld the Monroe Doctrine and reaffirmed the neutrality of the transisthmian route. Convinced that any territorial acquisitions linked to a canal project would result in war, Clayton further proposed that both nations pledge not to annex, settle, colonize, or fortify any part of Central America.

A sense of urgency prevailed in Washington but not in London. The British wanted a compromise if they could safeguard Belize and preserve their special privileges on the Mosquito coast. Viscount Henry John Temple Palmerston, accustomed to baiting Yankees, had more important concerns—the 1849 Turkish crisis, pecuniary claims against Greece, and the suppression of the Brazilian slave trade in 1850. He waited nine months before dispatching Sir Henry Lytton Bulwer across the Atlantic. By the time Bulwer arrived, Clayton's threats to submit the Squier treaties to the Senate for ratification and the earlier jingoism of the American press had been subsumed in the congressional debate over the question of slavery in the newly acquired Mexican territory. Alert to the sudden divisiveness in American politics, Bulwer remained firm in seeking a compromise that protected British rights and honor. These priorities safeguarded, he readily agreed to Clayton's proposal.

Clayton was a diplomat, not a politician. The Clayton-Bulwer Treaty was sufficiently ambiguous to persuade Americans that the British had been checked. The two governments pledged not to "assume or exercise any dominion over Nicaragua, Costa Rica, the Mosquito Coast, or any part of Central America."[9] Clayton naively believed (as did the Central Americans) that the British had surrendered their claim to the Mosquito coast and that the provisions ensured the benefits of the proposed canal would accrue to all nations.

Almost immediately after the treaty received the Senate's narrow approval, the political debate over Central America resumed. The catalysts for the conflict were the California gold rush and the talk about the isthmus as the fastest route from the east to the west coasts of the United States. From the east coast, travelers arrived at Greytown (then considered one of the prettiest places), and from there they sailed up the San Juan River on a *bongo* (a large, uncovered dugout made from a tree trunk) to Lake Nicaragua and beyond to the Pacific coast. Even as the number of travelers increased, Greytown did not grow beyond the opulent British waterfront.[10]

The opportunity to capitalize on the passenger traffic now beckoned new entrepreneurs. The most illustrious of them was Cornelius Vanderbilt, who envisioned a transit system from New York to San Francisco via Nicaragua. A beneficiary of concessions contained in the

Squier treaty, Vanderbilt dispatched his Accessory Transit Company steamboats to San Juan and Lakes Nicaragua and Managua. From there, a macadam road wound to Realejo on the Pacific coast. The trip across the isthmus took three days. Regular bimonthly service was introduced, and by 1852 an estimated ten thousand persons traveled this route. The increased passenger and commercial activity transformed Greytown into a spirited community, bustling with new bars, amusements, gambling houses, and hotels—all in all, a place more popular than the Panamanian hellhole of Chagres.[11]

The increased American presence inevitably brought confrontation with the British. Greytown, as the Clayton-Bulwer Treaty stipulated, became a free port, a status that deprived British authorities of duties on transitory cargoes. To compensate, the British began levying ship charges to cover harbor maintenance, freeing local revenues for public services only. Everyone—except Vanderbilt, who asserted that his settlement across the bay, at Puntarenas, did not use any of Greytown's facilities—paid the fees. The controversy climaxed on 21 November 1851, when Vanderbilt's *Prometheus* departed for New York without paying port charges. A British brig, HMS *Express,* fired three shots across its bow, forcing Vanderbilt, who was aboard the *Prometheus,* to comply. Washington protested, and the British instructed their naval commanders at Greytown not to enforce payment of duties until an adjustment was reached with the United States.[12]

However, the British hold on Mosquitia proved a difficult problem to solve. For one thing, both Washington and London, having resolved to negotiate about rather than fight over Central America, had seriously underestimated the Central Americans' resolve to resist the intruding powers' efforts to decide their fate. Costa Rica and Nicaragua had conflicting claims on the San Juan River. A tentative 1852 British-American agreement, which guaranteed Costa Rica all the territory south of the San Juan River, had been drawn up without the parties' consulting the foreign ministers of Costa Rica and Nicaragua. Understandably, the Costa Ricans were willing to accept the offer, but the Nicaraguans demurred. Acquisition of the San Juan River would have been a prize for the Costa Ricans, but this action would obviously have been a serious loss for the Nicaraguans, who invoked the Monroe Doctrine to review their demands for British evacuation from Greytown.[13]

On 20 March 1852, the British further complicated matters by proclaiming the "Colony of the Bay Islands" over Roatán, Bonacca, and four neighboring islands off the Honduran Caribbean coast. Anticipating the loss of Greytown and the need to secure another commercial and political position in the region, the British assumed such a move would not provoke the United States because the Bay Islands bore little importance for a transisthmian canal.[14] Here they misjudged the political climate in the United States, especially in the Senate, where the foreign relations committee characterized the takeover of the Bay Islands as a violation of both the Monroe Doctrine and the Clayton-Bulwer Treaty. In a superfluous gesture of defiance, the committee also determined that Belize was Guatemalan and demanded British withdrawal. When the new minister to London, James Buchanan, pressed the issue in September 1853, the British remained resolute.[15]

Events in Greytown were already straining U.S.–British relations. Greytown fell on hard times, as the Accessory Transit Company transformed Puntarenas from a utility base for housing workers into a self-sufficient community capable of monopolizing interoceanic traffic, and thus exceeding the original concessions granted by British administrators at Greytown. In 1853, when the company refused to honor a financial requisition, the infuriated British allegedly burned some of its buildings at Puntarenas, increasing the animosity between the residents of both enclaves.

Into this tense atmosphere arrived Solon Borland, U.S. minister to Nicaragua, who called the Greytown British "pirates and outlaws." Predictably, Borland exacerbated the situation. He offered protection to the commander of an American riverboat sought by Greytown officials in connection with the murder of a black native leader, and he later claimed diplomatic immunity when they tried to arrest him for interfering in the matter. The crisis intensified in July 1854 with the arrival of the SS *Cayne*, sent to collect reparations from the British for the damage they had inflicted a year earlier to Accessory Transit Company property at Puntarenas and to extract an apology for insults to Borland. When British officials refused both demands, the *Cayne's* captain ordered Greytown's destruction by bombardment and burning. The town never recovered.[16]

The William Walker Era

"Central America is destined to occupy an influential position in the family of nations," proclaimed the *New York Times* on 15 December 1854, particularly "if her advantages of location, climate and soil are availed of by a race of 'Northmen,' who shall supplant the tainted, mongrel and decaying race which now occupies the region." [17] Ambitious northmen had already discovered the isthmus. "Colonel" Henry L. Kinney had traveled to Washington to explain that the project of his Central America Land and Mining Company was a business venture, not a filibustering enterprise in violation of the nation's neutrality laws. Kinney's company, which held questionable title to 22.5 million acres, or 70 percent of Nicaragua's land area, began in the fall of 1854 a newspaper advertisement and solicitation campaign urging potential colonists to relocate to the Mosquito coast.

But the Yankee entrepreneur had already embittered Nicaraguans. Outraged by the company's hollow promises and false assurances and by the sudden presence of foreign adventurers, the Nicaraguan government declared the Kinney grant illegal and any occupation of its territory a violation of its sovereignty. Naively, it appealed to the U.S. government to prevent Kinney's company from carrying out its designs. The Costa Ricans quickly joined in the protest.

Expansionist Democrats had returned to power in Washington, and Secretary of State William L. Marcy, already embarrassed by revelations of the administration's bungled attempt to acquire Spanish Cuba as a slave territory, brushed the appeals aside with a curt statement that the government had no authority to prohibit a private company from the peaceful pursuit of its objectives. Neither a federal grand jury's indictment against Kinney for violating the 1818 neutrality law forbidding the organization of a military campaign nor an order to the Coast Guard to halt the sailing of Kinney's chartered steamer prevented the expedition's departure in April 1854. With only thirteen followers, Kinney arrived at Greytown and proclaimed himself governor. Once he landed in Nicaragua, however, his scheme quickly began to unravel. The United States abandoned him, and the British ignored him. Bankrupt, Kinney returned to the United States in 1856.[18] But the ease with which he had established his intrusion on Nicaragua's Caribbean coast was a sign of Central America's fractured unity and its vulnerability to a craftier and more ambitious man—William Walker.

Since the collapse of the United Provinces of Central America in 1839, disputes between Liberals and Conservatives, who were still bitterly divided over the issue of the state and the foreign entrepreneur, had plunged the five nations into political conflict and international war. Leaders from one country routinely intervened in the internal affairs of neighboring states, sometimes calling on the support of exile military forces. British meddling in Nicaragua, it was said, had by 1845 bequeathed two governments: the Conservatives, or "Legitimists," at Granada and the Liberals, or Democrats, at León. The economic and social legacies of these political conflicts left Nicaragua vulnerable to foreign exploitation.

William Walker and his generation of filibusters profited by Nicaragua's factional politics. Walker was the architect of a tropical empire. The highly intelligent son of a Tennessee merchant and insurance man, he completed college at the age of fourteen and later earned a medical degree from the University of Pennsylvania. Losing interest in medicine, Walker went to New Orleans, where he was admitted to the bar and dabbled in journalism as a part owner and an editor of the *Daily Crescent*. He subsequently found his way to California. From there, he led an unsuccessful filibustering expedition into Mexico's state of Sonora. The experience was a prelude to his more famous adventure in Central America.

His talents and daring appealed to a harassed band of Nicaraguan Liberals, who had tried, with Honduran aid, to seize power in 1854;

they had failed when Rafael Carrera of Guatemala had given their Conservative enemies some timely assistance. The conflict would have doubtless gone the way of earlier confrontations were it not for the work of Byron Cole, part owner of the Honduras Mining and Trading Company. Cole feared that, if Nicaragua came under Conservative rule, it would lead to a Conservative-dominated Honduras, which would limit the company's opportunities and open the door to British competition. But if the Nicaraguan Liberals hired American filibusters, they would triumph, and Nicaragua would be profitably opened to private investment from the United States. In the fall of 1854, Cole convinced Liberal leader Francisco Castellón that filibuster reinforcements would revivify his seemingly hopeless cause.

To his ultimate regret, Castellón agreed. Cole soon contracted with Walker, who set sail with his fifty-six "immortals" from San Francisco in May 1855. Their warm reception in Nicaragua, highlighted by Walker's quick promotion to colonel in the Nicaraguan army, rapidly disappeared when it became apparent that Walker had his own goals. Walker sought control of the country for himself, envisioning a trans-isthmian canal and modernization of the Nicaraguan economy.

Following their initial setbacks in the battlefield, Walker and the immortals reversed Liberal fortunes and persuaded the Conservatives—even though their army was not totally defeated—to sue for peace in October 1855. Walker then created a puppet government headed by the aging Patricio Rivas, who promptly appointed Walker commander in chief of the Nicaraguan army, thus giving Walker political and military power. He disbanded the conscripted "all-volunteer" peasant army and retained the filibusters as Nicaragua's military force. In farcical elections in June 1856, and in defiance of a constitutional prohibition, Walker became president of Nicaragua.

His plan called next for a Central American union, with Nicaragua at its core, to be governed by military principles. But the initial task was the attainment by U.S. citizens of the privileged position held by Nicaragua's social elite. To that end, in September 1956 Walker issued a series of land and labor decrees instituting forced labor for anyone not actively seeking employment, legalizing labor contracts for unlimited time periods (which, in effect, created indentured servitude), and rescinding the decrees abolishing slavery. A complicated land registration program began, and English became the country's second official language. Walker soon boasted that the majority of Nicaraguan territory would be "in the hands of the white race." His political enemies soon found their land titles forfeited and auctioned to purchasers paying with filibuster military scrip.[19]

Walker's seizure of political power, and especially the "reforms" he introduced, mobilized the isthmian elites. They soon had unexpected help from another American—Cornelius Vanderbilt.

While Walker was consolidating power in Nicaragua, Vanderbilt was engaged in a power struggle, with Cornelius K. Garrison and Charles Morgan, for control of the Accessory Transit Company. Under an 1849 agreement, the company was required to pay the Nicaraguan government $10,000 annually, plus $200,000 of the company's stock, plus 10 percent of its net profits, together with an annual account of the company's receipts and expenditures.[20] In 1852, the Nicaraguan government received nothing, but the company paid its stockholders a 25-percent dividend. Anticipating Nicaragua's hostile reaction, Walker struck a deal with Garrison and Morgan, whereby the company advanced him $20,000 in gold bullion against its debt to the Nicaraguan government and further agreed to ship immigrants to Nicaragua at $20 per head.

This arrangement, together with Garrison and Morgan's 1853 stock manipulation, which had caused Vanderbilt to suffer a considerable financial loss, touched off an intracompany struggle for power. In the midst of this struggle, Garrison convinced Walker to revoke the Accessory Transit Company's charter for not paying the royalties required by the 1849 concession and to reissue a new charter to him and Morgan. Walker ordered Rivas to carry out the plan in February 1856. Knowledgeable Nicaraguans were pleased with the annulment of one worthless concession and with the prospect of renewed payments from the transit company's successor. Unfortunately, nothing materialized.

The Garrison-Morgan deal remained a secret for a month, enabling both men to realize huge profits from the sale of their stock in the Accessory Transit Company. When Vanderbilt uncovered the deal, he diverted his Atlantic and Pacific steamers from Nicaragua to Panama to utilize the newly opened transisthmian railroad, and he then asked the United States to intervene on his behalf. Marcy refused, advising Vanderbilt to take his claim to Nicaragua, where the company was incorporated. Recognizing the futility of that approach, Vanderbilt turned his attention to supporting Walker's opponents.[21]

Neither the public nor the administration, evidently, identified with Commodore Vanderbilt in this matter. By contrast, Walker's scheme to Americanize Nicaragua came at a time when many Americans, mostly southerners, recognizing that slavery was illegal in the recently acquired Mexican territories, dreamed of an empire beyond the continental limits of the United States. The Democratic party appeared to champion the southern strategy. In 1856, when Walker came to power in Nicaragua, the Democratic platform boldly proclaimed, "In view of so commanding an interest, the people of the United States cannot but sympathize with the efforts which are being made by the people of Central America to regenerate that portion of the continent which covers the passage across the interoceanic isthmus."[22]

The expansionist press glorified Walker's cause just as he was launching an enthusiastic campaign to bring new recruits to Nicaragua, and detailed advertisements extolled the benefits of relocation. But the success of the effort was mixed. In New York City, William Appleton Oaksmith, a Walker admirer, worked with Brooklyn mayor George Hall to arrange the shipment of arms and recruits from the Atlantic states to Nicaragua. Walker's agents labored in New Orleans, Texas, and the Tennessee-Kentucky area, but the initial excitement rapidly diminished with the circulation of unsettling stories about the heavyhanded methods used by Walker's agents, the questionable legality of the Nicaraguan land grants, and a Nicaragua plagued with sickness, poverty, and death.[23]

The plan to introduce slavery into Nicaragua appealed to southerners and particularly to those in New Orleans, where there was also noticeable business support for a railroad across the isthmus.

Southern political ideologues of the "tropical empire"—Pierre Soulé, Jefferson Davis, J. D. B. DeBow, Sam Houston, and John A. Quitman—believed that Walker was sustaining the "peculiar institution," and they lauded his achievements. But their public enthusiasm was largely self-serving. They anticipated that Nicaraguan slavery would open the way to a lucrative slave trade and, in Texas, provide a labor base for the expected expansion of the cotton industry. A few, such as Soulé, may have looked for a greater southern destiny and a larger representation in Congress, but for the most part Walker's supporters seemed to be serving their own personal interests.[24]

As often happens where Central America is concerned, the U.S. government confronted a situation without first forming a coherent policy to deal with it. The administration of Franklin Pierce, though sympathetic to Walker's purpose, could not set aside the neutrality laws or reverse diplomatic practice. Thus, when Minister John H. Wheeler, who was part of the Conservative government at Granada, took it upon himself to extend recognition to the Liberal Rivas regime that Walker had imposed upon the country, Secretary Marcy rescinded recognition and reprimanded Wheeler. The chastised agent, an ardent supporter of Walker, remained in Nicaragua and kept up the pressure. He had an ally in President Pierce, who had already extended recognition to the Rivas regime on the specious reasoning that a Nicaraguan government must be recognized. By the time word reached Wheeler, however, Walker had been elected president. Again, acting without the State Department's instructions, Wheeler recognized Walker's government. His actions infuriated the Central American diplomatic corps in Washington, who, not unreasonably, thought that recognition of the Rivas-Walker government would only encourage illegitimate governments elsewhere.[25]

The Americans' failure to enforce neutrality laws also raised doubts about American intentions. In December 1855, the president had dutifully warned prospective recruits for a military enterprise in Nicaragua that they were not entitled to protection from the United States government. The apparent intention of the directive was to deny Walker military recruits and to enforce the nation's neutrality laws. But enforcement of the order was a different matter, especially in New York and San Francisco, the main ports of embarkation for Nicaragua. Arrests were rare because authorities had no ready proof that departing New York passengers were filibusters. Most of them were headed for California or were leaving with the legitimate intention of being Nicaraguan colonists. In San Francisco, officials reasoned that Walker had accepted an invitation to Nicaragua in order to aid the Liberal party against the Conservative party in a domestic revolution and that those who left the United States to join him were entering a foreign theater of operation. Although there was no enlistment facility in San Francisco, these officials incorrectly reasoned that neutrality laws were not being violated, yet their refusal to halt individuals from leaving the United States for Nicaragua brought no reprimand from Washington. Under these circumstances, Central America's ruling elite, alarmed at Walker's unchecked filibustering, concluded that the U.S. government intended to impose its will over the entire isthmus.[26]

Despite their fears, Central Americans remained divided. The ousted Honduran Liberal dictator, José Trinidad Cabañas, who, while exiled in Nicaragua, became disillusioned with Walker, declared against the filibusters. Guatemala declared its neutrality and El Salvador its sympathy. Only the historically aloof Costa Ricans, who had never accepted isthmian unity in spirit, now seemed willing to expunge the intruders. Their motives were both political and social. The Costa Rican president, Juan Rafael Mora, feared that Walker would support the Liberal opposition in his country and that the Americanization of Nicaragua would disturb his country's social structure. If that happened, and the United States extended recognition to Walker, "May God help us!" exclaimed Edward Wallerstein, Costa Rica's consul general in London.[27]

Mora took action on two fronts. In Washington, the Costa Rican minister pressed unsuccessfully for appropriate preventative measures against Walker, and in London, Wallerstein appealed for British sympathy and aid. Sensing they had an isthmian surrogate to check their American competitors, the British supplied the Ticos with two

thousand muskets, under the pretext that they were to be used to protect British lives, and also increased the naval squadron in the Gulf of
Mexico.[28] Mora prepared for battle with an offer to pardon filibusters
who surrendered, but he vowed to shoot any prisoners captured with
arms. When the offer went unanswered, Mora's troops attacked on
1 March 1856 and won an initial victory at La Virgin, but they did
not pursue the retreating filibusters because an outbreak of cholera in
Nicaragua took a heavy toll on the forces.[29]

With his Costa Rican adversary in retreat from the plague, Walker
had a few months to regroup. But his seizure of the Nicaraguan
presidency in June 1856 inspired additional opposition. Patricio Rivas
and his cabinet deserted Walker to join with Conservative José María
Estrada at Chinandega. From there, the coalition issued to Nicaragua's
neighbors a joint plea for help in evicting the Yankee usurper. Central American Conservatives, mobilized by their alarm over Walker's
apparent intentions and the apparent pro-Walker sentiment in Washington, encouraged Walker's rapidly growing internal opposition. On
16 July 1856, Guatemala, Honduras, and El Salvador recognized the
Rivas government at Chinandega and pledged to unify their forces to
oust Walker. Mora and the Costa Ricans, reinforced with a timely loan
from a vengeful Cornelius Vanderbilt, joined them.

The invading forces entered Nicaragua in September 1856. There
ensued what Central Americans proudly call the National War—a
campaign of unprecedented destructiveness in which Walker, retreating from Granada, ordered the burning of one of the isthmus's loveli-
est cities, leaving behind a sign that read, "Here Was Granada." By
the end of the year, a British blockade shut off Walker's supply of
recruits. Isolated, Walker and his troops retreated to Rivas, which
came under siege in March 1857. Two months later he surrendered
to Commander Charles E. Davis of the warship *Saint Mary's*, which
had been dispatched to San Juan del Sur to protect American citizens.
Davis offered safe conduct out of Nicaragua for Walker and his remaining army. Though divided over the proposal, most of the Central
American commanders wanted to end the war and avoid possible U.S.

intervention. They allowed Walker to depart from Nicaragua in the benevolent custody of a U.S. naval officer, and the Central American allied armies returned home.

Walker arrived in New Orleans to a hero's welcome, but elsewhere his support and popularity had ebbed. Much had changed since 1854 and the onset of his filibustering. The end of the California gold rush contributed to a decline in transisthmian traffic, and the Panama Railroad, opened in 1855, now made the Nicaragua route less attractive. Once lionized as a model of the "Young America," Walker read disbelievingly as Jefferson Davis and Stephen A. Douglas denigrated his actions in congressional debates over the expansion of slavery. "I have no sympathy for such expeditions," Davis asserted, while Douglas disavowed any "fancy for this system of filibustering."[30]

Although money and recruits were difficult to come by, Walker launched two more expeditions—one in 1858, when he was intercepted at Greytown and sent back to the United States, and one in 1860, when he landed on Roatán, lured there by Bay Islanders with a scheme to prevent the British from transferring the islands to Honduras and the prospect of an alliance with Honduran Liberals. The British were still on Roatán, however, and Walker sailed for Trujillo, Honduras, which he captured and held until a regiment of British marines landed. His cause hopeless, he surrendered to the captain of a patrolling British warship and was turned over to the Hondurans. They quickly tried, sentenced, and executed the "Green-Eyed Man of Destiny."[31]

Newspapers throughout the south carried stories of his death without editorial expression of regret. President James Buchanan, however, retained the faith of "Young America": "It is beyond question the destiny of our race to spread themselves over the continent of North America, and this at no distant day, should events be permitted to take their natural course. . . . Central America will contain an American population which will confer blessings and benefits . . . upon the natives."[32] But a former ally, Patricio Rivas, had already written Walker's epitaph: "God will condemn his arrogance and protect our cause."[33]

Ebbing Interests: The 1860s

Even in victory, the Central Americans remained apprehensive about U.S. intentions in the isthmus. The British, by contrast, had drawn more precise limits in their ambitions. As the Walker era drew to a close, Great Britain, distracted by the Crimean War and the reminder of greater commitments to the eastern Mediterranean, had already settled on a policy of accommodation with the United States in the western Caribbean. Britain would not be pushed out of any territory it already occupied on the isthmus, but it "would not give three coppers to retain any post on Central American territory or coast from which she could not honorably retire."[34] U.S. inflexibility regarding the Clayton-Bulwer Treaty had apparently prompted British officials to negotiate their own settlement with the Central American nations. With their conciliatory mood being praised in Washington, the British dispatched a less combative agent, Charles Wycke, to treat with the Central Americans. In 1859, he eased tensions with Guatemala over the boundary of British Honduras by promising Carrera that the British would undertake the construction of a railroad connecting the Caribbean coast with the nation's interior. Wycke moved on to Honduras and negotiated a treaty recognizing the Bay Islands as Honduran territory. On their part, the Hondurans agreed not to transfer the islands to a third party or to interfere with the religion or property of the British already residing there. Britain abandoned the Mosquito Indians in Honduras to Honduran control. And in the Treaty of Managua, Britain relinquished its protectorate over the Mosquito territory, including Greytown, which became a free port under Nicaraguan sovereignty. Within Nicaragua, the Mosquitos enjoyed self-government.[35]

However, the British treaties and Walker's death did not free Central America of North American influence. Immediately after the outbreak of the American Civil War in April 1861, President Abraham Lincoln determined to deny the Confederacy the legal status that would be obtained through recognition by a foreign government. Anticipating that a Confederate victory would advance southern and foreign involvement in Central America, Lincoln sought to prevent any linkage between the Confederacy and Central America. The isthmian governments generally complied. They withheld recognition from the Confederacy and denied its privateers use of isthmian ports, but their motives owed more to regional factors than to diplomatic pressures. Central American leaders believed that a grant of recognition to the Confederacy encouraged rebellion at home. Lacking a navy to shield their coastline, they could ill afford to open their Caribbean ports to Confederate privateers and risk confrontation with U.S. gunboats.[36]

Their initial accommodation of U.S. wishes may have prompted one of the most bizarre episodes in U.S.–Central American relations. In 1861, Lincoln recommended a search for a congenial climate for the colonization of free blacks. The idea of a colony for freed slaves was not new. Since the early nineteenth century, various schemes had been concocted to effect the emigration of blacks abroad. The most feasible called for a colony in Panama, where shipbuilding magnate Ambrose W. Thompson had acquired several thousand acres. But Lincoln also viewed Central America as a prospective site, in part on the questionable assumption that transplanted blacks from the United States would blunt European intervention on the isthmus. When the new U.S. minister Elisha O. Crosby arrived in Guatemala in 1861, he sounded out Carrera on the colonization subject. The aging Carrera rejected the notion, as did Honduran president Santos Guardiola. Undeterred, Crosby continued to pursue the project on his own and a year later was touting plans for a colony at Livingston, on Guatemala's isolated Atlantic coast, where blacks already resided.

Uniformly ignorant of Central American racial sensibilities, American diplomats continued to push the plan. Secretary of State William H. Seward, for example, argued that freed blacks would find ready employment on the isthmian plantations and enjoy the protection of their civil rights. In 1862, he initiated another round of inquiries for the colonization project. Again, the Central Americans responded negatively. The minister for Guatemala and El Salvador, A. J. Irisarri, was shocked at Lincoln's reference to blacks as equals and predicted they would not be allowed to settle in either country. The

Costa Ricans, more European in their makeup, were even more adamant in their disapproval. The U.S. minister in San José, Charles N.
Riotte, urged his government not to spend "one cent for the purchase of land for negro colonization" there. From Comayagua, Honduran minister Thomas Partridge reported that Hondurans wanted
white colonists (preferably Germans), not freed blacks, in order to improve the national economy. From León, Nicaraguan minister A. B.
Dickinson wrote that the Nicaraguans were "extremely jealous of their
national character, and feel indignant at the idea of being ranked with
the North American Negro."[37]

Obviously, officials in Washington did not understand race relations
in Central America, even though slavery had been banned immediately after independence in 1823. Since Central America's colonial
days, blacks were Hispanicized, adopting Catholicism and the Spanish language, and intermarrying with whites and Indians. The exact
number of blacks throughout the isthmus was not known at the time
of Lincoln's plan, although those identified as black appeared to suffer a separatism largely unknown to mixed races. Washington's officials apparently learned nothing from the furor caused by Walker's
reinstatement of slavery in Nicaragua in 1856.

Central American leaders also questioned American motives. A
familiar query, put to one U.S. emissary, was, "If the U.S. want [sic]
to colonize the free blacks on territory themselves, why dont [sic] they
appropriate some of their own sparsely populated territory to this
purpose and keep them themselves?"[38] The experience of the Walker
era gnawed at them. Colonization of free blacks, Costa Rican Luis
Molina wrote, was another form of "filibustering," and El Salvador's
Gaceta Oficial alerted its readers to the "dangers of establishing colonies beneath the protection of a foreign and very powerful nation,
whose sons had already revealed their tendencies in the aggressions
of [William] Walker."[39]

In effect, the *Gaceta* asserted that Central America should distance
itself from the United States, and for good reason. In the years after
1850, the isthmian republics became little more than pawns on Washington's foreign policy chessboard. Central America was not consulted

about the Clayton-Bulwer Treaty, nor was it given any consideration in the diplomatic maneuvering that followed. Washington's ambivalence toward William Walker's activities and its subsequent plans for a black colony on the isthmus demonstrated both Washington's insensitivity to Central America's cultural and social heritage and Washington's intention to dominate diplomatic relations. It seemed to the Central Americans that the United States had replaced Great Britain as the aggressive interloper in their affairs.

3 Relationships Established, 1865–1903

In 1881, journalist John A. Kasson, anticipating a transisthmian canal, asserted, "No chance should be left to convert a weak Central American state into another distracted Egypt by means of foreign possessory rights in another isthmian canal." The European presence in Central America, he continued, threatened the United States both militarily and economically and warranted a vigorous reaffirmation of the Monroe Doctrine.[1] Alert to the commercial benefits of the heightened American interest, Guatemalan president Justo Rufino Barrios gave voice to a political sentiment widespread in Central America when he declared, "I am decidedly American and prefer the advantages of that industrious race if they are able to increase and multiply among us."[2] Thus the Americans determined to preserve the region for their own security and economic advantage, while the Central Americans foresaw American intrusion, and especially that accompanied by venture capital, as a route to the modernization of their economy. But the Central Americans did not readily perceive that along with a generation of ambitious entrepreneurs and capitalists came American leaders who viewed the isthmian canal not as a means to developing Central America's economy but as the stepping-stone to major power status in world affairs.

Reestablishing Interests, 1865–1885

As U.S. interest in Central America heightened after 1865, American officials believed that unification of the five republics was the most effective means to advancing isthmian economic development and more efficient management of its foreign affairs. State rivalries had condemned the region to backwardness, observed the U.S. minister to Costa Rica, Charles N. Riotte, in 1861: "Family feuds become affairs of State, and the ascendancy to political preponderance is often sullied with acts of unwarrantable cruelty, practiced not so much against the political adversary as upon the enemy of the tribe. It is seldom the greediness of gain which causes the outbreak of hostilities, but rather the desire for influence and power."[3]

The bitter conflict between Conservative Guatemalan president Rafael Carrera (whose struggle with Francisco Morazán had virtually destroyed the earlier union) and Liberal Salvadoran president Gerardo Barrios appeared to validate Riotte's lugubrious assessment. Their war of words rapidly escalated into a blood feud. In February 1863, the United States became involved when Carrera sought its mediation of the conflict and guarantee of the resultant peace. Secretary of State William H. Seward agreed to the first but wisely demurred from the second, arguing persuasively that Central America's tumultuous history precluded any lasting peace settlement. The United States, he noted, could not police the isthmus without becoming involved in its conflicts. When both Carrera and Barrios died in 1865, Riotte happily noted, "Humanity . . . it seems to me has on the whole gained in losing both of them."[4] For nearly a generation after their deaths, Central America enjoyed relative political tranquility.

Liberals, who had suffered by their close identification with William Walker, slowly reemerged as political leaders across the isthmus. Their political rebirth brought renewed interest in isthmian unity, a trend openly encouraged by Washington. Secretary of State Hamilton Fish therefore directed George A. Williamson, who was appointed minister to all five republics in 1874, to work constructively for their union. But Williamson was typically insensitive to regional politics and soon became disillusioned with Central American leaders who professed faith in isthmian unity but would do little to bring it about.[5] As with later generations of Americans, Williamson had little patience with political figures who valued—and were judged by—their ability to articulate unachievable goals and not compromise in their quest for a settlement. His assessment did not apply to Justo Rufino Barrios, a Liberal who became president of Guatemala in 1871 and who struggled for isthmian unity until his death in 1885. Joined by kindred spirits in El Salvador and Honduras, Barrios fashioned a political alliance among the three governments to combat their Conservative enemies. Little came of their endeavors until February 1885, when Barrios proclaimed the unification of Central America, by force if necessary. The Honduran government quickly approved the Barrios plan in order to shield itself from internal opposition. Traditionally aloof to regional political intrigue, the Costa Ricans demurred. The Salvadorans and Nicaraguans resented Barrios's political interference in their internal affairs. Fearing that a strong union might encourage Barrios to reclaim the state of Chiapas, Mexican president Porfirio Díaz offered to assist Costa Rica and Nicaragua, and assembled troops in Chiapas.[6]

Explaining that his government could not accept a forced union, Secretary of State Thomas Bayard announced that the United States would use its influence to avert a conflict and promote peace. He took measures to ensure that the nation's neutrality laws were not violated and dispatched five warships to the region, ostensibly to protect American lives and property. In the meantime, the minister to Guatemala, Henry C. Hall, worked to prevent an open conflict.[7] Despite these efforts, war broke out on 31 March 1885. Two days later, in the fighting at Chalchuapa, El Salvador, Barrios lost his life. His death brought a quick armistice and revocation of his union decree by the Guatemalan government. In 1887, his successor revived the movement in a conference of the five republics in Guatemala City. The conference achieved several agreements—recognition of each nation's territorial integrity, noninterference in each other's internal affairs, arbitration of mutual international disputes, and establishment of free trade among them by 1890—but failed to craft another union. Their failure, wrote a journalist for *The Nation*, was the inevitable legacy of "jealous officials, unscrupulous rulers [and an] ignorant and hopeless population."[8]

Central Americans failed to achieve political unity, but in twenty years the United States had fashioned tentative but important commercial ties.[9] Though outnumbered and outclassed by British and German merchants, North American commercial venturers, reinforced by increasingly vocal U.S. agents, systematically railed against higher shipping and insurance charges, unfavorable exchange rates, and especially Central America's high tariffs (the chief source of government income) and bemoaned the inadequacy of Caribbean ports.[10]

Commerce, of course, was inextricably tied to foreign markets, which U.S. manufacturing and agricultural interests were already aggressively pursuing, and to the prospects for an isthmian canal.[11] Politics, even more than economics, dictated a more assertive U.S. role in the isthmus and, more consequentially, a departure from the older notion of a neutral waterway. Central Americans wanted a canal; Americans had already begun thinking about a U.S.-controlled canal.

In fact, Washington had signaled its changed priorities in 1867, when it negotiated with Nicaragua a treaty that granted the United States the right of transit on any route across Nicaragua in return for the United States' guaranteeing the route and overseeing its peaceful use.[12] Two years later, President Ulysses S. Grant determined that an American-owned canal was essential to the nation's security and prosperity.[13] He therefore ordered a survey of a possible canal route at Panama, named the Interoceanic Canal Commission to study the entire project, and declared inapplicable the Clayton-Bulwer Treaty's proviso that disavowed exclusive control of a transisthmian passageway. A stronger indication of the singularity of American purpose in Central America was the announcement (prompted by Nicaraguan overtures to London bankers for canal financing) that any large European investment on the isthmus violated the Monroe Doctrine.[14] In 1876, the Interoceanic Canal Commission recommended a canal crossing Nicaragua and using the San Juan River, which was considered less vulnerable to natural disasters and, with its shorter distance between Atlantic and Pacific coastal ports, represented (at an estimated cost of $100 million) a $50 million savings over the Panama route.[15]

Almost unnoticed was the commission's observation that the Clayton-Bulwer Treaty covered only Central America, thus leaving both of the routes at Tehuantepec, Mexico, and Panama open to foreign canal speculators. Americans also gave little credence to reports about a possible French project at Panama. However, in 1879 a French company headed by Ferdinand de Lesseps, who had built the Suez Canal, concluded an agreement with Colombia to construct a canal through Panama, and only then did the U.S. government begin to insist that a transisthmian canal be a U.S. project.[16] President Rutherford B. Hayes reflected Washington's more militant approach when he emphatically declared, "The policy of this country is a canal under American control." The United States, he averred, "cannot consent to the surrender of this to any European power or to any combination of European powers."[17]

As before, Central American Liberals sensed an opportunity in this U.S. assertiveness. In 1880, caught up in the jingoism of the time, the U.S. minister to Central America, Cornelius A. Logan, proposed to the Guatemalan president, Justo Rufino Barrios, the notion that a U.S. protectorate over a unified Central America under Barrios's leadership would not only reinforce the Monroe Doctrine but also clear the way for the construction of a canal by an American concern. Barrios was heartened by the plan, pledged Guatemala's cooperation, and sent a special negotiator scurrying off to Washington. There he found President Hayes resolved to build an American canal but unwilling to support Barrios's unity plan in return for a canal concession.[18]

Despite U.S. reluctance to become involved in Central America's internal politics, three successive secretaries of state, William M. Evarts, James G. Blaine, and Frederick T. Frelinghuysen, repeated the call for a United States–owned canal and the abrogation of the Clayton-Bulwer Treaty, and they charged that any European canal adventure in the Western Hemisphere violated the Monroe Doctrine. The height of the nation's canal euphoria came in 1884, when Frelinghuysen completed a treaty with Nicaragua's envoy to Washington, Joaquín Zavala, by which Nicaragua permitted the United States to construct and jointly administer a canal in return for the latter's safeguarding of Nicaragua's national "integrity." The lopsidedness of the pact, observed the *New York Times*, was understandable: "It is unquestionably true that the Nicaraguan Government did not desire to make this present treaty [but] . . . the will of a mighty nation of 55,000,000 of homogeneous, progressive, and patriotic people is of course irresistible when it runs counter to the wishes of feeble and unstable Governments like those of Central and South America." [19]

President Barrios was characteristically alert to the opportunity. He promised Frelinghuysen that he would personally convey "your final canal proposal" to Nicaragua and guaranteed its approval. As it had done four years earlier with the ambitious Guatemalan leader, the United States, unwilling to become more deeply involved in Central America's fractious politics, demurred. However, the episode clearly indicated that Nicaragua could be readily intimidated. Fearing that Barrios might force its participation in a Central American union in order to achieve a canal treaty, Nicaragua's senate reluctantly approved the Frelinghuysen-Zavala canal treaty. The newly inaugurated Democratic president, Grover Cleveland, who had an apparent distaste for his predecessor's aggressive isthmian diplomacy, withdrew it from consideration in 1885 on the grounds that a commitment to protect Nicaraguan territory contradicted the long-standing principle of avoiding entangling alliances.[20] For the time being, the United States opposed European efforts to construct a canal, retaining the exclusive right of construction, but it was unwilling to become involved in Central American political affairs. The United States intended to benefit from Central America's geographical advantages but not to take on the burden of its problems.

On being reappointed as secretary of state in March 1889 (he had served earlier in 1881), James G. Blaine promoted a Central American union because it supported his continental system, which was designed to end wars between nations in the Western Hemisphere and to advance U.S. commercial and economic influence among them. A tentative beginning in Guatemala ran afoul of Costa Rican, Honduran, and Nicaraguan opposition. Whisked away to Washington for the Pan American Conference and a tour of America's industrial heartland, the delegates appeared amenable to the scheme. They returned to Central America, promptly crafted the Republic of Central America, and then watched in dismay as the effort collapsed in 1890 in yet another isthmian interstate conflict.[21]

Commerce, Investments, and Markets, 1885–1895

As the intrusion of American capital and entrepreneurs into Central America accelerated, the United States government continued to oppose undertaking a canal project itself and, instead, enthusiastically supported private efforts to achieve the same end. In March 1887, A. G. Menocal, a U.S. Navy civil engineer representing the Nicaraguan Canal Association, reached with the Nicaraguan government an agreement that both provided a ninety-nine-year lease on a canal with extensive land grants and freed company employees from forced loans or military exactions. In a concession later considered essential by American entrepreneurs, the company received permission to import, duty-free, materials needed for the canal's construction. Anticipating a spillover of economic benefits, the governments of El Salvador, Guatemala, and Honduras expressed their approval of the project.[22] Only Costa Rica, which had a territorial dispute with Nicaragua, objected. The Ticos got a hearing from the avuncular Grover Cleveland, who judged that they were entitled to compensation but not to any of the canal's toll revenues. With all apparent roadblocks cleared, Menocal's Maritime Canal Company began construction at Greytown in 1890. Three years later, with approximately $4 million spent on dredging the Greytown harbor, clearing the jungle, and doing other preliminary work, the project collapsed, the victim of underfunding, corruption, and Nicaragua's political turmoil.[23]

But other Yankee promoters followed, and they came to a Central America where Liberals and liberalism again flourished. Isthmian Liberals professed faith in positivism, a blend of Auguste Comte's "sociocracy" and Herbert Spencer's Darwinian evolutionary theory. The positivists held that economic growth and prosperity were necessary before true political democracy could take hold. Well into the twentieth century, these "republican dictatorships" remained characterized by their obsession with material development, faith in scientific and technical education, imitation of the values of the United States and western Europe, and, increasingly, postponement of political democracy and insensitivity to workers' needs. President Barrios of Guatemala best expressed their philosophy on how to deal with the Yankee newcomers and those beneath them: "I am not like many Central Americans who think that North American intervention in enterprises . . . is dangerous to the independence and integrity of Central America. . . . What more should we desire if the entire country should go forward in every respect because of that powerful element destroying the ignorance of these masses, . . . redeeming through the stimulus of work and making them understand their rights and duties?"[24]

Central America's Liberals, now politically dominant, enthusiastically promoted diversification of agriculture and development of an export economy, mining, transportation, communication, and even manufacturing. In an effort to advertise their products, the Central American nations participated in world trade congresses such as the industrial and cotton centennial exposition in New Orleans in 1884 and 1885. After 1880, New Orleans's commercial promoters eagerly expanded the city's economic ties with the isthmus, an effort that contributed to its eventual preeminent trade position with the region and, early in the twentieth century, to the Crescent City's being called the "capital of Central America." To attract badly needed foreign capital, the Liberals granted generous concessions, modified tax laws, and suppressed labor. The foreigners who came quickly identified and melded with the local elites.[25]

Except in Honduras, where conditions were not conducive to its production, coffee received the most attention. Governments in the other four countries took steps to stimulate existing coffee production. In Guatemala, for example, President Barrios exempted coffee from export taxes and established government nurseries to grow and distribute coffee plants free of charge to farmers who could not afford to buy them. These steps encouraged increased coffee production, and after 1880 a further impetus came from a worldwide rise in coffee consumption. As a result, the number of acres in coffee production more than doubled, reaching 750,000 acres, between 1880 and 1889. There was a corresponding increase in the demand for an adequate labor supply. Government vagrancy laws forced Indians to enter into contractual relations with *finca* owners.[26]

To avoid the pitfalls of monoagriculture, the Liberals also promoted the production of sugar, cotton, chicle, cocoa, rubber, and timber. Generous concessions, however, continued to favor foreign invest-ment, as typified a rapidly growing economy lacking sufficient internal capital. Thus, in 1894, the H. C. Emery Company of Boston obtained the exclusive five-year privilege to cut mahogany, cedar, and rose-wood in eastern Nicaragua at the modest cost of one gold peso for each log exported and the planting of two seedlings for every tree cut.[27] But for foreigners, mining was the quickest route to profit, especially in the mining boom of the 1880s that swept mountainous Honduras. The mining entrepreneurs' Honduran political benefactor was Presi-dent Marco Aureilio Soto, who exempted from import duties virtually everything they required (machinery, equipment, and materials), ex-cluded ore from export duties and all municipal and national taxes, and granted water and timber requisition rights on adjacent proper-ties. President Luis Bográn subsequently instituted the *mandamiento* press-gang labor system to meet the labor demands of the mining companies. Mining's ancillary economic activities brought little bene-fit to Honduras. Merchants imported most of their supplies from New York. Although local hotel, transportation, charcoal, and salt indus-tries grew, they were considered essential for the mine's daily opera-tions and thus avoided taxation.[28]

In the 1880s, the Honduran government granted a total of 129 min-ing commissions; in the following decade, it granted another 58. At the peak of the boom period, 1888, there were 57 working mines in Honduras. Among the earliest U.S. concerns were Thomas Lombard's Yuseman Mining Company and the Chicago Honduran Mining Com-pany. As the older mines declined and civil war plagued Honduras in the 1890s, foreign investment shrunk drastically, and the country gained the reputation of an investment "rat hole." The most successful operation was the New York and Honduran Rosario Mining Company. The moving force behind Rosario, Washington S. Valentine, wielded sufficient political influence into the twentieth century to earn the title "The King of Honduras."[29]

Each Central American nation needed to develop an internal trans-portation network and ports to advance its economic development.

Private enterprise accomplished much, but it also contributed to local corruption. Foreign companies that received railroad concessions repeatedly failed to raise sufficient capital to complete the project because they repeatedly misjudged the effects of the steep terrain, dense vegetation, and torrential rains. Only in Costa Rica did the North Americans gain immediate profits from railroads.

While North American entrepreneurs could be found in each isthmian country, the most notable railroad man was Minor C. Keith, who supervised the construction of a railroad that by 1911 connected the Caribbean port of Limón with San José. Keith also supervised the completion of the nation's telegraph system, was a leading stockholder in the national telephone company, and financed the electrification of railways and streetcars. He secured his position by marrying the daughter of the prominent Costa Rican José María Castro.[30]

Ports were opened on Central America's Pacific coast, but those on the Atlantic—Livingston, La Ceiba, Puerto Cortés, Bluefields, and Limón—remained dreary clusters of wooden shacks and warehouses with rusting roofs and did not provide regular steamship service to the United States and Europe.[31]

Nonetheless, Americans who settled in Central America chose the isolated Mosquito coast, where Nicaragua's Mosquito Indians proved equally as generous as the Liberal politicians in granting North Americans concessions at low cost and freedom to operate without economic restraints throughout the reserve. They acquired tracts of land for banana growing along the Escondido River and built plantation houses that often rivaled the gracious homes along the Mississippi and other southern rivers in the United States. The land grants were generous, each with three-mile-wide river frontage. Despite poor labor and haphazard planting patterns, by 1885, bananas shipped from Bluefields competed favorably in markets from New York to New Orleans. By 1893, U.S. private interests controlled over 90 percent of the reserve's wealth, enterprise, and commerce, with an estimated value of $6 million.

With the broad privileges received and the pliable Mosquito leadership, North Americans were able to recreate the life-style of any

American town. They had their own churches and newspaper. Their schools, run by Moravian missionaries, were considered as good as any in the States. Bluefields had a bottling plant that produced ginger ale, ginger beer, potass water, champagne, lemonade, sarsaparilla, and seltzer. Patrons of the numerous restaurants and hotel dining rooms enjoyed high-quality wines, liquors, cigars, and "fancy eatables." A German club boasted spacious lounging, reading, and smoking rooms along with a gymnasium. In the midst of the Mosquito kingdom, still under British protection but with titular Nicaraguan sovereignty, the American colony thrived.

Its future became entwined with Nicaraguan politics after 1893, when the Conservatives, who had governed for thirty years, were ousted in a Liberal revolt headed by a young Managuan politician, José Santos Zelaya. Capitalizing on the anti-British sentiment that had been stirred by the British violation of the 1860 Treaty of Managua and on the resentment over the generous concessions made to the Americans, the *Zelayistas* made the Mosquitia, seen as vital to Nicaragua's economic future, a national issue. They advocated running the British out and eliminating the American economic hold.

Under the pretext of a Honduran invasion in February 1894, Zelaya ordered troops to Bluefields to impose martial law. While Zelaya's action brought the British protectorate and the Nicaraguan legal claims into conflict, the American residents at Bluefields either feared for their lives or believed that they would be expelled from the Mosquito reserve. Nicaraguan martial law severely affected U.S. citizens in the reserve. Under its terms, the Nicaraguan government did not recognize any of the concessions made to foreigners by the Mosquito Indians. Further, U.S. insurance firms voided contracts where martial law existed. The Zelaya government also imposed the national export tax on bananas, an action that so infuriated the American residents that they appealed to the State Department for help. Washington hesitated, but London did not. Asserting their right to protect Mosquito Indians from Nicaraguan force, British troops arrived at Bluefields on 2 March to a warm reception provided in part by the Americans residing there. One U.S. resident asserted that "the Monroe Doctrine did not mean to deprive the United States citizens of their rights, or to assist a despotic nation to control a weak and liberal government like the Mosquito." [32]

Two related issues, observed the *New York Tribune*, confronted the United States. Washington "ought not to support Great Britain's right to intervene in Nicaragua's affairs, for that will involve a repudiation of the Monroe Doctrine . . . [and] is in direct violation of the Clayton-Bulwer Treaty." The reality, however, the *Tribune* pointed out, was that American economic interests on the Mosquito coast "will be damaged by the permanent administration of the country" by Nicaraguan authorities. [33]

Nicaragua's foreign minister, José Madriz, denied any hostile intentions toward the Americans but confirmed his government's determination to exert Nicaragua's legal rights over the Mosquito coast. In an effort to assuage American fears and bring acceptance of Nicaraguan authority, Madriz visited the reserve, where he gained the goodwill of the Indians, who were discriminated against by the Jamaican administrators but not by the American and British consuls and citizens. Madriz's vote of confidence to the military government at Bluefields further antagonized the foreigners, who believed that the military's presence threatened their privileged position.

Madriz also failed to impress Washington policymakers, who reluctantly supported the Nicaraguan claim over the reserve. Because of a renewed interest in an American-controlled transisthmian canal through Nicaragua, removal of the British from the region, not the interests of some fifteen hundred Americans residing in the reserve, became Washington's paramount objective. The United States would intervene only to assure the citizens' safety and just treatment in accordance with the policies adopted toward its citizens in other foreign countries. In a curious turn of events, the British invasion had, predictably, aroused American concerns about its own role in Central America, yet Americans living in the reserve passed resolutions denouncing the Nicaraguans for intervening and pledging their support to the deposed Mosquito government.

While the U.S. government took a strong posture, the British became increasingly uneasy about their dealings with the Mosquito kingdom. Their caution was evidenced by their withdrawal of ships from Bluefields and their refusal to support an estimated six hundred Jamaicans ousted from Bluefields in August 1894. In the course of the year, both Washington and Managua were mollified. The Nicaraguan government became more tactful in dealing with the Indians and gained some of their confidence, but the Jamaicans and foreigners remained recalcitrant.

The improved atmosphere provided for the implementation of the 1860 Treaty of Managua and the absorption of the reserve into Nicaragua. In November 1894, delegates from all of the reserve's tribes unanimously consented to incorporation, which permitted Nicaragua to officially take control of the reserve. The act of incorporation was generous. It exempted the Mosquito Indians from Nicaraguan military service and from personal taxes. Furthermore, only Mosquito Indians could hold elected office in the reserve communities and municipalities. Because the Mosquito representatives were unable to write, the U.S. consul and three American officials of the Bluefields city government signed the document for them. With the stroke of a pen, an estimated six thousand Mosquito Indians and fifteen hundred other residents finally came under Nicaraguan authority. The British quietly withdrew, to the satisfaction of the governments at Managua and Washington. The American residents, however, remained at the mercy of President Zelaya.

A Canal under United States Control, 1895–1903

In Central America, the Liberal crusade for foreign investment and the British withdrawal from the Mosquito coast came at a time when several different pressure groups, organizations more powerful than individual entrepreneurs and politicians, surged to the forefront in the United States.

When William McKinley took the presidential oath in March 1897, he quickly found himself pressed upon by a vocal coterie of imperialists, among them Assistant Secretary of the Navy Theodore Roosevelt, Admiral Alfred T. Mahan, and Senators Henry Cabot Lodge, Sr., and Cushman Davis. Their "large policy" advocated a program to make the United States "indisputably dominant over the western hemisphere, possessed of a great navy, owning and controlling an Isthmian canal, holding naval bases in the Caribbean and the Pacific, and contesting, on at least even terms, with the great powers, the naval and commercial supremacy of the Pacific Ocean and the Far East."[34] Two major prizes, Asia and the west coast of Latin America, would not be colonized but economically developed and given the benefits of Western culture. An interoceanic canal became the communications link to these strategic areas.

Mahan became the group's most articulate spokesman. He viewed the acquisition of Hawaii and a transisthmian canal as essential for the operation of a great navy. In 1898, during the Spanish-American War, the ninety-eight-day voyage of the USS *Oregon* around the tip of South America from the Puget Sound to Cuban waters dramatized the need from a strategic position. Chambers of commerce, boards of trade, and resolutions in state legislatures (those of California, Louisiana, New York, and South Carolina) endorsed a transisthmian canal as being in the nation's commercial interests. A common theme to their rhetoric emphasized that a canal would enhance the capabilities of the United States to market its wares in Asia and on the west coast of Latin America. Little was said about potential markets in Central America.[35]

But the isthmus was still vulnerable to the foreign intruder and incapable of sustaining political unity. In 1895, Nicaragua, El Salvador, and Honduras, prompted by the concerns of a nationalistic *hondureño* and suspicious of American entrepreneurs, created a loose federation, the Greater Republic of Central America, but none of the states surrendered its autonomy to the central government. It expired in 1898 with the defection of El Salvador.[36] The continued lack of an effective central government and political democracy only reinforced Washington's century-long impression that Central America's landed elites who contested for political office were motivated merely by greed.

Lacking effective political unity and desperate for foreign capital,

Central Americans again turned to outsiders, yielding to the Liberal insistence on economies based on exports—on coffee, which had both native and foreign producers, and, more important for the development of the Caribbean coast, on bananas. There were feeble attempts to encourage the production of basic foodstuffs to offset the dependence on imports for these necessities, but coffee and subsequently bananas came to dominate isthmian economic life and shape Central America's politics and culture.

Few could have foreseen the "empire of green and gold," [37] because the banana industry had inauspicious beginnings. First introduced to the United States in 1866, bananas wrapped in tinfoil sold for ten cents each at the Philadelphia Centennial Exposition of American Independence ten years later. By the nineties, it had ceased being a curiosity and found a limited market in large cities. By then, two business groups dominated the banana trade from the tropics: Boston Fruit Company, founded by Lorenzo Baker and Andrew Preston, which established seven subsidiaries throughout the Caribbean and marketed bananas in the mid-Atlantic and northeastern regions of the United States; and a consortium of small companies, owned by railroad magnate Minor C. Keith, which shipped fruit from Colombia, Costa Rica, Panama, and Nicaragua to New Orleans and Mobile.

The crucial year for the banana industry was 1899, when the three men created a business alliance of necessity. Their operations hampered by the vicissitudes of weather and Central American politics, they realized that a more constant and reliable flow of fruits could be achieved by spreading their production base to several areas, so that a disaster in one area could be counterbalanced by adequate production in another. Thus the United Fruit Company (UFCO) was born. Within a few years, UFCO became the world's largest banana producer, owning land in Central America and the Caribbean, operating the Great White Fleet, which consisted of nearly forty ships it owned or chartered, and holding title to 112 miles of Central American railroad track, most of it linking the banana plantations to the sea. Early in the twentieth century, UFCO controlled 80 to 90 percent of the bananas shipped to the United States. [38]

By 1900, Central America's export-oriented economies produced a

Table 3.1

United States–Central American Trade, 1870–1900

Year	U.S. Exports to Central America	Percent of Total U.S. Exports	U.S. Imports from Central America	Percent of Total U.S. Imports
1870	$232,478	0.05	$734,565	0.16
1875	784,232	0.15	2,435,151	0.46
1880	1,784,855	0.21	3,313,469	0.50
1885	2,762,531	0.37	6,409,015	1.11
1890	5,296,478	0.62	8,052,444	1.02
1895	6,629,369	0.82	11,580,761	1.58
1900	5,866,579	0.42	8,630,554	1.02

Source: Thomas Schoonover, Department of History, University of Southwest Louisiana, "Compilation of Statistics," Typescript. Used with permission.

favorable balance of trade with the United States (see Table 3.1), but it did not have a positive impact upon the region. While British merchants remained the largest transporters of cargo to and from Central America, they found themselves increasingly challenged by German and American carriers. Only the French share of the market declined. American merchants still realized their greatest profits in trade between the eastern and western coasts of the United States; trade with Central America ranked second.

The ruling Liberals in Central America believed that the development of an export economy would inspire an industrial revolution, which, in turn, would create a society modeled on those of the United States and western Europe. Regrettably, this did not happen. Native capital went into coffee production or investment abroad. Skilled labor and technology were absent. The combined effect was to reinforce Central America's debilitating reliance on the foreigner, who, as one diplomat observed, had the capacity to develop "foundations of control of this rich little country." Many Americans apparently shared this vision. In 1896 the U.S. consul in Nicaragua reported over fourteen hundred inquiries about investment opportunities in Nicaragua.[39] Despite the growing number of U.S. entrepreneurs, the British continued to dominate Central America's foreign community. Yet for both, the rate of return was poor: 4.7 percent during good years in El Salvador, 3.7 percent in Costa Rica, and 1.6 percent in Guatemala. Mining brought few economic rewards, and investment in public utilities yielded income only on outstanding debentures. The aggregate British investment in Central America seldom brought more than 3 percent, and for most of the century it yielded less than 2 percent or no return at all.[40] By comparison, Minor Keith's ventures were handsomely profitable.

Nor did Central America's favorable trade balances bring prosperity to the isthmus. Foreigners dominated not only trade and shipping but also banking, making capital available at high interest rates. Concessionaires controlled the local market for consumer goods, to the exclusion of native residents. As a result, those at the apex of Central America's political and economic structures realized some benefit from the foreign investors, while those at the bottom remained at the subsistence level. Thus, despite the Liberal publicizing, Central America still had the characteristics of a premodern society. In 1898, William E. Curtis told his *Forum* readers that, with the exception of limited advances in Costa Rica, modernity had not yet reached Central America. Misgovernment remained the greatest obstacle to the region's development. Revolutions were a game among the elite, Curtis observed, and the masses, "if left alone[,] may never rebel." Locals with any money invested it abroad to avoid the risks of political turmoil at home. Constitutions, such as El Salvador's, were meaningless, because the country was ruled by a "small group of politicians who maintain their power by military force and are overthrown as often as the opposition can form and carry out a conspiracy."[41]

But to the fin de siècle American strategists, commercial publicists, and missionary diplomats, Central America, even though it was politically corrupt, economically backward, and socially stagnant, posed an irresistible challenge. The quest for a transisthmian canal provided the catalyst for action. By now the move for a canal was fast becoming a national obsession. In 1898, President William McKinley emphatically told Congress, "Our national policy now more imperatively than ever calls for [the canal's] control by this government."[42]

By 1898 the formerly competitive environment of canal building had dramatically changed in favor of the United States. Confronted with the defiant Boers in South Africa and the challenge of imperial Germany, the British retrenched in Central America, yielding to U.S. domination of canal construction. The failure of Ferdinand de Lesseps's project at Panama soured French enthusiasm. With the decline of foreign interest, the debate in the United States now focused on the canal's location. Nicaragua was the perennial favorite and was advocated by the powerful senator John Tyler Morgan of Alabama, considered the most knowledgeable student of isthmian geography. Even so, in March 1899, Congress authorized another canal study by a commission that consisted mostly of engineers. Popularly known as the Walker Commission, its task was a scientific study of potential canal sites.

In November 1901 the Walker Commission issued its first report. As expected, it recommended the Nicaraguan route at an estimated cost of $189 million, as opposed to $149 million for a route across Panama. The figure did not include the $109 million that the New Panama Canal Company, successor to the de Lesseps company, wanted for its rights and properties there. Shortly afterward, the Senate approved the second Hay-Pauncefote Treaty with Great Britain, which, unlike the first treaty in 1900, permitted the United States government to not only construct but fortify a canal.

In early 1902, the House approved the Hepburn bill, putting it on record as favoring the Nicaraguan site. Given this favorable ambience, Secretary of State John Hay, also an advocate of the Nicaraguan route, and William L. Merry, the minister assigned to both Costa Rica and Nicaragua, began negotiations in both Washington and Central America. In the beginning they encountered a hospitable diplomatic climate. Like many of their predecessors, both President Zelaya and Costa Rican president Rafael Igesias believed that a canal would bring economic prosperity to their countries. Zelaya, especially, favored a U.S.-sponsored project on the plausible assumption that, unlike previous private projects, it would come to fruition. Merry shuttled between Managua and San José, promoting the project, suggesting possible treaty provisions, and even disseminating copies of the proposed

Hepburn bill to both presidents. Meanwhile, Hay signed protocols with their governments, for $5 million and $2.5 million to Nicaragua and Costa Rica, respectively, and the United States thus gained the exclusive right to build a canal along their common border and then through Nicaragua.

While Hay and Merry busied themselves with the Nicaraguans and Costa Ricans, forces favoring the Panama route crystallized, particularly after the New Panama Canal Company dropped its asking price to $40 million. In response to the decision, the Walker Commission issued a supplemental report favoring the Panama route, and the Senate Committee on Interoceanic Canals expressed its approval of the Panama location. The increased interest in the Panama site prompted Hay to step up the diplomatic pressure on Costa Rica and Nicaragua, but, just as the Costa Ricans prepared to debate the proposal, Zelaya declared that Nicaragua would not surrender civil jurisdiction in the proposed canal zone. In the meantime, Hay received from Colombia a promising proposal for the Panama route.

The stage was set for a great debate on Capitol Hill, and it began in June 1902. On the Senate floor, Mark Hanna led the cause for Panama, while Morgan appeared to stand alone in favor of the Nicaraguan route. The controversy focused on the physical advantages and cost of each route and the cost of acquiring the French properties. Only occasionally did isthmian politics enter the debate. In the end, the Spooner amendment to the Hepburn bill received narrow approval. It authorized the president to pursue the Panama route first and, only if unsuccessful, to turn to Nicaragua.[43]

Theodore Roosevelt was now president, and he determined to set his own mark by bringing the canal project to fruition. He instructed Hay to commence negotiations with Colombia to obtain the Panama route. The resultant Hay-Herran Treaty in January 1903 granted the United States the rights to build a canal in a six-mile-wide zone across Panama in return for a $10 million cash payment and an annual payment of $250,000. The Colombian senate rejected the treaty in August but instructed renewal of negotiations in the hopes of wringing a greater financial concession from the United States.

The displeased Americans found a willing ally in Panama, where the local citizens unhappily endured Bogotá's political domination. The Panamanians received encouragement from Philippe Bunau-Varilla, who feared losses for the New Panama Canal Company, which he represented. The upshot of their intrigue was a revolt in Panama on 2 November 1903, independence two days later, and U.S. recognition two days after that. Roosevelt did little to conceal his joy at the revolutionary plot, which he at least tacitly encouraged. Bunau-Varilla then negotiated a treaty with Hay in the Waldorf-Astoria Hotel in New York City. When completed on 18 November 1903, without Panamanian representation, the Hay–Bunau-Varilla Treaty gave the United States the same privileges as the Herran Treaty, except the canal zone was widened to ten miles.[44]

Democrats in the United States and leaders in Europe generally criticized Roosevelt's cowboy diplomacy, but there was no public outcry against the U.S. action. *Public Opinion* best summarized the national sentiment when it wrote that the Americans wanted a canal even though "this course of action [cannot] be justified on moral grounds."[45] Latin Americans who had grown impatient with Colombian dalliance acquiesced in Roosevelt's precipitous diplomacy. While some castigated his questionable tactics, commercial interests generally condemned Colombia, congratulated Panama, and condoned the United States.[46]

But in Central America, and especially in Costa Rica and Nicaragua, the abrupt change of canal venue revived a latent anti-Americanism. Costa Rica retreated to its traditional isolation from regional affairs, but the mercurial Zelaya reacted with a vengeance. At first he interfered with the diplomatic mail, discriminated against American businessmen, and resisted settling pecuniary claims. Secure in his position at home, Zelaya correctly assumed that the United States would not intervene in these domestic issues. But when he vowed to unite Central America under his leadership, it meant inevitable confrontation with the United States, whose relationship with the isthmian republics now took on new meaning.

4   The Search for Stability, 1903–1920

The acquisition of the Panama Canal Zone marked a major turning point in the United States' relations with Central America. Under three presidents—Theodore Roosevelt, William Howard Taft, and Woodrow Wilson—the United States encouraged political and financial stability on the isthmus and discouraged foreign intervention in the region, which it now considered vital to its security. Meddling and interfering in Central America's internal politics antagonized virtually every political sector save Nicaragua's Conservative party, which owed its prominence and survival to American bankers and marines.

The U.S. Navy played an important part in carrying out Washington's assertive Caribbean policies. To secure the Panama Canal and the sea-lanes approaching it, naval facilities at Guantánamo, Môle St. Nicole, Samana Bay, the Corn Islands, and Panama took on new importance. The Caribbean squadron, initially consisting of four cruisers and two gunboats, was stationed at Panama and commanded by officers who disdained the region's culture and people. They stood ready to use force to implement Washington's policies and protect American lives and property.

In the same era, Central America experienced significant progress as a result of the Liberal programs initiated during the late nineteenth century. In addition to the building of railroads and port facilities, there were gains in foreign exchange, tax revenues, the exploitation of coastal lowlands, and the eradication of many tropical diseases. Capital cities took on a modern, even European appearance, and national universities received significant attention. Newspaper publication expanded to meet the interests of the growing professional and middle classes. However, the price for progress proved enormous. Foreign

Table 4.1
Central American Trade, 1913–1938

Year	Percentage with Great Britain	Percentage with Germany	Percentage with United States
1913	17.6	21.0	44.6
1929	13.0	17.5	53.4
1938	6.7	18.4	55.8

Source: Ralph Lee Woodward, Jr., *Central America: A Nation Divided*, 2d ed. (New York, 1985), 184.

investors received generous concessions, including monopolies, tariff reductions, and land grants, and they paid little, if any, income tax and, through undervaluation of their properties, minimal real estate taxes. The foreign businessmen mingled with the local elites and, like them, sought to preserve their special status in the economic order by opposing political change. Often, the foreigner became involved in the region's political intrigues.

In contrast to the vibrant capital cities were the outlying provincial towns, such as León, Comayagua, and Totonicapán, which remained isolated and backward. The lowland coastal port cities, such as Puerto Limón, Puerto Cortés, and Puerto Barrios, were cluttered with wooden buildings, ravaged by disease, and populated by imported black Jamaicans and West Indians who built the docks, warehouses, and railroads and became the labor force for the banana industry.

Liberal programs, however, failed to bring industrial advancement, leaving Central America in a dependent economic position. World market conditions dictated the price of its produce, largely coffee and bananas, and the profits went mostly to companies incorporated abroad. The United States increased its share of the Central American trade at the expense of Great Britain and Germany, which tightened the bond of their relationship.

Teddy Roosevelt and the "Big Stick" Era

In 1901, President Theodore Roosevelt set the tone of the United States' policy toward Central America for the next generation when he declared, "Every failure on their part to maintain social order, every economic distress which might give rise to domestic disturbance, every discord between them which could impede their industries, menace their stability, or bring upon them the calamity of foreign intervention would be a misfortune to us."[1] His remarks reflected the understanding of Central America formed by the Americans who visited the region during the nineteenth century and reaffirmed a basic principle of U.S. policy since Monroe's pronouncement in 1823.

Roosevelt was also anticipating new challenges from Europe. Three years later, in the aftermath of a debt crisis that had brought an Anglo-German blockade of the Venezuelan coast, The Hague's Court of Permanent Arbitration upheld the right of creditor nations to use force, if necessary, to collect debts from recalcitrant debtor states. The prospect that European creditors might intervene in the politically corrupt and financially bankrupt Dominican Republic left Roosevelt, as he saw matters, with the choice of either accepting European intervention or assuming responsibility for foreign nationals throughout the region. With the Panama Canal under construction and the assessment that after one hundred years of independence these "incompetent" states would inevitably come under U.S. protection and regulation, Roosevelt chose the latter course. In December 1904, he added a corollary to the Monroe Doctrine, declaring that "chronic wrongdoing" in the Western Hemisphere would force the United States to act as an "international police power."[2] A month later, a protocol with the Dominican Republic permitted the United States Marine Corps to occupy Dominican customhouses. A formal treaty in 1907 created a financial protectorate and the vehicle for an American effort to modernize Dominican society.[3] The Dominican experience became a model for Central American policy.

In Central America, Roosevelt's dicta meant that the inter- and intrastate rivalries and fiscal irresponsibilities that begged European intervention would no longer be tolerated because of their potential threat to the Panama Canal. To ward off the dangers, the Roosevelt administration determined to establish constitutional governments across the isthmus.

Roosevelt had already encountered a defiantly nationalistic and ambitious *centroamericano* in Nicaraguan president José Santos Zelaya, who envisioned himself as head of a Central American union. As Roosevelt began to favor Panama as a canal route, a plan that boded ill for Nicaragua, Zelaya began charting a separatist policy that ultimately conflicted with U.S. prescriptions for Central America. In January 1902, he convened a conference at Corinto, Nicaragua, where the heads of state (except for Manuel Estrada Cabrera of Guatemala, his unrelenting adversary) initialed a treaty requiring compulsory arbitration of regional disputes by the Central Americans themselves. Cognizant of their precarious fiscal status, the leaders rationalized that this agreement would prevent Europeans from forcibly collecting debts in their countries. Zelaya also promised not to aid revolutionary movements in the neighboring republics.[4] As a result, his prestige across the isthmus increased, and four years of a fragile political tranquility followed.

The calm was shattered in May 1906, when a group of Guatemalan exiles, with Salvadoran assistance, invaded their homeland in an effort to oust Estrada Cabrera. Although the rebellion failed, Roosevelt sensed an opportunity to dictate the course of events. Following a futile mediation effort by Minister Lewis Combs, the president arranged for a peace conference aboard the USS *Marblehead,* where representatives agreed to convene a regional peace conference in San José, Costa Rica. Still fuming over the selection of Panama for the canal and citing the 1902 Corinto agreement, Zelaya denounced the interference and refused to attend, but the other leaders, who were on friendly terms with each other and who mistrusted Zelaya's scheming, framed a set of treaties designed to lay the basis for a more permanent peace. Zelaya's resistance to the U.S. peace effort and his apparent desire to dominate isthmian affairs lowered his status in Washington.

The peace was short-lived. Responding to border skirmishes with

Honduran troops in early 1907, Zelaya ordered an invasion. Nicaraguan troops reached Tegucigalpa by the end of March and forced President Manuel Bonilla into exile aboard a U.S. warship. Fearing that the crisis would escalate into a regional conflict and still hopeful of establishing a constitutional government in Honduras, the State Department permitted Washington S. Valentine, an American with extensive mining interests in Honduras, to assist U.S. diplomats in the region in working for a settlement. To their dismay, Valentine suggested that Zelaya be permitted to establish a military government in Honduras as the only means of preventing continued foreign interference in its political affairs. His proposal not only angered the State Department but also united El Salvador and Guatemala against Nicaragua and Honduras.

When Zelaya discovered that the State Department did not approve Valentine's suggestion, he accepted the call by Roosevelt and Mexican president Porfirio Díaz for a general peace conference in Washington, D.C. Zelaya was determined to maintain his prominence in Central American affairs and to prevent the two foreign powers from dictating the course of events, and he tried unsuccessfully to persuade his presidential counterparts to bury their past differences and act in unison in Washington. He also suggested a postconference meeting to broaden the scope of any agreements reached in Washington. Zelaya's actions further contributed to his lowered standing both in the Central American capitals and in Washington. The Washington conference produced several agreements, three of which satisfied the United States' desire for constitutional governments across the isthmus.

The General Treaty of Peace and Amity provided for the nonrecognition of governments that came to power by coup d'état. Further, the treaty banned Central American governments from intervening in each other's internal affairs. Honduras, as the weakest and most vulnerable to outside interference in its domestic politics, was declared neutral. Another accord established the Central American Court of Justice, which was envisioned as a nonpolitical instrument for settling disputes among the five nations. The Americans were pleased with these agreements because they promised regional political stability guaranteed by a treaty system. The Central Americans, on the other hand, were pleased more by the accords that pointed toward union and considered the Central American bureau as most important because it intended to increase cooperation by introducing modern education facilities, developing trade, agriculture, and industry, and reforming legal institutions. Although the Washington conference brought momentary peace to the isthmus, the agreements illustrated the differences between U.S. and Central American policy objectives.

Before Roosevelt left office, the treaty system collapsed when separate revolutionary groups, one supported by Manuel Estrada Cabrera and the other by the former president of Honduras, Manuel Bonilla, sought to oust Honduran president Miguel R. Dávila, Zelaya's protégé. Costa Rica, which was not involved in the dispute, took the issue to the newly established Central American Court of Justice, whose judgment reflected the interests of each country rather than the merits of the case.[5] The decision proved the court's ineffectiveness and put to rest Roosevelt's aspiration to bring constitutional government to Central America through a treaty system.

William Howard Taft and Dollar Diplomacy

Save for the Panamanian intervention and the brief landing of U.S. troops in Caribbean ports, Roosevelt had not used the military to assure isthmian stability, but the apparent failure of the treaty system seemed to call for more drastic measures. In 1909, when Roosevelt left office, there were two "models" for Caribbean protectorates— Cuba and the Dominican Republic—that invited comparison with the Central American states and their attendant political turmoils and financial uncertainties. Roosevelt's successor, William Howard Taft, and his secretary of state, Philander C. Knox, were doubtful about the Cuban model, which in 1906 had required a formal military occupation for order to be restored. They elected the Dominican example of a financial protectorate. As Knox explained, U.S. security interests required the extension "to those little countries that measure of assistance which will render their governments stable and keep them from European intervention."[6] Ignoring the security aspect, critics labeled Knox's refunding projects in Central America "dollar diplomacy" because they benefited U.S. bankers. In its quest for fiscal responsibility, the Taft administration found itself confronted with both regional political intrigues and the self-serving interests of North American entrepreneurs.

In this scheme of things, the nationalist José Santos Zelaya was, of course, a menace. Because of his link to revolutionary plots in Costa Rica, El Salvador, and Honduras, Zelaya became a persona non grata among Washington's policymakers. In 1909, Taft informed Congress that on several occasions the United States had been called upon to defend the 1907 treaties and that "nearly every complaint has been against the Zelaya government of Nicaragua, which has kept Central America in constant tension and turmoil."[7] In addition to threatening regional stability, Zelaya challenged the Monroe Doctrine by allegedly making secret advances to the Japanese in 1909 for a canal treaty and by contracting a loan for £1.25 million with Ethelburga, a British investment syndicate. Secretary Knox reflected Washington's anger toward Zelaya when he implied that the United States might support any nation or alliance of nations willing to oust the Nicaraguan from office.

Knox's call for revolution inspired Nicaraguan Conservatives unable to legally gain political office and businessmen limited in their pursuits by Zelaya's habit of selling monopolistic concessions to his friends. When the governor of the Bluefields district, Juan B. Estrada, with Conservative support, raised the flag of rebellion, the foreign business community extended both sympathy and support to the rebels. Adolfo Díaz, a Nicaraguan employee of the Pennsylvania-based United States–Nicaraguan Commission, served as the conduit for a donation of two hundred thousand dollars from foreign business interests to the rebels. The American consul at Bluefields, Thomas Moffat, also declared in favor of the revolutionaries, and when events turned against the Conservative army, it found refuge in Bluefields under Moffat, the foreign community, and a contingent of American marines brought ashore to protect foreign nationals and property in the town.

Matters worsened when Zelaya ordered the execution of two Americans, Lee Roy Cannon and Leonard Groce, who were accused of planting dynamite charges that killed several *Zelayistas*. In November 1909, Knox rejected a peace initiative put forth by the Mexican president, Porfirio Díaz. Though the initiative provided for Zelaya's replacement with a pro-American Liberal, Dr. José Madriz, Knox was suspicious of Díaz's intentions and the link between Zelaya and Madriz. By a parallel logic, the United States refused to extend recognition to Madriz following Zelaya's abrupt resignation and departure from the country in December 1909. Afterward, however, the United States slowly increased its involvement in Nicaraguan affairs, convinced that each new step would be the last. Instead, the United States sank deeper into a quagmire from which it did not extricate itself until 1933.

The civil war continued until August 1910, when Estrada triumphantly marched into Managua. Despite Estrada's promises to hold new elections and restructure the national finances, the United States withheld recognition on the grounds that Estrada lacked sufficient political support from the feuding factions. In order to bring about a solution that was more satisfactory to the United States, Knox dispatched Thomas C. Dawson to Nicaragua. In November 1910, he negotiated a series of agreements that provided for the abolishment of Zelaya's monopolies and the establishment of a customs receivership and a mixed-claims commission to settle damages to foreign properties. Dawson also completed a political arrangement that named the Liberal Juan B. Estrada as president and the Conservative Adolfo Díaz as vice-president.[8]

Knox maintained that Nicaragua's unstable financial condition encouraged foreign intervention. To correct the problem, in early 1911, the State Department arranged the invitation of Ernst H. Wands to survey the nation's finances. His discouraging report contributed to the subsequent Knox-Castrillo convention, which provided for the refinancing of Nicaragua's foreign and domestic debts with a loan made by U.S. banking interests and secured with customs receipts collected by a third party approved by the president of the United States. Despite the administration's enthusiasm for the plan, the Senate Foreign Relations Committee opposed further involvement in Nicaragua's internal affairs. The full Senate failed to take any action. The ratification of the Knox-Castrillo convention by Nicaragua's constituent assembly did not conceal the nation's growing anti-American sentiment, which boiled over into demonstrations when Knox arrived in the country on a goodwill visit on 5–6 March 1912.[9]

In addition to its financial problems, Nicaragua was plagued by continued political intrigue between Liberals and Conservatives, which eventually led to the resignation of President Estrada in May 1911. The conflict continued between Díaz, the Conservative who followed Estrada in the presidency, and the army's commander in chief, General Luis Mena, whose Liberal followers were decidedly anti-American. War broke out in July 1912, when Díaz, confident of the United States' support, attempted to replace Mena with Conservative Emiliano Chamorro. When the fighting began, Thomas O'Connell and Bundy Cole, the American managers of the Nicaraguan railroad and the National Bank, respectively, convinced the U.S. minister, George Weitzel, that their properties needed protection from the warring factions. Weitzel had little difficulty persuading the compliant Díaz to approve the landing of an estimated twenty-seven hundred marines, for Díaz saw the marines as his savior. The State Department claimed that it had a moral mandate to preserve the general peace under the terms of the 1907 Washington accords, and it also asserted that Mena's forces had taken on the character of bandits who committed uncivilized and savage actions.

The U.S. military officers who played key roles in the intervention—Commander Smedley Butler, Colonel Joseph H. Pendleton, and Admiral W. H. H. Southerland—drew their inspiration from the Boxer Rebellion of 1900, when antiforeign outbursts in China had menaced the social order and were crushed by U.S. and European forces. Butler led a contingent of troops into the country in August 1912, and a month later he accepted Mena's capitulation. Despite the military victory, the United States did not secure the peace. The American presence ensured the scheduled presidential election on 2 November 1912. Díaz won the uncontested race, but he had little popular support. Still, Weitzel remained optimistic that U.S. moral suasion would ensure the safety of civil order, life, and property, but the minister failed to understand that intervention only fueled the anti-American aspect of Nicaraguan nationalism.[10]

While U.S. involvement in Nicaraguan affairs increased, the Taft administration feared a similar situation in Honduras. The most impoverished country in Central America, Honduras was also burdened with the oldest foreign debt—it dated to 1867, much of it accumulated in a succession of efforts to build a rail system. By 1909, the debt, with accrued interest, had climbed to more than $120 million, an amount nearly triple the original obligation. Given the government's annual revenues of approximately $1.65 million, there was little chance for the debt's recovery. In return for the investment, Honduras counted only sixty miles of railroad track, which lay in the banana-growing region of the north coast and was leased to the American businessman Washington S. Valentine. The U.S. government generally ignored the issue of the Honduran debt until 1908, when the British minister to Central America, Lionel Carden, proposed that the debt be restructured over a forty-year period, with the railroad and the dock facilities at Puerto Cortés serving as collateral. Secretary Knox envisioned the loan as a stepping-stone toward a permanent British presence in Honduras, at the expense of U.S. interests. In 1909, in an effort to ward off the British government, Knox persuaded the British creditors to accept a proposal, put forth by J. P. Morgan, that permitted Morgan's banking interests to purchase the outstanding British bonds at 15 percent of their face value. Honduran president Miguel R. Dávila subsequently sent a mission to Washington to deal with the issue. The resultant Knox-Paredes convention provided for refinancing the national debt, establishing a customs receivership, and appointing a U.S. customs collector. President Taft justified the agreement on the grounds that it fell within the purview of the U.S. security and constitutional objectives for Central America, but the Honduran legislature resoundingly rejected the agreement on the grounds that it would turn the country into a U.S. colony.[11]

The debt issue then became entwined in the intrigues of Honduran politics and the ambitions of American entrepreneurs. Ousted president Manuel Bonilla, anxious to return to the presidential palace, teamed up with Lee Christmas, an American adventurer and soldier of fortune equally anxious for military fame and reward. Together they found a financier in Samuel Zemurray, a Bessarabian Jew who arrived in Puerto Cortés in 1905 with plans for building a successful banana plantation. Zemurray correctly assumed that any customs collectorship would prevent him from bringing into Honduras, duty-free, materials essential for the expansion of his Cuyamel Fruit Company, and Dávila's willingness to cozy up to the administration in Washington caused Zemurray to speculate that Dávila might grant more favorable concessions to his company's rival, the United Fruit Company. UFCO did not sit idly by; instead, it proposed its own financial scheme in return for concessions on wharves and railroads. The American minister in Honduras opposed the offer and reported to the State Department that UFCO was unpopular with the Hondurans and that its scheme would give the company too much control over Honduran communications. UFCO's proposal prompted Zemurray to act. Despite their diverse interests, Bonilla, Christmas, and Zemurray had enough in common to become bedfellows in a revolutionary scheme that evolved into a near circus before U.S. Special Agent Thomas Dawson worked out an agreement, in March 1911, that provided for the withdrawal of sitting president Dávila and for elections in October that confirmed Bonilla as president.

Once he gained the presidency, Bonilla tried to be his own man. He shortchanged Christmas by making him nothing more than chief commandant of Puerto Cortés. Bonilla joined a suspicious group of U.S. senators who had cooled to the Knox-Paredes agreement, which caused J. P. Morgan to withdraw his proposed bond purchase. In the process, Secretary Knox's hopes for financial stability in Honduras disappeared. Only the banana companies were left to pursue their own objectives.[12]

The Taft administration confronted greater resistance to dollar diplomacy in Guatemala, where Liberal president Manuel Estrada Cabrera seized the presidency in 1898 and retained power under the guise of a great reformer. By 1913, he boasted of preserving order, encouraging railroad and highway development, establishing compulsory primary education, and improving public health and sanitation. He welcomed foreign capital and granted generous port concessions to the United Fruit Company. According to one journalist, however, Estrada Cabrera, who ensured his control through an army of informers and secret police, was "a robber and a murderer, and his administration [was] to blame for keeping the Indians in peonage, for debauching the public treasury, for starving the army and for pocketing wholesale the public revenues." [13]

Since the 1870s, when Justo Rufino Barrios had encouraged the export of coffee, the health of the Guatemalan economy had become increasingly dependent upon it. Coffee production came under the control of a small group of large planters. The most extensive holdings were in foreign hands—largely German, but some American. Estrada Cabrera recognized that the planters preferred an inflated currency, because they paid their workers in cheap paper currency while they sold their product for gold on the world market. By 1909, the system of unconvertible paper had increased by over 600 percent since 1896, and the peso had dropped to five cents on a par value of one U.S. dollar.

During the same time period, the Guatemalan foreign-bond debt reached $10.5 million (including interest), and the government found it difficult to satisfy the foreign creditors with even the interest payments on short-term loans, much less on the debts' principle. The problem was further complicated by Estrada Cabrera's penchant for negotiating $3–5 million loans nearly every two years with Adolfo Stahl, an American banker residing in Guatemala City. Despite an 1895 government pledge to use coffee revenues to pay international obligations, Estrada Cabrera directed these funds to Stahl. Estrada Cabrera's failure to satisfy foreign creditors led to the establishment of the Corporation of Foreign Bondholders. Founded in London in 1909, it represented the European lenders, most of whom were British.

As early as 1905, Minister Leslie Combs argued that U.S. bankers should set up a financial trusteeship in Guatemala to prevent a violation of the Monroe Doctrine. Before the establishment of the European consortium in 1909, policymakers in Washington had dismissed Combs's suggestion. Afterward, three North American groups put forward fiscal restructuring plans for Guatemala. The first proposal, made by railroad tycoon Minor C. Keith, called for issuing $17.5 million in bonds, establishing a national bank to act as both fiscal agent for the bond sale and customs agent, and setting up an arbiter's role so that the United States could settle any disputes. In addition, Keith wanted some of the funds issued to be used for the construction of port facilities at Puerto Barrios to serve his own business interests. The second proposal, made by the New York banking group J. and W. Seligman, called for issuing $30 million in bonds, with no provision for internal improvements, and for the United States to play a stronger role, including appointing a customs collector. The third proposal, made by the Windsor Trust Company of New York, offered to make a $10–12 million loan, providing that the United States government agree to arbitrate any future disputes. The State Department encouraged Estrada Cabrera to accept one of the first two plans, but he instructed the national assembly to reject all three proposals on the grounds that they infringed upon national sovereignty. Estrada Cabrera then procrastinated. Although he carried on negotiations with the Seligman group, he continually opposed any role for the United States government.

At the same time, the State Department was not averse to outside pressure upon Estrada Cabrera. In 1910, for example, the department refused to become involved with the German demand for claims settlements and a new commercial treaty. Frustrated at Estrada Cabrera's behavior, the chief of the division for Latin American affairs, Percival Dodge, suggested, "I think that we should do nothing to hinder them, provided that they do not go too far." Meanwhile, British impatience increased, prompting its chargé d'affaires in Washington, Mitchell Innes, to assert, "Nothing except a pistol held at Cabrera's head would move such a rascal." The *South American Journal*, a London financial publication, went further: "No one would object to the interests of the world at large, if the United States were to clear out, neck and crop this financial brigand, Estrada Cabrera." Only the threat of British force moved Estrada Cabrera to acquiesce. In May 1913, as the British minister in Guatemala City, Lionel Carden, began preparations to close the legation and the HMS *Aeolus* arrived in Belize, Estrada Cabrera capitulated and agreed both to restore current service on the bonds and to negotiate back interest.[14]

There was no outcry in the United States over the alleged British violation of the Monroe Doctrine, because in this case Estrada Cabrera was even more unpopular than British interference in the Western Hemisphere. Secretary of State William Jennings Bryan sympathized with the British claims against Estrada Cabrera, but he recognized that, if he invoked the Monroe Doctrine, he would be supporting the dictator against Great Britain. The *New York Times Magazine* asserted that Estrada Cabrera should not be protected "behind our coattails." In effect, British action served the purpose of dollar diplomacy.[15]

Looking back, Taft saw dollar diplomacy as an extension of the Monroe Doctrine and a way to secure the Panama Canal, and he was pleased that the American bankers were "willing to lend a helping hand."[16] The Central Americans did not share his view. To them, the schemes proposed by the American bankers, the marines in Nicaragua, the mercenaries in Honduras, and the British gunboats threatening Guatemala all smacked of imperialism.

Woodrow Wilson and the Politics of Morality

In the 1912 presidential election campaign, Woodrow Wilson renounced dollar diplomacy and the special interests that had influenced Latin American policy. Instead, he called for cooperation by hemispheric governments to deter foreign threats. Just as quickly, however, he dashed Latin American hopes for a real change in U.S. policy with his intervention in the Mexican Revolution and continued involvement in Central American affairs.[17]

Despite his professed support of a new Pan-Americanism, Wilson favored constitutional government and disdained the revolutionary turbulence he thought was endemic to Latin America. Thus, when confronted with revolutionary activities in Mexico a week after his inauguration, he reaffirmed the traditional policy: "Just government rests upon the consent of the governed, and that there can be no freedom without order based upon law and upon the public conscience and approval. We shall look forward to make these principles the basis of mutual intercourse, respect and helpfulness between our sister republics and ourselves. . . . We can have no sympathy with those who seek to seize the power of government to advance their own personal interests." [18]

When the outbreak of World War I in Europe in August 1914 raised the possibility of a German threat to the region, Wilson reaffirmed the Monroe Doctrine: "Any foreign influence . . . from outside the hemisphere," he argued, that would be "broadened or extended [so] as to constitute a control, either in whole or in part," of a Caribbean nation was unacceptable to the United States. [19]

Wilson's immediate problem in Central America lay in Nicaragua, where financial difficulties continued despite the considerable influence of American bankers. By 1912, government operating expenses and salaries were again in arrears, and most of the money advanced under the 1911 loan agreement went to pay the fictitious claims of political leaders. American bankers made additional loans in 1913 and 1917 in return for control of 51 percent of the country's national bank and Pacific railroad and the right to manage government expenditures. The bankers also negotiated, on behalf of the Nicaraguan government, a reduction in the interest due British bondholders.

The possibility that Nicaragua might sell canal rights to a foreign nation contributed to a further extension of U.S. involvement in its affairs. Another transisthmian canal under foreign control challenged both the Monroe Doctrine and the U.S. project at Panama. Rumors circulated in 1908 that President Zelaya had encouraged the Japanese to undertake a canal project, and President Madriz's offer in 1910 to cede the Corn Islands to the British caused policymakers in Washington to conclude that Nicaragua, under constant financial strain, might very well strike a deal with a foreign nation. This concern led to the 1911 treaty concluded between the American minister, George T. Weitzel, and Nicaragua's foreign minister, Diego Chamorro. For a one-time payment of $3 million, the United States received the exclusive right to build a canal across Nicaragua, a ninety-nine-year renewable lease on the Corn Islands, and a site for a naval base in the Gulf of Fonseca. Washington officials concluded that the $3 million would stave off European creditors, a small price to pay for securing the Nicaraguan canal route.

The agreement also included the Platt Amendment feature, which permitted the United States to supervise Nicaragua's foreign policy and intervene in its internal affairs. The idea originated with President Adolfo Díaz, who saw it as a means of securing his own position. Emiliano Chamorro (who had aided the Americans in the 1912 intervention) understood Díaz's intentions, too, when he reportedly boasted that the treaty would ensure Conservative party rule in Nicaragua for one hundred years.[20] More to the point was the charge made by Bundy Cole, manager of Nicaragua's national bank: "I think the present government would last until the last coach of marines left the Managua station, and I think President Díaz would be on that coach."[21] The Senate Foreign Relations Committee held the same opinion when it informed the State Department that it would consider the treaty only after the removal of the Platt Amendment.

The canal issue moved to center stage again in June 1914, when Chamorro boasted that Germany had offered to pay up to $9 million for a canal monopoly. Chamorro's claim took on a more serious meaning two months later with the outbreak of war in Europe and the opening of the Panama Canal. Anxious to secure the region from any foreign intruder, the State Department revived discussions with Nicaragua, and the countries arrived at the Bryan-Chamorro Treaty, which contained the same provisions that were part of the Weitzel pact but excluded the provisions of the Platt Amendment feature. When the Senate considered the treaty in November 1915, the public debates focused upon the character of the Nicaraguan government, not the German threat. Senators with diverse interests, such as isolationist William Borah, Republican senator from Idaho, and former secretary of state and internationalist Elihu Root, Republican senator from New York, questioned the legality of Nicaragua's Conservative government and whether it could survive without the United States Marine Corps. Both feared that if the Liberals came to power, they might overturn the agreement with the United States. Only in executive session, in February 1916, did the full Senate debate the aspect of a German canal across the isthmus, and then it did approve the Bryan-Chamorro Treaty. In contrast, the Nicaraguan legislature acted quickly in anticipation of a financial windfall. However, the Nicaraguan government in fact gained little. After the British claims were paid, it received an estimated 30 percent of the $3 million, a small amount for a generous concession.[22] The American presence in Nicaragua—symbolized by the one-hundred-marine legation guard—also made that nation's 1916 presidential election meaningless. Conservative Emiliano Chamorro ran unopposed, because the Liberals boycotted the election when they learned that the United States would not extend recognition to their candidate even if he was legitimately victorious. The Liberals also feared U.S. intervention if they took the presidential palace by force.

Shortly after Wilson took office in March 1913, the fragile Honduran political structure fractured. The death of President Manuel Bonilla was followed by rumors predicting the forced ouster of his successor, Francisco Bertrand. The head of the State Department's Latin American division, Boaz Long, traced the crisis to the nation's history of chronic revolutions, its illiterate and malnourished population, and its lack of political leaders capable of properly exploiting the country's resources and avoiding debt. Believing that dollar diplomacy was the only U.S. option, Long urged Secretary Bryan to endorse one of the financial plans, put forth by American private investors—Minor C. Keith, Samuel Zemurray, and a New Orleans syndicate—to refund the national debt and refinance international obligations in return for concessions that would open the Honduran interior to railroad development and, in turn, contribute to political stability.[23] Both the State Department and the Senate, however, were reluctant to become entangled in another Central American financial adventure.

In addition, Bertrand had reason to mistrust the United Fruit Company, Cuyamel Fruit Company, and the Vaccaro Brothers Fruit Company, whose large tracts of land and generous railroad concessions had enabled them to dominate the Honduran economy. Convinced that the fruit companies had instigated at least two revolts against him, Bertrand determined to secure his own position by allying himself to the Wilson administration. He therefore supported Wilson's call for Pan-Americanism, signed one of Bryan's "cooling off" treaties, and refrained from criticizing the Nicaraguan canal treaty, although many prominent Hondurans saw it as another act of imperialism. In return, Bertrand found solace in the U.S. response to the violence that threatened to surface in 1915, after he announced his intention to stand for reelection despite a constitutional provision forbidding it. Secretary of State Robert Lansing pressured Guatemalan President Estrada Cabrera to guarantee that the neutrality provisions of the 1907 treaty would be upheld in order to prevent the crisis from escalating into an isthmian affair. Lansing also promised to prevent arms shipments to any Central American revolutionary and had the navy send two ships to cruise the Honduran coast. Subsequently, Lansing commissioned a military attaché and asked the Federal Bureau of Investigation (FBI) to investigate charges that the fruit companies were linked to plots against Bertrand, including an alleged invasion of the country led by Lee Christmas.[24] Following his reelection in 1915, Bertrand continued to applaud the United States. His pro-American attitude was not generally shared outside the presidential palace in Tegucigalpa, as evidenced by several revolutionary plots involving the fruit companies. The presence of U.S. naval cruisers in Honduran waters helped to secure Bertrand's presidency until 1919 and also contributed to increased anti-American sentiment in the country.

As the U.S. intervention in Nicaragua and Honduras rankled the opposition in those countries, the Bryan-Chamorro Treaty provoked Costa Rican and El Salvadoran leaders, who asserted that the treaty violated the 1907 agreement prohibiting secret negotiations, the granting of leases on the Corn Islands, and guaranteeing the free use of each nation's territorial waters. The Costa Ricans added that the Bryan-

Chamorro Treaty also violated their rights under the 1858 Cañaz-Jerez Treaty and the 1888 Cleveland Award, both of which prevented Nicaragua from making any canal concessions without consulting Costa Rica. President Alfredo González Flores dismissed Bryan's explanation that the United States purchased only an option to build a canal through Nicaragua, not the actual right to construct one. The Salvadorans protested the bartering away of their rights in the Gulf of Fonseca, which it jointly shared with Nicaragua and Honduras. The Salvadorans also feared that a U.S. canal and naval station in the region would draw Central America into a future war. Both nations took their cases to the Central American Court of Justice, asking it to invalidate the Bryan-Chamorro Treaty and to reestablish the status quo ante.[25]

Considered the centerpiece of the 1907 treaties, the court was weakened by justices who were appointed and paid by their home governments. Its decisions in 1916 and 1917 with respect to the Bryan-Chamorro Treaty reflected both the self-interest of each nation and the general anti-American sentiment across the isthmus. Only the Nicaraguan justice, Daniel Gutiérrez Navas, dissented when the court announced that it lacked the authority to rule on the Bryan-Chamorro Treaty because one of the signatories, the United States, did not sign the 1907 agreement that created the court. The court then affirmed the Costa Rican and Salvadoran claims and ordered Nicaragua to return to the status quo ante. Encouraged by the United States, Nicaragua refused. The Central Americans, embittered at the U.S. interference, made no effort to reconsider the convention establishing the court when it came up for renewal in 1918.[26]

Relations with Costa Rica were further strained by Wilson's response to Frederico Tinoco, who seized the presidency on 27 January 1917. Until then, Costa Rica appeared to be a model for the other isthmian republics. Since the 1880s, it had not experienced the political turmoil of its neighbors. Government expenditures on education and public works gave it the ambience of a progressive nation. Often unnoticed was the pervasive influence exercised by the coffee barons, United Fruit Company, and Minor C. Keith, who depended on political stability to maintain their privileged economic position. Nor did Costa Rica escape the arm of dollar diplomacy. In 1910, the State Department approved a $13 million refinancing scheme, devised by Minor Keith and his associates, to pay British creditors. In return, the businessmen gained the right to appoint a customs collector in case Costa Rica defaulted.[27]

The immediate cause of the coup was the economic adversity brought about by the loss of European markets after World War I began. In response to the economic decline and concomitant loss of government revenues, President González Flores proposed to increase taxes and establish a national bank, both of which struck at wealth of the privileged few, including UFCO. When González Flores was ousted, the State Department learned of the coup from UFCO, rather than its minister in San José. UFCO also recommended the immediate recognition of Tinoco and advised that troops were not necessary because American lives and property were not threatened. Wilson rejected UFCO's advice and determined that Tinoco violated the standards of good government that he expected in Central America, an opinion substantiated in a State Department paper prepared by G. Herbert Stabler. Although Stabler understood that the Tinoco coup was a family affair, he repeated a basic pattern of U.S. policy: recognition of Tinoco might encourage revolution elsewhere on the isthmus, which in turn would threaten the security of the Panama Canal. Moreover, Stabler was convinced that UFCO and Keith had at least prior knowledge of the coup and that they understood that the withholding of recognition also left private business interests in Costa Rica unprotected. Determined to restore constitutional order, Wilson set out to dislodge Tinoco from the presidential palace, but he underestimated the general's support from the landed oligarchy and foreign investors.

Not everyone agreed with Wilson's position. Secretary of State Lansing and the military personnel in the Panama Canal Zone recognized the need for Costa Rican cooperation in World War I. Military authorities in the Panama Canal Zone and John Foster Dulles, sent on a special mission to Costa Rica in May 1917, argued that the withholding of recognition only encouraged German activities in the country. Tinoco also raised the German issue when he capitalized upon his friendship with *New York Times* correspondent Modesto Martínez to plant stories of alleged pro-German plots in Costa Rica, none of which squared with the State Department's assessment of German influence there. Several private lobbying efforts on behalf of Tinoco, including one by John Popham, president of the Costa Rica Mining Company, and another by former secretary of state Bryan, failed to budge Wilson. The president remained adamant: "This is a test case and I am sure that my yielding in it would break down the whole morale of our relations, particularly with Central America." [28]

The Costa Rican economy suffered severely under the weight of nonrecognition. Several New York banks suspended operations in the country, and Washington's influence kept Britain and France from extending loans. Scarcity of consumer goods soon contributed to inflation, which resulted in the issuance of unbacked paper currency. In the face of this adversity, Keith and other prominent Americans purchased the major portion of a bond issue of 2.5 million *colones* in 1917.

Not U.S. diplomatic and financial pressure or the economic adversity brought on by the war but an unauthorized act by U.S. naval commander L. B. Porterfield prompted Tinoco to leave office. Porterfield took the USS *Castine* to the port of Limón on 14 June 1919 and threatened to land marines. Tinoco feared the worst and resigned. Following Tinoco's departure and another show of U.S. force in September, preparations were made for a presidential election in December. It was won by Julio Acosta, who quickly received recognition from the United States.[29] Throughout the crisis, only Nicaragua, whose Conservative government owed its existence to the United States, withheld recognition from Tinoco. On the other hand, El Salvador, Guatemala, and Honduras, all critical of American interventionist policies, extended recognition to the Tinoco administration.

A similar pattern characterized Central America's response to the European war. Only Nicaragua forthrightly molded its policy to conform with Washington's. At first it took only a pro-Allied stance, but four days after the United States declared war against Germany, it did the same. Throughout the war, German nationals and their descendants residing in Nicaragua experienced little discrimination.

Elsewhere, governments were hesitant to follow the American lead. Despite Washington's acquiescence in the British pressure for debt collecting in 1913, Guatemalan president Estrada Cabrera continued to profess friendship toward the United States. He unsuccessfully invited Wilson to visit Guatemala in August 1914 en route to or from Panama for the canal's opening, praised Wilson's Pan-Americanism, signed a "cooling off" treaty as suggested by Secretary of State Bryan, and refused to become involved in the United States' disputes with Mexico. These manifestations did not prevent Estrada Cabrera from declaring his nation's neutrality immediately after the outbreak of World War I. His decision was influenced, not by German submarines threatening the Guatemalan coast or the lingering bitterness over British debt collection, but by the extensive German influence in the Guatemalan economy, particularly in the coffee sector. Some estimates placed 60 percent of the national wealth in the hands of German nationals or descendants. Germany also received the greatest share of Guatemala's exports: in 1913, Guatemalan exports were valued at $14.4 million, of which Germany took $7.6 million, the United States $3.9 million, and Britain $1.6 million. In Germany, Hamburg and Bremen received the largest portion of the Guatemalan coffee crop. In the years preceding the war, German investors controlled one railroad and two electric companies, including Empresa Electrica, Guatemala City's utility.

Events between 1914 and 1917, however, moved Estrada Cabrera into the Allied camp. The German minister to Central America, Kurt Lehman, who worked out of Guatemala City, allegedly developed an espionage system on the isthmus, distributed German propaganda, and was linked to a series of plots aimed at diverting U.S. interests away from Europe. Immediately after the war began, Guatemala lost access to the German market, which contributed to Estrada Cabrera's support for the U.S. call for an inter-American conference to deal with mutual economic problems and his refusal to renew the 1887 commercial agreement with Germany. The economic adversity caused by the war prompted Estrada Cabrera to denounce Germany's resumption of unrestricted submarine warfare in February 1917 and to sever diplomatic relations with Berlin. In the meantime, Estrada Cabrera unsuccessfully attempted to use his pro-Allied stance to gain special advantages from the United States. The Treasury Department denied his request for wartime loans on the grounds that Guatemala was not a belligerent and that it intended the money for nonmilitary use. In September 1917, the Guatemalan president failed to obtain American support in his dispute with neighboring El Salvador and Mexico. Before the year was out, he sent Joaquim Mendez on a special mission to Washington in an effort to circumvent the War Trade Board's proscription list so that surplus coffee and sugar could be sold in the United States and so that spare parts for Empresa Electrica be purchased. The Mendez mission failed because the War Trade Board refused to issue import licenses until the Guatemalan government placed all of its German-owned properties under the control of a U.S.-appointed alien property custodian.

Finally, on 22 April 1918, Estrada Cabrera yielded. Citing "continental solidarity . . . and the bonds . . . existing between" the United States and Guatemala, he declared war on Germany.[30] Immediately, German nationals and descendants became subjected to surveillance and restrictions on their movements. Pro-German propaganda was suppressed. On the economic front, concessions were rescinded; German properties, including plantations, were sequestered; and public utilities were taken over by the government. The State Department forced the acceptance of Edward W. Ames as special agent to deal with enemy alien property. Although he arrived after the war ended, Ames was still responsible for a February 1919 law that provided for the disposal of property owned by Germans. However, by controlling the subsequent negotiations, Estrada Cabrera allegedly profited from the return of most German properties to their original owners, except Empresa Electrica, which was sold to Electric Bond and Share Company, a subsidiary of United Fruit Company.

El Salvador, the country least affected by U.S. intervention but most embittered by American meddling in isthmian affairs and the Bryan-Chamorro Treaty, did little more than declare its "benevolent neutrality." Owing to American intervention in its political affairs, the

Honduran legislature delayed its declaration of war until 19 July 1918, a move designed by President Bertrand to ferret out his political opponents.[31]

Central America's distrust of the United States prompted all the republics, save Costa Rica, to join the League of Nations as a means of curbing Washington's meddling in their internal affairs. The Honduran representative to the Paris peace talks, Policarpo Bonilla, an opponent of U.S. political meddling in his country, best stated the isthmian position when he asked for a clarification of the league covenant regarding the Monroe Doctrine (article 21). Bonilla did not intend to internationalize the doctrine but rather to weaken it in order to deny the United States a justification for future intervention in Latin America. The issue became moot when the United States failed to join the league, a factor that contributed to Central America's dwindling interest in the international organization.[32]

In 1922, Dana G. Munro of the State Department's Latin American affairs division assessed relations with Central America since early in the century. He naively commented that "the energetic insistence by the United States government that these principles [in the 1907 treaties] be observed . . . put an end to the international wars" that plagued Central America.[33] Munro failed to take note of regional political dynamics or the role of American capitalists, which brought together people with different self-serving motives. Often, such political leaders as Adolfo Díaz in Nicaragua and Francisco Bertrand in Honduras allied themselves with U.S. policy objectives for the sole purpose of securing their own political positions. Likewise, American businessmen—Minor C. Keith, Washington S. Valentine, and Samuel Zemurray, for example—allied themselves with local political factions and cozied up to U.S. ministers in order to protect their own investments. This uneasy trilateral relationship only increased Central America's political fragility and heightened anti-American sentiment. Moreover, none of the participants took note of the growing socioeconomic disparities between the elite and the masses in Central America.

5 Abandoning Intervention, 1920–1940

In 1933, Secretary of State Cordell Hull told the delegates assembled at the seventh inter-American conference in Montevideo, Uruguay, that "no government need fear any intervention on the part of the United States under the Roosevelt administration."[1] Hull's pronouncement reflected a decade of changing thought regarding the wisdom of attempting to impose constitutional order upon Central America. With the threat of European intervention sharply diminished, and wearied by its own interventionist policies, the United States was presented with the opportunity to lessen its direct involvement in the region's internal affairs.

As the United States slowly disengaged, new and more dynamic forces surfaced in Central America as the impact of previous Liberal policies took hold. Nationalist groups decried the political legacy of U.S. intervention and the economic and social disparities wrought by the operations of foreign capitalists. For the moment, the protest against U.S. interference remained in the hands of diplomats and journalists, but the outcry against economic imperialism soon became violent. In the late 1920s and early 1930s, Augusto C. Sandino and Augustín Farabundo Martí, with their armed followers, crossed the Nicaraguan and Salvadoran landscape, calling attention to the plight of the exploited masses. Local ruling elites, opposed to any change in the established order, moved to crush both revolts. They found sympathy among foreign businessmen anxious to protect their investments and among U.S. policymakers anxious to promote constitutional order.

The High-Water Mark of Constitutionalism:
The 1923 Central American Conference

After World War I, the sense of regional unity that had developed in response to the United States' policies from 1900 to 1917 contributed to the renewed desire for a Central American union. To that end, in late 1920 isthmian presidents gathered in San José, Costa Rica, where the Guatemalans, Hondurans, and Salvadorans agreed upon a federal constitution. Nicaragua, prodded by the United States, subsequently approved the agreement. Only Costa Rica remained noncommittal. Although President Warren G. Harding believed that the proposed union would contribute to regional political stability, facilitate U.S. investment, and limit Mexican influence, he withheld recognition until the unified government demonstrated its ability to function effectively.[2] Unfortunately, the attempt at union shortly collapsed. For nearly fifteen years after World War I, the Central American republics returned to their historical pattern of state rivalries, with the exception of Costa Rica, which returned to its traditional aloofness from regional affairs.

After the overthrow of Guatemalan president Carlos Herrera in 1921 began a new round of political intrigue that eventually pitted the Liberal governments in Tegucigalpa and Guatemala City against the Conservative governments in San Salvador and Managua. When a series of border incidents threatened to embroil the entire isthmus, the United States persuaded the presidents of El Salvador, Nicaragua, and Honduras to meet on the cruiser *Tacoma* in the Gulf of Fonseca in August 1922. There they reached a peaceful settlement and, at the United States' encouragement, called for a meeting of representatives from the five Central American countries to convene in Washington in December 1922.[3]

U.S. policymakers saw the conference as an opportunity to reinforce the 1907 treaties, adopt an arms limitation agreement, and create tribunals of inquiry to settle disputes that could not be resolved through normal diplomatic channels. The goal was the same as it had been since 1903: the establishment of political stability in Central America by inculcating respect for constitutional government and discouraging political change obtained through revolution. Aware of the region's historical record of failure in introducing unionist schemes, the State Department discouraged discussion of that subject at the conference. Central America's political history also prompted Secretary of State Charles Evans Hughes to speculate that marines might be needed to ensure regional peace, but he wanted to avoid any treaty commitment, which he believed the Senate would in any case reject. In contrast, the rivalrous Central American governments failed to develop any common set of objectives for the conference, an omission that contributed to the United States' domination of the proceedings.

The conference ended on 7 February 1923 with the signing of twelve agreements, five of which reflected American policy objectives. Washington's continued quest for constitutional order was spelled out in article 2 of the General Treaty of Peace and Amity, which provided for nonrecognition of governments that came to power by a coup d'état or revolution, even if eventually legitimized by free elections. Excluded from serving as heads of state were revolutionary leaders, their close relatives, and high-ranking civilian and military officials who had been in power six months before or after the event. The Central Americans further agreed not to interfere in each other's domestic affairs, assist exiles or contending parties, or harbor revolutionaries. The second accord established international commissions of inquiry that could be activated by any party to a dispute and that possessed the authority to conduct impartial inquiries and issue nonbinding reports, including recommended solutions to disputes among the Central American nations. The third accord created a new Central American tribunal to settle all disputes not reconciled through regular diplomatic channels. In an effort to eliminate the nationalistic politicking that had plagued the preceding court, the signatories agreed that the new tribunal would be composed of jurists selected from a list submitted by each signatory, including the United States. Next, an electoral projects commission was established to codify voting procedures and verify election returns in each nation. In effect, every threat to the established order that Central America had experienced after 1907 was declared illegal.

Influenced by the worldwide call for disarmament after World War I and the success of the 1922 Washington Naval Disarmament Conference, the United States insisted on the arms limitation agreement, confident that it would remove the military as an arbitrary domestic political force, relieve each nation from an excessive military budget, and bring an end to interference in each other's domestic affairs. The United States also wanted to replace the politicized standing armies with nonpolitical national constabularies. Although Central Americans agreed in principle to arms reduction, each state was concerned with its own needs for internal order and border defense and was reluctant to replace standing armies with national guards. In the end they agreed to a formula fixing the overall size of each military for a five-year period: Guatemala, 5,200 men; El Salvador, 4,200; Honduras, 2,500; Nicaragua, 2,500; and Costa Rica, 2,000.[4]

Hughes was satisfied with the new treaty system because it protected U.S. interests and improved upon the 1907 accords, but he pessimistically noted that coups d'état were "about the only reform measures available . . . to dislodge corruption" and that there was "considerable force in the argument that these peoples [Central Americans] are entitled to their revolutions." However, without the treaties, the door would be opened to perpetual revolutions, "thus forestalling the possibility of really democratic government" in Central America. Ominously, Hughes reminded the Central Americans that the United States could not "tolerate much disturbance in the Caribbean region because of the vital importance to our self-defense of the Panama Canal."[5]

The five treaties that the United States considered essential for the region's political stability had varied fates. Only two—the General Treaty of Peace and Amity and the arms limitation agreements—were ratified by all five Central American governments. El Salvador rejected both article 2 of the general treaty and the tribunal treaty. Costa Rica rejected the commissions of inquiry agreement. The electoral reform pact was approved by just Nicaragua and Honduras. Only after the United States Senate ratified the inquiry commissions convention in January 1925, Costa Rica, Guatemala, and Nicaragua followed suit.[6] If Central America's response to the 1923 treaty system was an omen, the future looked dim for constitutional order and political tranquility in the region.

Intervention Again, 1924–1933

Whereas Charles Evans Hughes had looked upon the 1923 treaty system as an opportunity to bring progress to Central America, the assistant chief of the State Department's Division of Latin American Affairs, Stokeley W. Morgan, did not. He pointed out that, historically, the party in power in any Central American country always supported a treaty system and sought U.S. assistance to enforce the treaty system, but the party typically wanted no interference in its control of elections. He suggested that the party out of power would want to be made an exception to the provisions of article 2 and would ask for U.S. supervision of elections.[7] For the decade after the Washington conference, Morgan's judgment proved correct.

The ink had barely dried on the 1923 treaties when a crisis developed in Honduras. The Liberal party of President López Gutiérrez was split over the issue of succession, and the exiled Conservatives, with Nicaraguan aid, were making border incursions. Secretary Hughes refused the Guatemalan suggestion that a conference be convened to settle the issue, because he knew that Guatemala would work for the Liberals, Nicaragua and El Salvador, for the Conservatives. Hughes also warned that whoever gained power would have to satisfy article 2 of the 1923 treaty. Subsequently, Conservative Tiburcio Carías won the October 1923 election by a plurality, but not a majority, over his two Liberal opponents, Policarpo Bonilla and Juan Angel Arias. When the Honduran congress failed to come to grips with the issue, Carías took to the countryside with an armed force and declared himself president.

In the civil war that followed, American lives and property were threatened. The U.S. legation in Tegucigalpa was fired upon. Along the north coast, from Puerto Cortés to La Ceiba, the property of the foreign fruit companies and American-owned homes and shops were attacked and looted. Much of the anti-American sentiment could be traced to the United Fruit Company, Cuyamel Fruit Company, and Vaccaro Brothers Fruit Company, whose economic exploitation was made possible by the generous concessions they had received. In the face of the violence, the companies wanted to know which faction the U.S. government intended to support so that they could do the same in order to protect their own privileged positions in the Honduran economy. UFCO, which supported Carías during the 1923 election campaign, continued to do so once war erupted. The Cuyamel Fruit Company provided assistance to the opposition Liberal faction, and a U.S. government embargo on arms shipments to Honduras did not prevent Cuyamel from shipping arms through Nicaragua. Shortly after the fighting broke out, U.S. naval ships patrolled the north coast, but as the violence continued, the consuls at Puerto Cortés and La Ceiba asked for bluejackets to come on land and protect the property of the fruit companies that supported the warring factions. Meanwhile, in Tegucigalpa, the inexperienced U.S. minister, Franklin T. Morales, requested the marines to protect foreign lives and property there.

Finally, in April 1924, Sumner Welles was dispatched to Honduras to bring the crisis to an end. He issued only a mild rebuke to the fruit companies for their political intrigue and proceeded to work out an agreement aboard the USS *Milwaukee* on 28 April. The agreement paved the way for the election of Conservative Paz Barahona in December 1924, but only because the Liberals abstained. Acceptable under the terms of the 1923 treaty, the United States and the other four Central American countries extended recognition to Paz Barahona and for the next eight years Honduras enjoyed political tranquility.[8]

Already wearied of its commitment to guarantee orderly government in Nicaragua, the United States determined to withdraw the marines from the country following the implementation of electoral reforms that would ensure a graft-free presidential contest in 1924. To that end, the State Department sent the president of Princeton University, Harry W. Dodds, to Nicaragua. The Dodds mission was destined to fail because the Conservatives viewed reform as a threat to their position, while the Liberals saw it as their opportunity to return to the presidential palace for the first time in thirteen years. In the end, a ticket combining Conservative Carlos Solórzano for president and Liberal Juan B. Sacasa for vice-president won the tainted 1924 election. The election, however, did not bring an end to other problems that contributed to Nicaragua's volatile political atmosphere. The government's refusal to establish a constabulary meant that the politicization of the army continued, and at a heavy cost to the national treasury. Moreover, the rising tide of nationalism demanded that the government reclaim ownership of its main railroads and national bank and that it become financially independent of the United States. Still, the United States extended recognition to the Solórzano administration and scheduled the marines' withdrawal for August 1925. As expected, soon after the marines departed, the forces of the Conservative general Emiliano Chamorro struck, forcing the beleaguered Solórzano to resign and Sacasa to flee to Honduras in 1926. For the moment, the State Department refused to intervene beyond withholding recognition from Chamorro in accordance with the provisions of article 2 of the 1923 treaty.[9]

By this time Mexico had emerged as a factor in Nicaraguan politics and concomitantly in U.S. policy. Following the conclusion of the Mexican Revolution in 1917, President Venustiano Carranza extended encouragement and aid to Liberals across the isthmus in their quest to overthrow Conservative governments supported by the United States. In Nicaragua, the "Carranza Doctrine" meant support for the followers of the former president, José Santos Zelaya. In addition to these political considerations, the socialist ideas that sparked the Mexican Revolution found expression in the Nicaraguan labor movement, which was represented in the government by Vice-President Sacasa. When Sacasa was forced into exile, Mexican president Plutarco Calles supported his return home. In June 1926 the two reached an agreement under which Sacasa's invading army received Mexican arms.

While the U.S. Marines expelled Sacasa's troops from Puerto Cabezas, in Washington, President Calvin Coolidge and Secretary of State Frank B. Kellogg concluded that Mexican assistance to Sacasa was part of a larger scheme to spread Bolshevism across the isthmus and ultimately to threaten the Panama Canal.[10]

Mexico's interest in Nicaragua provided a rare moment for cooperation between the United States, Costa Rica, Guatemala, and El Salvador. The leaders of the Central American countries shared Washington's belief that socialist Mexico intended to use Nicaragua as a base from which to spread its influence throughout the region and in so doing threaten the established order. While the Salvadoran government did little more than express its regret at extending recognition to Nicaragua, Costa Rica and Guatemala went further. Costa Rican president Ricardo Jiménez, reflecting both his country's long-standing mistrust of Nicaragua and his awareness that its military was insufficient for resisting external aggression, secretly encouraged the United States to take some action against Mexico. When it did, however, he failed to publicly embrace the U.S. interference. Costa Rica and Guatemala subsequently offered to mediate the conflict, only to be rebuffed by the Nicaraguan government because neither had extended recognition to it.[11]

Confronted with opposition at home and abroad, the embattled Chamorro accepted a U.S. offer of twenty thousand dollars and safe transit to Europe, an event that permitted Conservative Adolfo Díaz to complete his presidential term. Díaz received U.S. recognition after assenting to Washington's demand that a U.S. military mission organize and train a national constabulary. The Conservative governments in Honduras and El Salvador followed the American lead, while the Liberal administration in Guatemala withheld recognition. President Jiménez correctly observed that the whole affair violated the nonintervention provisions contained in the 1923 Central American treaties.

The installation of the Díaz administration failed to solve Nicaragua's political crisis, and it also contributed to the United States' deepening involvement in its internal affairs. Continued civil strife prompted President Coolidge to order the return of marines to Managua on 6 January 1927 on the grounds that continued Mexican influence in Nicaragua "put in jeopardy the rights granted . . . to the United States for the construction of a canal, [and threatened] large investments in lumbering, mining, coffee growing, banana culture, shipping and also in general mercantile and other collateral businesses," as well as foreign-owned bonds.[12] State Department analysts believed that Coolidge overemphasized the business component of the problem and that he missed the overriding issue, which was, as explained by Under Secretary Robert Olds, that the Nicaraguan crisis was a test as to "whether we shall tolerate the interference of any other power [i.e., Mexico] in Central American affairs or insist upon our own dominant position there."[13] By April 1927, some two thousand marines were in the country, allegedly to protect American property, but they were also exchanging gunfire with the combatants.

Despite being confronted with increased complications in Nicaragua, Coolidge remained determined to restore constitutional order and eliminate foreign influence. He selected former secretary of war Henry L. Stimson to seek a negotiated settlement of the political crisis. Stimson fully understood that if he failed in his assignment, the only alternative was a solution imposed by the U.S. military. Both Díaz and opposition leader General José Maria Moncada also understood this. "The forces of the United States are . . . sufficient to do what they please with our little country," Moncada admitted.[14]

Stimson worked out a truce acceptable to all the factions except that led by Augusto C. Sandino, who took to the hills in defiant resistance. Stimson's agreement provided for the U.S. Marines' supervision of the 1928 election, won by the Liberal José Maria Moncada. By stretching its interpretation of article 2 of the 1923 treaty, the United States extended recognition to Moncada's administration, but it failed to prevent him from instituting repressive measures that led to the U.S. Marines' supervision of the 1930 congressional election as well.[15] Just as it had done seventeen years before, the United States sought to impose order, and in the process it violated the spirit, if not the text, of the treaties it had crafted.

Moncada's acquiescence apparently validated Washington's deci-

sion to intervene. Over the next four years the United States dominated Nicaraguan politics through a number of vantage points and
offices—the American embassy, the high commissioner of customs,
the directors of the railway and National Bank, army and marine officers, and the National Guard.

But Sandino's defiance was symptomatic of the anti-Americanism
that had been taking shape in Nicaragua since the 1912 intervention.
Sandino had left Nicaragua in 1920 to escape arrest for his shooting of another man. He first went to La Ceiba, Honduras, where he
worked for three years as a mechanic and warehouseman for the
Vaccaro Brothers Fruit Company (subsequently Standard Fruit Company). From La Ceiba, Sandino went to Tampico, Mexico, a modern
and bustling city populated by a mix of people from around the world
who had been attracted there by the lure of oil wealth. In Tampico,
Sandino joined the Masonic order and encountered new political and
social ideas that later shaped his own attitudes. Nor was the efferves-
cence of ideas characterizing the Mexican Revolution lost on him. In
Mexico, labor unions demanded economic and social justice for the
workers at the expense of the American-owned oil companies. Mexican nationalism, especially the exaltation of the country's Indian heritage, inspired him. Sandino also suffered the taunts of Mexicans, who
saw his native Nicaragua subjugated by the same Yankee imperialism
from which Mexico had escaped in its revolution. The Mexican experience influenced Sandino's ideas regarding the rights of the working
man and government's social responsibility and nurtured in him a
strong anti-American sentiment. Indeed, Sandino later claimed that
he told fellow oil field workers of his intention to return home to take
up arms against the United States.

Responding to his father's request that he come home, Sandino arrived in Niquinhomo in June 1926 with approximately five hundred
dollars in his pocket. After a brief visit with his family, Sandino set
out for the Nueva Segovia district, where he found employment with
the American-owned San Albino gold mine as an assistant paymaster
"because he was too well educated to work as a peon."[16] At San
Albino, Sandino lectured to the workers about the injustices under

which they labored and about Mexican social legislation that had improved the workers' quality of life. Sandino's agitation earned him a following, and he was encouraged to take action. With three hundred dollars of his savings, Sandino armed a band of twenty-six men that on 2 November 1926 struck at the government garrison at Jarico, near San Albino, and were decisively beaten. From the defeat Sandino learned that he and his small band of followers could not act alone, and they therefore set out for the constitutionalist stronghold at Puerto Cabezas. There they were rejected by both President Sacasa and his war minister, General Moncada, because Moncada distrusted Sandino's talk of "the necessity for the workers to struggle against the rich and other things that were the principles of communism." As for Sandino, he was not surprised at Moncada's acceptance of Henry L. Stimson's peace offering in May 1927, because Sandino had always thought that Moncada would "at the very first opportunity sell out to the Americans." [17]

Tired of the United States' imposing its solutions, Sandino became convinced that he was "the one called to protest the betrayal of the Fatherland." [18] With his followers, he slipped off to San Rafael del Norte to take up his cause. A strong argument can be made that Sandino had a twofold purpose in his war: one was to defeat Moncada, for his submitting to the Americans and returning the country to its traditionally corrupt political practices, and the other was to free his country of the Yankee imperialists.

The war lasted for six years, waxing and waning from mid-1927 until 1933. Sandino's forces, never more than a thousand strong, usually averaged half that number. Despite their superior number and firepower, however, the government troops never gained control of the battlefield. The U.S. Marines remained in Nicaragua to supplement the neutralized National Guard, a move that so frustrated the government that, after winning the 1928 election, Moncada organized "volunteer" groups to chase Sandino. But the volunteers' terrorist tactics only served to increase Sandino's local popularity and, with it, anti-American sentiment. As time passed, the Sandino affair drained the Nicaraguan national budget.

Initially, U.S. officials described Sandino as a "bandit" who could be quickly defeated. Stimson claimed that Sandino and his men were "common outlaws" whose "activities cannot be considered to have had any political significance whatsoever." In June 1927, Captain G. D. Hatfield of the U.S. Marines warned Sandino that if he did not surrender, the marines would "finish you and your forces once and for all." Two months later, U.S. officials in Nicaragua believed that Sandino's troops had disbanded and fled down the Coco River. But American confidence was shattered by year's end: American mining engineers reported that their workers, having been converted to "radicalism and Bolshevism," had become increasingly anti-American; coffee and cattle barons in northern Nicaragua asked for marine protection; and the Standard Fruit Company, operating on the Atlantic coast, was forced to hire guards at annual salaries of ten thousand dollars in order to protect their properties.[19] This last measure was to no avail. Standard Fruit's properties at Cabo Gracias a Dios and Puerto Cabezas were looted and its radio station put out of commission by Sandinista forces. In response to the company's appeal for protection, Secretary of War Stimson authorized the landing of troops at Puerto Cabezas.

The U.S. Marines subsequently warned all travelers and pack trains in Nicaragua's northern region to give prior notice of their movements to avoid being bombed by patrolling aircraft. But Sandino remained elusive, even slipping away from the marines in January 1928, when they assaulted his headquarters at El Chipote. Sandino's success caused American officials to drop the bandit classification in 1928 and label Sandino and his followers as guerrillas. Although Sandino survived, the national revolution he hoped for never materialized.

The United States found itself alone in pursuing Sandino. Journalists throughout Central America unanimously opposed U.S. intervention in Nicaragua, although they did not portray Sandino in favorable terms. The search for stability was viewed as an act of political imperialism that only promised greater turmoil. The governments in Central America did not want to become involved in Nicaragua's domestic affairs, fearing that such action might encourage revolutionaries at home. Nor did the United States gain support from the other Latin

American nations at the sixth inter-American conference meeting in Havana in 1928.

At home, opposition to the administration's interventionist policies in Nicaragua surfaced near the end of the decade. In 1928 the Democratic party denounced all forms of imperialism, including the supervision of elections in foreign countries and executive agreements that drew American forces into foreign wars. Sandino's crusade also drew public attention. Writing in *The Nation,* Carleton Beals portrayed him as a national hero struggling against foreign oppressors.[20] The All-America Anti-Imperialist League sponsored emotional meetings featuring Sandino's half brother Socrates, who compared the Nicaraguan rebel to George Washington, Simón Bolívar, and José de San Martín. President Herbert Hoover was confronted with, in addition to the increasingly vociferous opposition, continuing lists of dead marines and a stalemate on the battlefield. Finally, in 1930, Hoover concluded that it was time for the United States to withdraw from Nicaragua. Admitting to a hopeless situation, the State Department announced on 13 February 1931 that the United States would end its occupation shortly after its supervision of the 1932 Nicaraguan presidential election. On 2 January 1932, the same day the marines departed from Nicaragua, the State Department announced "the termination of the special relationship" with that Central American country.[21]

The end of the special relationship, however, did not terminate the social impact of the U.S. Marines. They had brought baseball to Nicaragua, and the sport's popularity led to the organization of a league that included teams from Managua, León, and Masaya, with the marines acting as umpires. Despite the commingling, most Nicaraguans still disliked seeing their Catholic daughters accompanied by Protestant nonbelievers.[22] Fascination with American games and gadgetry was tempered by mistrust of American social values.

The marine withdrawal was followed by a peace agreement signed on 2 February 1933 by Sandino and the newly elected president, Juan B. Sacasa, a Liberal. The agreement provided for, in addition to an immediate bilateral cease-fire, amnesty for Sandino's forces and a land cession to them in the Coco River region for the establishment of a cooperative farm. To the former foreign interloper, Sandino asserted, "I have nothing against the North Americans personally, . . . so let them come here to work. However, I will not accept them coming as bosses again. . . . I send my greetings to the American people." In a subsequent letter to the *New York Herald Tribune*, Sandino offered his condolences to the families of Americans killed in Nicaragua.[23]

While the Nicaraguan crisis drew the most attention, events in Guatemala and El Salvador brought an end to the work of the 1923 Washington conference. The Guatemalan political climate enabled the United Fruit Company to expand its holdings. In 1926, President José María Orellana granted the company legal status in the country, a twenty-five-year, tax-exempt lease on additional territory along the Caribbean coast, and a monopoly on the region's maritime trade. By the end of the decade, UFCO dominated Guatemala's banana industry. At the same time, the nation's political tranquility and the company's privileged position became threatened. In December 1930, Guatemalan president Lázaro Chacón became incapacitated by a cerebral hemorrhage, prompting the cabinet to select and congress to confirm second designate Baudillo Palma as provisional president. Political rivals continually threatened his position and led to a coup d'état engineered by General Manuel Orellana on 16 December 1930. The United States immediately withdrew recognition on the grounds that Orellana had violated article 2 of the 1923 treaty. Secretary of State Henry L. Stimson persuaded the other Central American governments to do the same.

Determined to influence events in Guatemala, the State Department instructed Minister Sheldon Whitehouse to work for the restoration of what it considered constitutional government. Whitehouse subsequently persuaded Orellana to resign and the legislature to appoint José Maria Reina Andrade as provisional president. Although Reina Andrade's appointment was technically unconstitutional, he was acceptable to Washington because his appointment did not violate the 1923 treaty. Whitehouse then arranged the presidential election held on 14 February 1934. The candidate for the Liberal Progressive party, Jorge Ubico, ran unopposed because both Conservatives and Liberals remained on the sidelines in protest of the U.S. interference. Since Ubico was not identified with Orellana's revolt and his election to the presidency did not violate any of the provisions in article 2 of the 1923 treaty, the United States extended recognition to him. Throughout the crisis, Samuel Zemurray, who had replaced Minor C. Keith as UFCO's chief executive officer, remained neutral in order not to antagonize any of the rivals. When Ubico emerged victorious, with U.S. approval, Zemurray championed his cause, confident that the company's privileged position was again secure.[24]

If Washington had its way in Guatemala, it did not in El Salvador. There, the 1931 presidential campaign became an acrimonious affair when the incumbent president, Pio Romero Bosque, failed to name a successor. The fraudulent election, won by candidates Arturo Araujo and Maximiliano Hernández Martínez, only contributed to increased tensions until a coup in December 1931 forced Araujo to flee to Guatemala. A military directorate, headed by vice-president and war secretary Maximiliano Hernández Martínez, took over the government, and Hernández Martínez announced his assumption of the presidency in accordance with the constitution. He dissolved the military directorate and formed a new cabinet, approved by congress. The State Department did not hesitate to withhold recognition from Hernández Martínez, despite its failure to link him to the coup and the fact that El Salvador had not ratified article 2 of the 1923 treaty. In January 1932, the State Department dispatched Jefferson Caffrey to investigate the situation. Because Caffrey was already prejudiced against Hernández Martínez, he refused to discuss the legality of his administration, and his final report only reaffirmed the department's conclusion that Hernández Martínez had come to power through revolution and was therefore not entitled to recognition under the terms of article 2. Washington's position stiffened later that same year, after Hernández Martínez used an allegedly Communist revolt in the countryside to delay elections until at least 1935.[25]

In both instances the other Central American governments followed the United States' lead in withholding recognition. With the exception of Costa Rica, the other governments believed that, by upholding article 2 of the 1923 treaty, they secured themselves against revolutionary ferment at home.

American policymakers were preoccupied with the treaty system, not the challenge El Salvador faced because of its stagnant economic and social order. The symbol of change came to be Augustín Farabundo Martí, the son of a mestizo hacendado and, for a brief time, a student at the national university, where he became acquainted with socialist and Marxist-Leninist ideas. Following his expulsion from the country in 1920 for espousing radical ideas, Martí spent five years traveling in Central America and the United States. He became a founding member of the Central American Socialist party, established in Guatemala in 1925. Martí returned to El Salvador the same year to become a propagandist for the Regional Federation of Salvadoran Workers, a position that brought him a short sentence in jail. Afterward, Martí again left El Salvador to join Sandino in his fight against the United States, only to break with the Nicaraguan in 1929 because he "would not embrace my communist program. His banner was only that of national independence . . . not social revolution."[26] In the meantime, the Regional Federation of Salvadoran Workers organized an estimated eighty thousand peasants, an action that resulted in a government ban on leftist demonstrations, rallies, and propaganda. The decree failed to stem the tide of demonstrations, which provided the government with a reason for increasing its repression.

The December 1931 coup that had ousted Araujo galvanized the leftist opposition, including the Communist party, which was now convinced it could never legally gain political power in El Salvador. It organized an insurrection to take place on 22 January 1932 in several towns and army barracks, but the government learned of the plan and arrested several purported leaders, including Martí. The arrests caused a breakdown in communications that prevented the rebels from calling off the insurrection and resulted in an unorganized uprising that brought a swift and brutal government response. In the *matanza* that followed, about thirty thousand people were killed, of which less than 10 percent participated in the rebellion. A firing squad executed Martí and several other leftist leaders. In the end, the landed oligarchy gained the political peace it wanted, but at the same time, the military tightened its grip on government, which subsequently outlawed peasant unions and all opposition political parties.[27]

The *matanza* frustrated policymakers in the United States. At the same time that they wanted to impose the 1923 treaty system upon El Salvador, they tended to view the peasant uprising as part of a global Communist conspiracy. Secretary of State Stimson appeared apologetic when he noted that Hernández Martínez "is the only pillar against the success of what seems to be a nasty proletarian revolution . . . [but] we are unable to recognize [him] under the 1923 rule."[28] During the crisis, the United States and Canada dispatched naval ships to nearby ports, but no troops landed on Salvadoran soil.

Sandino and Martí may have differed in their philosophies but not in their objectives. Both were convinced that the exploitation of the masses by the landed aristocracy and foreign investors needed to be reversed, a point not understood by the American press. Journalists debated whether Sandino was a bandit or a nationalist, but they agreed that Martí was a Communist. The United States was not alone in its thinking. The elitist governments across Central America applauded Hernández Martínez's anti-Communist crusade.[29] Nearly two generations later, their causes would be taken up by new groups bearing their names, and the same confusion regarding labels would reemerge.

Just as the political objectives of the 1923 treaty system met with failure, so too did the arms limitation agreement. With the exception of Costa Rica, the military remained a high-priced and potent political force. Only Nicaragua permitted the United States to organize, train, and supply a national constabulary, or National Guard, which by 1930 replaced the local police, assumed most army functions, and controlled Nicaragua's liquor and tobacco traffic at a cost equal to that of the army it had replaced.[30]

While in 1923 the United States may have been motivated by the highest intentions, that is, to end Central American revolutions, in 1932 Nicaragua's *La Prensa* correctly observed that "under the protection of the Washington Pacts there have been more revolutions in Central America than ever before"—revolutions that opened the doors to increased U.S. intervention.[31] That same year, Costa Rican president Jiménez, motivated by the failure of the 1923 treaty system and the continuing U.S. involvement in isthmian affairs, called for a Central American conference for the sole purpose of discrediting the 1923 treaties. However, influenced by the need to protect themselves from political opponents, the Guatemalan, Honduran, and Nicaraguan governments rejected Jiménez's call. Guatemala's foreign minister, Alfredo Skinner-Klee, clearly illustrated their point when he noted that "never were the treaties more necessary in Central America than at the present moment."[32] Jiménez, frustrated by the response, gave the required year's notice to abrogate the treaties in order to extend recognition to Hernández Martínez. The Salvadoran government was pleased with Costa Rica's action and also renounced the 1923 treaties.

In 1933, presidents Ubico and Sacasa, confronted with increased political opposition at home, sought a Central American conference to reaffirm the principles of legal government as provided for in the 1923 treaty. The United States did not play a part in the conference's preparations or deliberations, which began on 15 February 1934. Secretary of State Cordell Hull only hoped that the five isthmian nations would reach an agreement "to encourage orderly constitutional government, and a continuance of friendly relations among them." Hull could not have been satisfied with the conference declaration, on 14 April 1934, in which all the participants proclaimed that the 1923 treaty system was still in force except for those nations "which have denounced them," namely, Costa Rica and El Salvador. Furthermore, the Central American governments extended recognition to Hernández Martínez.[33] While the declaration demonstrated the conflicting policy objectives of the Central American leaders, it also demonstrated their determination to prevent the United States from dominating their political affairs.

The Political Good Neighbor in Central America

During the 1920s, as Washington sought to foster political order in Central America, there slowly emerged new attitudes that resulted in policy changes. After World War I, the public was tired of conflict and wary of obligations to other governments, and it favored withdrawal from world affairs, including the League of Nations. The war also momentarily ended the European threat to the Western Hemisphere, a fact that contributed to Secretary of State Charles Evans Hughes's belief that inter-American conferences could be gala affairs demonstrating the harmonious relations among the hemispheric neighbors. The mood change found its way into the 1924 and 1928 platforms of the Democratic party, which condemned intervention, a position repeated by Franklin D. Roosevelt in the December 1928 issue of *Foreign Affairs*. President-elect Herbert Hoover's goodwill visit to Central and South America in late 1928 was followed by J. Reuben Clark's *Memorandum on the Monroe Doctrine*, which renounced U.S. intervention in Latin American domestic affairs under the terms of the Roosevelt Corollary to the Monroe Doctrine.[34]

Within the State Department there was a growing sentiment against involvement in Central American affairs. Successive heads of the Latin American affairs division, Francis G. White and Edwin C. Wilson, believed that it was no longer necessary to meddle in Central American politics. Stokeley W. Morgan, the division's assistant chief, asserted in 1925 that "as long as the people of Central America feel that the 'last word' comes from the Department, the attainment of political stability will be postponed." A year later, Dana G. Munro indicated that some of his State Department colleagues wished that the government was not so committed to the 1923 Central American treaties. By 1930, Secretary of State Stimson privately expressed doubts about the wisdom of the nonrecognition policy used in Central America, and Lawrence Dennis, who had served in both Honduras and Nicaragua, argued that the nonrecognition policy could be more embarrassing than useful should a revolutionary government come to power and defy Washington.[35]

The shift in policy culminated with President Franklin D. Roosevelt's inaugural address on 4 March 1933, when he announced that henceforth the United States would be a "Good Neighbor" in the Western Hemisphere. The policy was reaffirmed later in 1933 when the U.S. delegation to the Montevideo conference approved the Convention on Rights and Duties of States, which proclaimed that "no state has the right to intervene in the internal or external affairs of another."[36] Three years later, at Buenos Aires, the U.S. delegation to the Inter-American Conference for the Maintenance of Peace affirmed a protocol denouncing direct or indirect intervention in the affairs of any Latin American state. From 1933 until 1954, the State Department used three criteria to determine the recognition of a given government: the government must control the nation's territory and administrative machinery, including the maintenance of public order; it must express a willingness and possess an ability to meet its international obligations; and it must have the willing support of the populace.[37]

The new policy was tested in Central America during the 1930s. In Guatemala and Honduras, Jorge Ubico and Tiburcio Carías were elected prior to the 1933 Montevideo conference and were accorded recognition at the time of their elections. After 1934, however, both men used extralegal means to extend their presidential terms. Ubico initiated a nationwide plebiscite in 1935, which prodded the national assembly to amend the constitution, effectively extending Ubico's presidential term to 1943. The United States verbally attempted to dissuade Ubico from taking these actions but, given its noninterventionist policy, did nothing more. Subsequently, Washington only acknowledged his inauguration. In 1935, three years after Carías's election to a four-year presidential term, a compliant constituent assembly amended the 1924 constitution, permitting him to remain in office until 1939. As it had done with Ubico, Washington did little more than register its displeasure with Carías's extended tenure. The United States continued to withhold recognition from Hernández Martínez until his administration was given an air of legitimacy in the January 1935 presidential election. Although Hernández Martínez ran unopposed, the United States extended recognition to his government.[38]

Washington's reaction to Anastasio Somoza's path to the Nicaraguan presidency in 1937 confirmed its adherence to its noninterventionist policy. Following the withdrawal of United States Marines in 1932, the National Guard, under Somoza's leadership, became increasingly politicized. Despite the fact that Somoza, a former used-car salesman with a dubious legal record, and his uncle, President Sacasa, filled *Guardia* posts with loyal Liberals, the two were at odds. In November 1933, Somoza told the American minister, Arthur Bliss Lane, that he was frustrated with Sacasa's refusal to let the *Guardia* finish off Sandino, whom Somoza considered a political threat. Somoza was also infuriated by Sacasa's failure to keep the *Guardia*'s pay current, a situation that threatened to undermine Somoza's personal following within the organization. By early 1934, Sacasa clearly understood the *Guardia*'s potential and Somoza's willingness to use it in order to gain political power for himself. At the same time, Sandino's mistrust of the *Guardia* as an institution and Somoza's potential use of it prompted him to repeat the charge that the *Guardia* was an unconstitutional institution that needed to be disbanded. Only Minister Lane appeared oblivious to the *Guardia*'s potential. In early 1934 he cabled Washington, "I have grave doubts as to the efficiency and discipline of the organization [*Guardia*] as a whole, and as to whether Somoza really controls his men."[39]

Somoza was not secure in his own position. When Sandino and Sacasa conferred at the presidential palace on the evening of 18 February 1934, they reached an agreement to reorganize the *Guardia*. Hoping to protect himself, Somoza, on 21 February, sought out Minister Lane, who had only to "wink [his] eye" to approve any action that Somoza might take. Instead, Lane counseled patience. If Lane intended to act, he never had the opportunity. Immediately after leaving the U.S. minister, Somoza conferred with National Guard officers at the Campo de Marte military compound, where all in attendance signed a resolution sharing responsibility for Sandino's assassination. Later that evening, as Somoza listened to a poetry reading at the national theater, Sandino and colleagues Francisco Estrada and Juan Pablo Umanzar, as they left the president's residence, were picked up by a contingent of guardsmen and taken to the edge of Managua's airport, where, in the glare of truck headlights, they were machine-gunned to death.[40]

Although frustrated, the United States failed to condemn Sandino's assassination. Nor did it respond to the overtures made by all Nicaraguan political parties between 1934 and 1937, which called for U.S. intervention to forestall Somoza's presidential designs. In fact, during 1935 and 1936, the State Department instructed its ministers in Managua, Lane and Boaz Long, to avoid any involvement in the political crisis. The United States did not respond in 1936, when Somoza temporarily placed Brenes Jarquin in the presidential palace, or on 1 January 1937, when Somoza himself moved in. Although a few State Department officers expressed a desire to do something, reaction after the fact was considered ineffective. Any form of intervention violated the pledges made at the seventh inter-American conference in Montevideo.[41]

Afterward, U.S. officials did little more than scorn the constitutional maneuverings whereby Carías, Hernández Martínez, and Somoza extended their presidential terms. Each dictator satisfied Washington's three prerequisites for receiving recognition. Each controlled the nation's administrative machinery, expressed a willingness to meet international obligations, and apparently enjoyed popular support, despite his silencing of political opposition. Technically, article 2 of the 1923 Central American treaty was not violated, for it made no mention of constitutional manipulation.[42]

Just as the United States' interventionist policies of the past failed to produce constitutional governments in Central America, its Good Neighbor policy of the 1930s failed to prevent the emergence of dictators in all the isthmian countries except Costa Rica, where the traditional elite continued to vie for political power. However, the United States had no alternative except to watch these events unfold. Having abandoned its interventionist practices, Washington could not support the political factions opposed to the dictators, nor did American policymakers have many friends among the articulate middle sector, which retained its strongly anti-imperialist feelings.

Washington's failure to impose political modernity upon Central America did not prevent American entrepreneurs from exploiting the local economies and melding with the upper class. Against this system of political, economic, and social elitism, Sandino and Martí stood alone. At the time, no one understood what ingredients were necessary for a social revolution.

6   Incorporating Central America into Global Strategies, 1933–1948

For fifteen years after Franklin D. Roosevelt announced his Good Neighbor policy, three successive world crises—the global depression, World War II, and the onset of the cold war—vaulted the United States into the leadership role in international affairs. Its policies toward Central America reflected the changed priorities dictated by these larger issues. As the United States formulated a reciprocal trade policy for its own benefit during the Great Depression, developed strategies during World War II to fit the needs of the European and Asian theaters, and designed containment policies to thwart Communist expansion, the Central American caudillos cooperated with the United States in the belief that cooperation guaranteed their *continuismo*. Washington's failure to dislodge the caudillos, however, only strengthened the perception that the United States approved of them. Even more important was the growing pressure exercised by lower- and middle-sector groups who demanded political and socioeconomic reforms; preoccupied with its worldwide responsibilities, the United States largely ignored them, even while the region's oligarchs sought to suppress them.

The Economic Good Neighbor: Reciprocal Trade Agreements

The world staggered under economic collapse when Franklin D. Roosevelt took the presidential oath in March 1933. Since 1929, world trade had declined 25 percent in volume and 66 percent in value, and

U.S. trade had declined 48 percent in volume and 68 percent in value. Trade with Latin America had dropped even more drastically: exports declined 78 percent in value, and imports, 68 percent. Washington's response to the economic calamity was not imaginative. In fact, the Smoot-Hawley Tariff of 1930 exacerbated the trade problem by increasing the cost of foreign imports. The nationalistic practices of many Latin American countries also contributed to trade stagnation. Governments sought protection from falling prices by establishing a complicated web of monetary devaluations, currency restrictions, higher tariffs, import licensing, exchange controls, quotas, embargoes, and bilateral arrangements with European trading partners. None of these measures, however, stimulated commerce.

Convinced that economic nationalism worsened the depression, Secretary of State Cordell Hull sought the liberalization of trade policies to improve the world's economy and to ease world tensions. At home, Hull found a gallery of supporters, including the assistant secretary of state for Latin American affairs, Adolf A. Berle; the Secretary of Commerce, Henry A. Wallace; the International Chamber of Commerce; and the American Automobile Association. Abroad, at the 1933 Montevideo conference, Hull secured a resolution calling for liberalized trade policies, including the negotiation of reciprocal trade agreements. Congress resisted until June 1934, when it passed the Reciprocal Trade Agreements Act, which provided for the use of the unconditional most-favored-nation clause and the principle of active tariff bargaining through reciprocal agreements. It also empowered the president to raise or lower tariff duties by 50 percent and enabled him to move goods on and off the duty-free list.[1]

Latin America fit into the plan because it did not have a competitive industrial sector, nor did its major exports (flaxseed, cane sugar, cocoa, castor beans, bananas, crude rubber, manganese, bauxite, and platinum) compete with U.S. commodities. In comparison, the United States was in a stronger bargaining position because it could serve as Latin America's chief supplier of manufactured goods, and, given the fact that reciprocal trade agreements favored the principal supplier, tariff negotiations would focus only on those products that constituted the chief source of supply.[2] In sum, the act placed the State Department in a nonconcessionary negotiating position.

The Great Depression struck hard at Central America's export-oriented economy, and the subsequent policies of the United Fruit Company exacerbated the situation. By 1933 the drop in commodity prices for the region's chief exports—bananas and coffee—could not be offset by increases in volume. The sharp decline in external trade caused defaults on the public external debt after 1931. Costa Rica and El Salvador, forced off the international gold standard, experienced a depreciated currency. At first, wages for both private- and public-sector workers declined, but by 1933 unemployment rapidly accelerated, causing labor unrest across the isthmus.[3]

The banana industry, and particularly UFCO, benefited from the crisis at the expense of their hosts. The banana industry suffered, in addition to the decline in worldwide demand, an epidemic of Sigatoka disease in the 1930s. The Standard Fruit Company responded by cutting its operations in Honduras, but UFCO did not. The industry's plight provided Samuel Zemurray with the opportunity to reemerge in Central America. In 1929 Zemurray transferred the Cuyamel Fruit Company to UFCO for three hundred thousand shares of stock, making him UFCO's largest stockholder. When the depression caused the value of his stock to drop by 85 percent, he easily convinced his partners to name him managing director.

Because Sigatoka disease struck in the Atlantic lowlands, Zemurray moved UFCO's operation to Central America's Pacific slopes. In an atmosphere of economic adversity, both Costa Rica and Guatemala were compelled to offer generous contracts. Costa Rica permitted the development of seven thousand acres on its Pacific coast on the same privileged conditions UFCO enjoyed on the Atlantic. But neither the government nor the company provided for the relocation of the black labor force, leaving it to fend for itself on the Caribbean coast.

UFCO's right to develop banana plantations on Guatemala's Pacific coast dated to a 1930 agreement that also obligated the company to develop a Pacific port. Zemurray wanted out of that agreement because the International Railway of Central America (IRCA), partly owned by UFCO and whose track stretched to Puerto Barrios on the Atlantic, would be bankrupted by a seaport serving the Pacific plantations. In a new contract, completed in 1936 with President Jorge Ubico, Zemurray reneged on UFCO's commitment to construct a Pacific port by extending a $1 million loan to the financially strapped government and agreed to an increase in the banana export tax, from 1.0 to 1.5 U.S. cents per bunch, a small price to pay for a generous concession. In the aftermath, IRCA charged UFCO's competitors more than double to move their produce to Puerto Barrios, at a time when UFCO had cut the wages of its field-workers in half. Under these conditions, banana exports from Costa Rica and Guatemala increased by the mid-1930s, while Honduras and Nicaragua continued to record steady declines. In all countries the workers' standard of living worsened, and they understandably blamed the fruit companies.[4]

Despite the economic misfortune across the isthmus, the State Department faced a difficult task in its negotiations with the Central Americans, who did not believe that reciprocity was mutually advantageous because the bulk of their primary exports already came into the United States duty-free. Further, the United States extended unconditional most-favored-nation treaties to all countries, which meant that the Central Americans already received the benefits provided to Haiti and Colombia, whose exports paralleled those from the five republics. The Central Americans also resisted Hull's advances because they sensed a degree of political independence stemming from the nonintervention pledge at the Montevideo conference and a degree of economic independence stemming from the bilateral arrangements made with Germany and Italy in the early 1930s.[5] Nevertheless, before the decade ended, all five republics completed reciprocal trade agreements with the United States, largely for political, not economic, reasons.

Guatemala became the first Central American nation to conclude such an agreement, but it did not do so without hesitation. Guatemalan politics, not pressure from Washington, broke the impasse. In 1936, when Jorge Ubico determined to extend his presidential term, he measured Washington's record of intervention against its recent promises to the contrary and decided it was in his best interests to take a conciliatory path. To gain Washington's friendship, Ubico first denounced Guatemala's most-favored-nation treaty with Great Britain and then established a maximum-minimum tariff schedule that permitted the importation of U.S. goods at the minimum rate but imposed higher tariffs on German and Japanese products. This set the stage for the reciprocity agreement that was concluded in April 1936. While the pact demonstrated Washington's willingness to make only limited concessions, it still implied recognition of Ubico's illegally extended administration. The pact also revealed Ubico's willingness to cooperate with foreign business interests at the expense of domestic development in order to serve his own political needs.[6]

Like Ubico, Honduran president Tiburcio Carías rationalized that a reciprocity agreement with the United States lessened the threat of its intervention in his nation's political affairs. Such a trade pact otherwise offered little advantage. Even during the depression, bananas, which accounted for 75 percent of Honduran exports to the United States, earned more in British and German markets, where Honduras had a favorable balance of trade. Carías did not want to jeopardize the latter two markets or place Japanese products at a competitive disadvantage, particularly cotton products and electrical goods. Yet, in 1935, as Carías prepared to illegally extend his presidential term, he wanted to placate the United States. The reciprocity agreement, concluded that December, did not favor Honduran domestic industry. While the United States received several tariff reductions ranging from 33 to 75 percent on its exports to Honduras, the isthmian republic received none.[7] Carías went a step further in 1937 when he denounced the most-favored-nation treaties with France and Germany, which led to the United States' purchase of 90 percent of the Honduran banana exports. Although these actions may have kept the United States from Carías's doorstep, they also increased Honduras's economic dependence upon the United States.

Political considerations also played a significant role in the events leading to the 1936 reciprocity agreement with Nicaragua. To prevent the ambitious chief of the National Guard, Anastasio Somoza, from seizing the reins of government, president Juan B. Sacasa sought to establish close ties with the United States. Although Sacasa successfully lobbied the national congress, persuading it to ratify a reciprocal trade agreement in March 1936, Nicaragua suffered a double loss. Like the others, this treaty favored U.S. interests and, at the same time, did nothing to prevent Somoza from capturing the presidency. Somoza recognized the agreement's imbalance and sought its revision, not for the benefit of Nicaragua, but rather to enhance the financial coffers of his family and friends. The new agreement, concluded in 1938, did not change duty rates, but increased the rate of conversion between the paper and gold *córdobas*.[8] This financial manipulation raised the price of American exports, thus impeding their access to Nicaragua, which benefited Somoza's business allies.

While the United States tried to improve its trade position in El Salvador immediately following its recognition of Hernández Martínez in January 1935, the Salvadoran dictator resisted. Such an agreement would cost his country nearly $1 million annually in lost revenues and would jeopardize its trade with Europe, where over 50 percent of El Salvador's exports went. But there were political advantages. Hernández Martínez alertly sensed that reciprocity would obviate U.S. assistance to his political opponents, and he was therefore willing to sign an agreement in February 1937.[9] When Hernández Martínez decided to remain in the presidency in 1939, the reciprocity agreement worked to his advantage. Washington again paused at yet another opportunity to denounce isthmian dictatorship.

Costa Rica's primary agricultural exports were already free-listed, so it gained little in the 1936 agreement, which stipulated that Costa Rica reduce its tariffs by 8 to 65 percent over previous rates on more than two hundred items imported from the United States. In contrast, U.S. concessions, like those to other Central American countries, were on "distinctively" tropical products for which there were minimal demand and several supply sources.[10]

These reciprocity agreements illustrated the divergence of foreign policy objectives. The United States, anxious both to stimulate commerce through a reduction in trade barriers and to present a picture of hemispheric solidarity, seemed less concerned about the political intrigues of the isthmian dictators. Central Americans thought otherwise. With the exception of Costa Rica, the Central American countries viewed reciprocity agreements as a means to forestall U.S. intervention. Economically, the agreements did little for either side. Central America had little to offer in the way of commodities and, with its limited purchasing power, could buy little from the United States. State Department counselor Laurence Duggan correctly observed that "the political achievements of the Good Neighbor policy were not matched in the economic field."[11]

A Strategic Outpost: Central America and World War II

By decade's end, strategic considerations dominated U.S. policy in the hemisphere. Washington's concern that increased German and Italian aggression posed a threat to the Western Hemisphere was not shared by the Latin American leaders. Most of them believed that Roosevelt was exploiting the trouble in Europe in order to circumvent the nonintervention promises made at the Seventh International Conference of American States in Montevideo, Uruguay. Thus, at the 1936 Inter-American Conference for Maintenance of Peace at Buenos Aires, the United States obtained little beyond an innocuous agreement calling for consultation when an emergency threatened the hemisphere.[12]

Only after the German invasion of Poland in September 1939 and especially the fall of France in June 1940 did the Latin American nations feel a sense of urgency about the hemispheric defense. At a special conference in Panama in 1939, they accepted a three-hundred-mile neutrality zone around the Americas, and at Havana in 1940, they approved measures for the occupation of European possessions in the Western Hemisphere (in order to prevent their seizure by the Axis powers) and adopted measures to deal with fifth-column activities in the hemisphere.

Latin America's more cooperative attitude enabled the United States to outline its hemispheric defense policy before the Pearl Harbor attack on 7 December 1941. First, Washington officials concluded that military assistance to Latin America should be sufficient to enable its military to resist an attack until U.S. troops could be mobilized. As a follow-up measure, the United States placed missions in each Latin American country to supervise the training of local forces. Military staff met with their counterparts from the Latin American nations (except Bolivia, Panama, and Paraguay) to discuss the use of naval, land, and air bases, air transit rights, and the exchange of security information. The Uruguayan pact, completed in November 1940, assuaged regional nationalism and became the model for subsequent agreements, all of which provided for U.S. funding of facilities that remained under the host country's sovereignty, were manned by the host country's military (with American technical assistance), and were available to all the nations in the Western Hemisphere engaged in the common defense. The Lend-Lease Act, approved by Congress in March 1941, provided the funds to meet these needs. Following its passage, the board established to administer the program recommended an allocation of $400 million to Latin America over three years, with only $70 million to be sent in 1941–42 and the remainder in 1943 and after.[13] U.S. policy toward Central America in the prewar years fell within these broad parameters.

Washington's initial defense priority in Central America focused on subversion because of the large number of German nationals and descendants throughout the region and particularly in Guatemala, where the so-called German colony played a major role in the national economy. The second largest German colony was in Costa Rica, and there were smaller communities in Nicaragua, Honduras, and El Salvador. Admiral Harold R. Stark, chief of naval operations, believed that under these conditions it was just common sense for the United States to seek internal stability in Central America.

In Guatemala, whose president, Jorge Ubico, shared many political traits with Benito Mussolini, Adolf Hitler, and the populist Latin American leaders of the 1930s, U.S. observers failed to accept the fact that many of the traits were peculiar to the nature of Guatemalan politics. This perception contributed to Washington's offhanded dismissal of Ubico's 1935 draft proposal for hemispheric cooperation in response to an external attack. The following year, when Guatemala withdrew from the League of Nations, the American press emphasized the Italian claim that its economic pressure was responsible, when in fact Italy accounted for only 1 percent of Guatemalan trade and Guatemala lacked the financial resources to meet its obligations to the world organization. Ubico did not improve his image in the United States when he recognized the Franco regime in Spain in 1936.

Early in the following year, however, the Guatemalans began exhibiting pro-Allied sentiment. The press curtailed its coverage of Fascist activities in Europe, replacing it with a more obviously pro-American bias. Foreign Minister Carlos Salazar permitted the private publication of a pamphlet warning of the danger of the growing Nazi efforts to organize the German colony in Guatemala. American flight crews received warm receptions on their stopovers at Guatemala City en route from Texas and the Panama Canal Zone. At Ubico's request, a U.S. army officer was detailed to command the Guatemalan Military Academy. In May 1939 Ubico decreed that foreigners, under the threat of expulsion, were prohibited from political activities, including assemblies, the formation of political groups, the spreading of propaganda, and the use of uniforms and insignias of foreign political parties. When the European war began that September, Ubico followed Roosevelt's lead in declaring neutrality. He also granted the United States use of Guatemala's water ports and land facilities, and, as a defense measure, the government made a serious effort to complete the Atlantic-to-Pacific highway. A year later, Guatemala joined eight other Latin American nations in sending a military mission to inspect military facilities in the United States. These and other gestures persuaded the U.S. minister that, if war came, Guatemala would support the United States.[14]

There remained a concern with the extent of unchecked German influence in Guatemala. Despite Ubico's 1940 decree against political activities by foreigners, U.S. officials considered the German legation at Guatemala City the distribution point for propaganda to all Central

America. In July 1940, the U.S. military attaché in Guatemala, Colonel Joseph Pate, thought that the German influence was so pervasive that they could engineer the overthrow, not only of Ubico, but also of the other Central American governments, at a moment's notice.[15]

American officials were equally concerned with German influence in El Salvador, where the administration of President Hernández Martínez resembled that of Ubico's, including its institution of a military regime, strict disciplinary control of society, and a centralized government. He was attracted to the successes of Mussolini and, to a lesser degree, of Hitler, and, like them, he believed that he had saved his country from Communism. An admirer of Spain's Francisco Franco, Hernández Martínez was among the first to extend recognition to him in 1938. Officials in Washington did not consider Hernández Martínez's Fascist sympathies within the context of Salvadoran nationalism or as a response to previous U.S. interference in El Salvador's domestic affairs.

The increased German economic presence also gave cause for concern. From 1930 to 1934 only 9 percent of El Salvador's imports came from Germany, but from 1934 to 1937 German imports increased to 25 percent of the national total. The appointment of Baron Wilhelm von Hundelhausen as head of El Salvador's Mortgage Bank in 1935, despite his lack of qualifications for the position, raised eyebrows in Washington even higher. Hundelhausen reputedly distributed Nazi propaganda in El Salvador, having arrived in the country from the German legation at Guatemala City. From the Panama Canal Zone, Commander W. R. Phillips reported in 1937 that Hundelhausen supported the Nazi's suggestion that Hernández Martínez overthrow Carías in Honduras, thereby becoming president of both countries, and from there absorb all of Central America through the twenty-five thousand German *bunds* said to be in the region. Hernández Martínez did not help his cause in Washington when he reprimanded newspaper editors for criticizing government officials' pro-Nazi attitudes and the unchecked German influence in the country or when he praised Axis troops following their early victories in Europe. Despite these actions, he did not appear to be in tune with the majority of Salvadorans. In addition to the newspaper editors, middle-sector groups also demonstrated against the spreading of Nazi and Fascist ideas. Hundelhausen was subjected to physical threats, including the stoning of his home and car, until his resignation shortly after the outbreak of war in Europe in September 1939.

The Italian military presence, rather than the economic link, was visible from the 1920s, when military missions began to make regular appearances in El Salvador. Salvadoran officers received flight and gunnery training in Italy. Italian guns and munitions were regularly purchased by the Salvadoran military until 1939, when European war demands forced Mussolini to cancel the contract. When the North American Aircraft Corporation refused to accept partial payment in coffee in 1938, the Salvadoran government purchased four Italian Caproni light bombers for thirty-nine thousand dollars each, with payments being made partly in cash and partly in coffee exports. Following the outbreak of war, Hernández Martínez slowly shifted to a more pro-Allied position: he spoke in favor of democracy and Pan-Americanism and against totalitarianism, and he instituted anti-Nazi measures at home, including a prohibition on the dissemination of foreign propaganda. Nazi sympathizers were forced underground. Subsequently, Foreign Minister Miguel Araujo refused to meet with the German representatives assigned to the country.[16]

Immediately after he seized the Nicaraguan presidency, Somoza began a campaign to get U.S. approval for his regime, and he rapidly accepted President Roosevelt's invitation to visit the United States. At their meeting in 1939, Roosevelt agreed to have the Army Corps of Engineers undertake a study of the proposed San Juan River canal project, a highway linking Nicaragua's east and west coasts, and the assignment of an army officer to head the National Guard school. While these initiatives fell within the parameters of the United States' defense needs, they also contributed to the myth that Somoza and Roosevelt were close friends.

The Army Corps of Engineers eventually abandoned the canal project at the San Juan River in favor of a road to Rama, which linked the west coast to the headwaters of the Escondido River and which reached to the east-coast port of Bluefields. The initial estimated cost of $2 million climbed to $4.5 million in 1942 and continued to escalate until the road's completion nearly a generation later. In the summer of 1939, Major Charles L. Mullins became the director of the guard's military school. Although the U.S. legation at Managua directed Mullins's activities, he faced an uphill battle in convincing Somoza to refurbish the school and to accept a three-year officer training program. Once these goals were accomplished, Somoza was obviously satisfied, because he augmented Mullins's regular army salary with a $385 monthly stipend.[17] In addition to cooperating with Washington's defense measures, Somoza continually expressed pro-Allied sympathies. More than once, he stated that "a small country such as Nicaragua needed the protection of the United States and could not progress without it."[18]

Nearly twenty months before the United States entered the war, Costa Rican president Rafael Calderón Guardia warned that a German victory in Europe meant the doom of democracy in America. Throughout the year he took a number of steps against Nazi influence, including expelling Nazi leader Karl Bayer and dismissing German nationals and Costa Ricans of German descent from government posts. In September 1940, Calderón Guardia ordered that the German consulate be closed. Despite Calderón Guardia's actions and his concern with German propaganda and Nazi influence in Costa Rica, Washington dismissed as "boyish glee" Calderón Guardia's assertion in July 1940 that a coup attempt against him originated at the German legation in Guatemala City. Beginning in early 1940, Calderón Guardia cooperated with the United States in preparing for the defense of the Panama Canal. He offered sites on Cocos Island, four hundred miles west of the canal, for the establishment of naval and air bases. He welcomed the arrival of military personnel to supervise the training of the nation's military police force, fifteen thousand men strong, and a small loan to purchase arms for them.[19]

Honduran president Tiburcio Carías had spoken of the need to defend the Western Hemisphere prior to Pearl Harbor, and he was confident that the United States would take the lead in hemispheric defense. But, given the record of U.S. intervention in Honduras and Carías's wanting to secure his own political position, it is understandable that Carías was not anxious to link himself to Washington.

When war came in December 1941, the five Central American republics immediately pledged their support to the Allied effort against the Axis powers. They subsequently cooperated with the United States' wartime policies for regional defense, control of subversion, and economic priorities.

Defense of the Caribbean region was defined by the "Rainbow Plans" as they evolved. Under the terms of "Rainbow 5," put into effect immediately after the Pearl Harbor attack, the U.S. Navy assumed responsibility for the Caribbean defenses, while the army retained responsibility for securing the Panama Canal. In accordance with the general hemispheric policy, the Central Americans assumed responsibility for their security from an external attack. The apex of the German threat to the Caribbean shipping lanes and the Panama Canal came in 1942, when their U-boats sank 336 ships totaling 1.5 million tons.[20] To counter the German U-boats, the United States needed air and naval bases to support the antisubmarine patrols, to protect Caribbean oil fields and refineries, and to safeguard the Panama Canal.

Central American governments readily cooperated with the United States to meet the German challenge. They agreed to pacts patterned after the Uruguayan model for the construction of airstrips and port facilities, the granting of air rights, and the exchange of security information. An executive agreement between Roosevelt and Ubico in 1942 permitted the stationing of U.S. troops in Guatemala for the war's duration. Salvadoran president Hernández Martínez permitted U.S. patrol boats to use Salvadoran ports, considered important for the Pacific defense of the Panama Canal. Somoza allowed the construction of facilities for seaplanes and air artillery at the Nicaraguan naval base at Corinto. After 1942, the United States augmented the Guatemalan, Nicaraguan, and Salvadoran marine patrols with small boats, as they assumed responsibility for their own coastal defense. Only Honduras hesitated; it did not sign a military cooperation agreement until December 1945, after the war had ended.[21]

By the end of February 1942, the five republics had signed lend-lease agreements. Although the Central American states received less than 10 percent of all wartime lend-lease aid, the material provided illustrated the emphasis upon securing the Caribbean sea-lanes—water and air craft, associated spare parts, and appropriate ordnance and ammunition. Only token shipments of light arms, tanks, and planes were made. As mandated by the Joint Advisory Board, the bulk of the material came after 1942, at a time when the U-boat threat to the region had subsided. Central America proved a most willing wartime ally, even though it became a strategic outpost after 1942.[22]

Immediately after the Pearl Harbor attack, the Central American governments cooperated with the United States in controlling subversive activities. Ubico directed the enactment of a series of "emergency laws" that imposed restrictions upon enemy aliens, mostly Germans. Assets were frozen; travel was restricted; and registration with the national police was required. All telephone and telegraph communications had to be in Spanish or English. German schools were closed, and suspected enemy aliens were deported to the United States for wartime internment. Hernández Martínez also imposed restrictive measures on El Salvador's German colony, including its travel and communication. Some German-owned lands were confiscated, and some German nationals were sent to the United States for internment. The Costa Rican government took over the administration of German-owned businesses and expropriated German-owned farms. Although not as anxious about the German problem as were his neighbors, Honduran president Tiburcio Carías also took measures to restrict German activities and control German assets within the country. Somoza handled the Axis problem by simply suspending the constitution.[23] The U.S. fear of Axis influence throughout Central America may have been exaggerated, but the Central American governments cooperated in controlling it.

An argument can be made that the Central American leaders used the alleged Nazi threat and the lend-lease military assistance as a means to stymie their political opponents. Washington understood this. For example, in 1943, Hernández Martínez's request for one thousand submachine guns through the lend-lease program came at a time when he was preparing to extend his presidency. The State Department denied the request, because, as the assistant chief of the American republics affairs division, John Cabot, bluntly stated, "These lethal toys [are] more likely to be used for a very different purpose than they were intended." In the spring of 1945, the State Department denied Somoza's request for ten thousand rifles to drive alleged Communists out of Nicaragua. Acting Secretary of State Joseph C. Grew clearly understood Somoza's real intention: the suppression of the conservative political opposition.[24]

The outbreak of the war in Europe also disrupted Central American trade patterns. The loss of the European market adversely affected their economies and contributed to a scarcity of consumer goods across the isthmus. Central America's primary exports—bananas and coffee—were not among wartime shipping priorities, which further depressed the region's agricultural sector. Policy decisions in Washington did not provide a satisfactory solution to the problem. Although the 1940 International Coffee Agreement guaranteed isthmian producers a market at prices higher than those obtainable during the previous five years, it also increased the U.S. share of the Central American markets. For example, from 1940 to 1944, the United States received 77.2 percent of El Salvador's exports, a 13.6 percent increase over the preceding five years. Despite wartime demands, the United States bore the blame for shortages of food, oil, and quinine in the isthmus. There were riots in Costa Rica in 1945 due to severe food shortages. U.S.-sponsored programs also failed to offset the rising unemployment in Central America's agricultural sector and to stem the flow of unskilled agricultural workers to the cities. Grants and loans from the Export-Import Bank and the Reconstruction Finance Corporation for infrastructure projects, such as water, sewerage, and road construction, did not employ all the displaced workers. Agreements to purchase Guatemalan and Honduran exportable rubber did not drastically increase employment in that industry. Another agreement sent an estimated ten thousand Salvadoran workers to the Panama Canal Zone, where they replaced American military personnel in nonessential jobs. The Salvadoran laborers resisted the relocation and looked upon it as a penalty for wrongdoing at home. Efforts by the Inter-American Institute of Agricultural Sciences to train graduate students and to experiment with new types of livestock and tropical crops focused on long-range projects, not the immediate foodstuff shortages. In effect, the economic adversity caused by the war placed additional strains on the region's established political structure. This was most evident in Costa Rica, where President Rafael Calderón Guardia promised a revision in the nation's tax code, a land distribution program, urban housing, and particular attention to the areas abandoned by UFCO.

To discourage American firms from trading with Axis businesses abroad, the U.S. government issued its "Proclaimed List of Certain Blocked Neutrals" in July 1941. While all of Central America was affected, the list struck hardest at Guatemala, where some two hundred firms were blacklisted. In order to avoid Guatemala's economic collapse, the United States accepted Ubico's proposal permitting the central bank to assume control of the German firms and hold all profits except those essential for business operations. Because of the German influence in the Guatemalan banking system, a new agreement in 1943 reduced exports from the German-owned firms to the amount necessary for continuing operations only. The Guatemalan government was not alone in seizing German-owned property. In 1942, the United States' custodian of alien property seized the controlling stock of the Central American Plantations Corporation (CAPO), a German-owned company incorporated in Delaware. The seizure made the U.S. government owner of twelve huge Guatemalan *fincas* that produced significant amounts of the nation's coffee and sugar exports. Ubico's protests resulted in a subsequent agreement that granted the Guatemalan government 51 percent of the stock owned by the United States in return for a ten-year concession. Ubico used this agreement as a model to obtain other German properties until June 1944, when his government expropriated all domestic German holdings.[25] In effect, the war weakened, rather than stimulated, the Central American economies.

Following the invasion of Poland in September 1939, a wave of pro-

Allied sentiment swept the isthmus. The press curtailed its coverage of Axis activities in Europe, replacing it with a more obvious pro-American bias. The Monroe Doctrine received praise for the protection it offered, the Good Neighbor policy was described as a pleasant fact of life, and the virtues of the United States military were extolled. Carías, Hernández Martínez, Somoza, and Ubico signed the United Nations' declaration and continually expressed the need to support the United States in the crusade against European and Asian totalitarianism. In 1943, Ubico proudly announced the purchase of $2 million of U.S. war bonds. Somoza renamed Managua's main street after President Roosevelt. Through the Office of Inter-American Affairs, which opened regional offices in Costa Rica, Guatemala, and Nicaragua, the United States encouraged the dissemination of pro-Allied propaganda (motion pictures proved most effective). Educational projects attempted to reach the politically excluded poorer classes.[26]

The impact of the pro-Allied and democratic propaganda upon Central America's literate groups is difficult to determine, but opposition to local totalitarianism increased as the war progressed. In the waning months of World War II, Central America appeared destined for political change, and Washington anticipated it. Secretary of State Edward R. Stettinius, Jr., cautioned American missions in Central America to be prepared for political turmoil and advised them to distance themselves from it. He referred to the coming of age of the "generation of rising expectations," with its demands for political and social reform. In the four countries governed by dictators, the pressure was for political change, while in democratic Costa Rica social change was the dominant issue. In both cases, the oligarchy was under attack.

The generation of rising expectations had its origins in the late nineteenth century—in the region's liberal movement and its encouragement of the importation of foreign capital and culture. A product of this development was the rising middle sector, which included individuals possessing varying degrees of wealth—doctors, dentists, lawyers, small businessmen, white-collar management, university professors, students, and skilled urban laborers—united only by their desire for participation in the political process and an end to the oligarchical dictatorships that dominated each nation.[27] Influenced by the Allies' idealistic goals during World War II, the middle sector expressed its discontent with increasing vehemence and pressured for its objectives, but it met with varied success.

Middle-sector pressure in El Salvador and Guatemala resulted in the downfall of Maximiliano Hernández Martínez and Jorge Ubico. The crisis in El Salvador was precipitated on 1 March 1944, when the constituent assembly elected Hernández Martínez to another four-year presidential term. The event did not receive much public attention, nor did the editorial by José Quetglas in *La Prensa Gráfica*, which expressed dismay at the United States for declaring war against dictatorships in Europe and Asia but cooperating with them elsewhere in the world. The U.S. ambassador in San Salvador, Walter Thurston, described Quetglas's opinions as "representative of the more literate sector of the opposition," but he did not expect violence and therefore was surprised by a four-hour uprising on 2 April that left 53 persons dead, another 134 wounded, and two square blocks of the capital destroyed. Suppression of the uprising did not quell the call for Hernández Martínez's resignation, which now spread to the outlying towns. In mid-April dissident professional groups pressured Ambassador Thurston to have the United States provide for a general election. Thurston refused, pointing to the noninterventionist policy that had been in effect since 1933.

Finally, on the morning of 19 April, a shouting match between students and police at the entrance to the national university set in motion a chain of events that led to a general strike and Hernández Martínez's resignation on 8 May. The caudillo himself blamed middle-sector elements—"capitalists, agriculturalists, industrialists, merchants and professions"—for the confrontation that resulted in his departure. The interim government satisfied the middle sector's demands for civil and political rights, and these interests were represented by the newly founded *Unión Democrática* party, under the leadership of Dr. Arturo Romero.

The events in El Salvador soon repeated themselves in Guatemala. Active opposition to Ubico first surfaced in 1941, when the national assembly approved another extension of Ubico's presidential term. The opposition continued, and by 1943 Ubico himself feared three middle-sector groups—lawyers, skilled laborers, and small businessmen. But, as in El Salvador, the catalyst for change came from university students, in this case, a group of students demanding the ouster of the medical school's dean. In response, Ubico suspended constitutional rights—the right of assembly, freedom of speech and press, inviolability of correspondence, and protection from illegal arrest and search of one's domicile. None of these liberties had been practiced during Ubico's regime, but their suspension provided the student movement with a political issue. By the end of June, other middle-sector elements, mostly lawyers and doctors, picked up on the theme and implored Ubico to resign. What had begun as a demand for university reform blossomed into a call for Ubico's resignation, which came on 30 June. In the euphoria that followed, a multitude of political parties emerged. Five of them represented the middle sector.

In Nicaragua, Anastasio Somoza instigated a constitutional amendment in April 1944 that permitted him to seek another presidential term in 1947. His action ignited a crisis that was confined largely to the upper economic and social echelon, which wanted political power for itself. But their protest contained the democratic rhetoric found elsewhere on the isthmus. Speaking on behalf of the dissidents, Carlos Pasos charged that Somoza had become a political and economic dictator who violated civil rights, usurped judicial power, accumulated private wealth, and imposed excessive taxation, all at the nation's expense. Pasos dismissed as a sham Somoza's self-comparison to President Franklin D. Roosevelt. Nicaragua's small middle sector also engaged in the political protest. University students conducted a sympathy demonstration on behalf of their Salvadoran counterparts, while lawyers spoke out against the constitutional amendment that permitted Somoza to seek reelection. Somoza understood the extent of the opposition, and he agreed to veto the amendment, to permit a free press, and to provide for government reform. He also silenced the dissidents by threatening them with internment, an action that sent many into self-imposed exile.

In Honduras, where Carías tightly held the government's reins and where most of the opposition forces had been exiled to Mexico, Costa Rica, Guatemala, and El Salvador, the overthrows of Hernández Martínez and Ubico received little attention in the press, but they did contribute to a marked increase in exile propaganda distributed by university students and to a series of demonstrations that called for Carías's resignation, free elections, a free press, and the release of political prisoners. The Honduran Democratic Front, based in El Salvador, criticized the United States for not aiding its cause and permitting Carías to use lend-lease military equipment to suppress the demonstrators.

As a result of the 1944 political turbulence, the middle sector entered the isthmian political equation traditionally preserved for the Liberals and Conservatives, but only in Costa Rica did the lower socioeconomic groups make their presence felt. The election of Teodoro Picado to the presidency in 1944 not only ended the *personalismo* that had characterized preceding presidential contests but also brought to the presidential palace a reform-minded politician who won the election with support from the local Communist party. Because of the conservative legislature, however, Picado's program never got on track. Elsewhere on the isthmus, there were hints of an impending confrontation between the elite and the deprived masses. In Guatemala, for example, five political parties espousing social reform were founded in the aftermath of Ubico's resignation. The 1945 constitution in El Salvador gave the government potentially sweeping power over labor.[28]

Washington officials only observed these harbingers of change, reserving most of their attention for bringing World War II to a successful conclusion and seeking a just peace. Because it did not represent an immediate threat to U.S. security interests at the time, Central America remained on the periphery of U.S. policy considerations.

The Cold War Comes to Central America

Immediately after World War II, the Truman administration fashioned a Latin American policy that reflected its larger global strategy of containing Soviet aggression. Through a series of agreements, the

United States incorporated Latin America into its global security system. By the Act of Chapultepec, signed in Mexico City in 1945, the American republics agreed to consult before responding to aggressive acts upon any hemispheric nation. Two years later, at Rio de Janeiro, the Latin Americans agreed to provide for assistance against direct aggression prior to consultation and, when the threat was other than direct aggression, agreed to consult before taking joint action. At Bogotá in 1948, the Inter-American Defense Board was established and charged with developing hemispheric defense plans. In 1951, following six years of debate, the United States Congress approved the Mutual Security Act, initially providing $38 million for direct military assistance to Latin America for its participation in hemispheric defense.[29] Through these measures, the United States sought to secure the Western Hemisphere from an external attack, something whose chance of occurring Washington policymakers believed was remote.

During the same period, from 1945 to 1951, administration spokesmen—secretaries of state Dean Acheson and George C. Marshall and the assistant secretary for Latin American affairs Edward G. Miller—continued to espouse traditional themes regarding inter-American relations: pleas for political stability and faith in democracy and promises of nonintervention in the internal affairs of its southern neighbors.[30] While preaching such lofty ideals, the United States ignored many Latin Americans' demands for an end to dictatorship and an improvement in the quality of life for the less fortunate. The Communist threat in Europe and Asia was deemed more important.

That Central America fell within the broad purview of this policy was evident as early as January 1945, when the U.S. extended recognition to Salvadoran president Salvador Castañeda Castro. Although Castañeda did not have popular support, one of the State Department's criteria for granting recognition, recognition was nevertheless extended to him because the U.S. wanted to present a picture of hemispheric solidarity at the Inter-American Conference on the Problems of War and Peace, scheduled to convene in Mexico City that February. In 1947, Anastasio Somoza, under middle-sector pressure, stepped aside from the presidential election but paved the way for the selection of his seventy-one-year-old uncle, Leonardo Argüello. When Argüello attempted to oust Somoza as head of the National Guard, Argüello was deposed, and Somoza then arranged for the congressional election of another uncle, Victor Manuel Ramón Reyes, as president. The United States withheld recognition, pointing to the illegality of Somoza's maneuvering, but the need for hemispheric solidarity again prevailed. At the ninth inter-American conference at Bogotá in 1948, the United States accepted a resolution that denounced nonrecognition as a political tool and called for continued diplomatic relations whenever government leadership changed. Because the United States placed greater importance upon the inter-American defense system, Somoza survived the crisis.[31]

Central America was of scant use to the Soviets in the immediate postwar period, and so U.S. defense policy stressed the security of the Panama Canal and the Mexican and Venezuelan oil supplies. Economic improvement, policymakers promised, would come from the European Recovery Program, popularly known as the Marshall Plan, and the "Point Four" programs. The promises proved false. Central America remained on the periphery of cold war strategies, a place that would enable its leaders to solidify their position at the expense of the middle and lower classes. During the same time span, pressure for social change intensified and soon presented the leadership in both the United States and Central America with a new challenge.

7 Nationalism or Communism: Costa Rica and Guatemala

In the decade following the end of World War II, new factors entered Central America's political equation, challenging the established tradition and, in the process, its social order. Encouraged by the United States' leadership in the continued battle against totalitarianism, the middle sector pursued its quest for entrance into the political process. More important was the emerging debate that focused on the lower socioeconomic groups—farm laborers, small farmers, and, in urban areas, unskilled laborers—who remained the largest and most aggravated element in the political structure. The dictators who emerged in the 1930s played upon the sympathies of the poor but provided few practical benefits to them. With the land-owning elite as allies, the ruling oligarchs were determined not to permit the lower class from upsetting the region's socioeconomic and political status quo, and they labeled as Communist anyone who identified with the cause of the poor. In the immediate postwar years, U.S. diplomats stationed in Central America dismissed the oligarchs' charges and instead described the demands made by the lower socioeconomic groups as liberal, not radical.

After 1947, as the United States stiffened in its policy toward the Soviet Union, the Communist issue took on new meaning in Central America. Diplomats stationed in the region cautioned that poverty was a breeding ground for communism and attempted to distinguish between the "Mexican" variety, found in El Salvador, Nicaragua, and Honduras, and the presumably international brand, found in Costa Rica and Guatemala, which threatened U.S. interests. However, decision makers in Washington often failed to distinguish between Communists and leftist nationalists who were responding to the region's socioeconomic disparities. When that happened, the United States stood ready to forcefully intervene.

1948: Civil War in Costa Rica

Costa Rica was especially troublesome for U.S. analysts. Since 1920, it had gained the reputation of a model democracy where political offices were transferred from incumbents to elected successors at regular, four-year intervals. Although the coffee, banana, and cattle barons enjoyed the prestige of political office at the expense of the middle and lower sectors, most observers believed that this oligarchical system worked well for all Costa Ricans. But undercurrents of discontent moved beneath the surface of the apparent calm. The deprivations of the lower socioeconomic groups first drew the attention of the Reform party in the mid-1920s. They were subsequently championed by Manuel Mora, who, as a twenty-year-old law student, in 1930 organized the Marxist-oriented Workers and Peasants Bloc; a year later, he founded the Communist party in Costa Rica.

From its inception, the Communist party sought "to completely transform the [Costa Rican] economic system so that products would be distributed equally, and . . . that the practice of one group exploiting another would cease."[1] Such exhortations earned the wrath of the nation's economic and social elite. Still, the Communist party increased its political presence from 1932, when it polled 1,132 votes in the national election, to 1942, when its congressional candidates received 17,060 votes. In the 1940 presidential election, won by Rafael Angel Calderón Guardia, the Communist party received an estimated 15,000 of the 90,000 votes cast.[2]

The political significance of the Communist party grew during Calderón Guardia's administration. Mora reportedly wrote and directed through congress a labor code that contained three potentially important provisions: first, 90 percent of the employed laborers would be Costa Rican, and they would receive 80 percent of the payroll; second, a laborer who resigned or was dismissed would receive one month's pay for each year of his employment; and, third, all laborers, including household servants, would be covered by contracts. The Costa Rican Communist party was dissolved in 1943 (at the same time the Communist International disbanded), but it was reconstituted as the Popular Vanguard party, with the same platform and stewardship. Archbishop Victor Sanabria, influenced by his own liberal views and the party's divorce from Moscow, permitted Roman Catholics to join the organization without fear of church reprisal.[3]

The apex of Mora's political influence came on 22 September 1943, when he pledged to work for the election of the presidential candidate for the National Republican party, Teodoro Picado, in return for Picado's promise to carry out a program identical with the Popular Vanguard party's pledge to lower living costs, support labor and farm movements, and implement political reform. As election day approached, the consul at the U.S. embassy in San José, Edward G. Trueblood, predicted that Costa Rica was about to embark upon a new political path in which "the traditional political battling over the personalities of individuals is giving way . . . as elsewhere, to a struggle between two radically opposed philosophies."[4]

As expected, Picado won the February 1944 election, the most corrupt in Costa Rican history. Although the National Republican party retained control of congress, its twenty-eight delegates in the national legislature were more responsive to the political agenda of former president Calderón Guardia than the president elect. Picado failed to deliver on the social legislation he had promised, a fact that contributed to Mora's growing prestige as a spokesman for the laboring classes. He championed government control of industrial and agricultural production, land distribution, increased social security, low-cost housing, and quality education.

Opposition to Mora's growing political prominence came from the business community, represented by former president Calderón Guardia, and the landowners, led by former president Leon Cortés. Newspaper owner Otilio Ulate emerged as another spokesman for the upper class. Each described Mora's proposals as Communist. A third group, the Social Democratic party, represented the middle sector. Characterized by their youth, their opposition to traditional "personalism," and their lack of political experience, the Social Democrats sought honest elections and an end to corrupt government. As the church took up the laborers' cause toward 1948, Archbishop Sanabria began to distance himself from Mora and criticized his Communist leanings.[5] U.S. policymakers generally regarded the Popular Vanguard party as more interested in domestic reform than in the goals of international communism and thought that the party's proposals "would be defined in most countries as merely a liberal program."[6] Mora was depicted as both a political opportunist and a sincere reformist, but not as a Communist.

But after mid-1947, as U.S.–Soviet relations rapidly deteriorated the analysis of Mora and his Popular Vanguard party also changed. Policymakers began to describe the party as an extension of Leninism, as a practitioner of democratic centralism, and charged that it imitated the membership drives of the Cuban, French, and Italian Communist parties. The Popular Vanguard party's criticisms of U.S. and British foreign policy further indicated its attraction to international communism. Although the embassy in San José found little evidence to substantiate the charge, it concluded that Mora had pressured Calderón Guardia and Picado to appoint Communists to government posts and that their influence far outweighed their numbers. In such circumstances, Costa Rica was important to Moscow as a potential communications and training center for Communists in Central America. American officials discounted reports that Mora was becoming increasingly isolated and politically weak.[7]

Against this backdrop of internal strife, preparations for the 1948 election moved forward. The National Republican party nominated its standard-bearer, Rafael Calderón Guardia, and the other opposition groups united around Ulate. The acrimonious campaign, devoid of issues, focused on personalities. The opposition's allegations that communism permeated the National Republican party and that Calderón Guardia himself was a Communist became the campaign's most prominent topics. Political tensions intensified after the electoral tri-

bunal declared Ulate the winner of the 8 February election but asserted that only the national congress could deal with the charges of
fraud and corruption surrounding the election. Voting strictly on party
lines, the congress voided the presidential elections but at the same
time validated congressional elections, won by the National Republican party. Amidst the confusion existed the hope that a compromise
could be reached.

Instead, a civil war broke out. José Figueres and his followers,
joined by other disenchanted opposition groups, led a revolt against
the government on 12 March. The ill-prepared government force (with
its undisciplined *mariachis*) failed to dislodge the rebels from their
post at San Isidro del General, on Costa Rica's central plateau. From
there, Figueres contented himself with waging a war of attrition. The
civil war also took on an international dimension when Figueres received aid from the Guatemalans and the Caribbean Legion. While the
United States and Honduras ignored Picado's plea for military assistance, Nicaraguan president Anastasio Somoza offered his troops to
the beleaguered president. In the meantime, Mora called upon a well-
disciplined force of workers in San José and vowed to defend the right
of social change. His actions presented a picture of a Communist party
defending itself in a supposedly democratic country.[8]

Three days after Figueres launched his final offensive on 10 April, a
cease-fire was arranged, and the subsequent peace negotiations were
conducted by the papal nuncio, Luigi Centoz, and the U.S. ambassador, Nathaniel P. Davis. The peace agreement provided for an interim
president, Santos León Herrera, the departure of the leaders of the
National Republican and Popular Vanguard parties, and a guarantee of the leaders' lives and property, but not before Mora vowed to
continue the fight, a threat that raised the possibility of Nicaraguan
intervention and the assignment to Costa Rica of U.S. troops stationed
in the Panama Canal Zone.[9]

Following the peace settlement, Figueres moved swiftly. After arranging for a personally led junta to govern for eighteen months, he
dismissed National Republicans from government posts and university positions and froze their personal assets. Asserting that it was

impossible to deal with the Communists as "normal people," Figueres exiled or jailed Vanguard party leaders, closed their offices, and finally outlawed the party on 17 July. Under these circumstances, Mora chose exile. Although Figueres asserted that he had saved the country from communism, Ambassador Davis found little difference in the social philosophies of Mora and Figueres.

Later, in February 1949, Figueres and Ulate reached an accord that extended the junta's term until 8 May 1950, which provided time to write a new and modern constitution and to elect a new congress and two new vice-presidents. Satisfied with his accomplishments, Figueres relinquished power early and permitted Ulate to be inaugurated, as president, for a full four-year term on 8 November 1949.[10]

Occupied with more pressing issues in Europe and Asia, the United States did little more than express its opposition to the junta's usurpation of political power, but, with the restoration of constitutional government, the State Department expressed its satisfaction that Costa Rica had solved its problems "in a democratic manner fully consistent with the country's long traditions of liberty and devotion to the principles of representative government."[11]

Ulate's economic policies endeared him to the business community. As a conservative, he chose not to push forward with social reforms, which, in turn, contributed to Figueres's presidential victory in 1952 and the introduction of sweeping social programs in Costa Rica. Figueres's socialist leanings and his criticisms of the U.S. failure to deal with socioeconomic issues contributed to his unpopularity in Washington, where some officials linked Figueres to the Communist camp.[12]

1954: Communism in Guatemala?

In contrast to Costa Rica, with its history of relative political calm, Guatemala had endured a military dictatorship under Jorge Ubico since 1931. The unicameral Chamber of Deputies did nothing more than rubber-stamp Ubico's directives, and the national judiciary hesitated to oppose his wishes. Guatemala's twenty-two departments, or states, were administered by a political chief (*jefe político*) whom Ubico had appointed and who doubled as military commandant.

This arrangement did not long conceal an explosive situation. Guatemala's agricultural economy had fostered two distinct socioeconomic groups: a small, wealthy upper class, and a poverty-stricken, illiterate, and inert mass of peasants, composed chiefly of Indians. Sandwiched between the two was a small middle sector frustrated by its inability to participate in politics. In practice, politics perpetuated the privileged position of the elite and kept the largest section of the population politically helpless.[13]

The dichotomy of interests was found in the eleven new political parties that emerged following Ubico's ouster in June 1944. Five— the Social Democratic party, the National Action party, the National Democratic Front, the Democratic party, and the Constitutional Democratic party—largely represented the middle sector, which had played a decisive role in ousting Ubico but lacked the necessary experience in public administration to provide effective leadership. Four other new parties—the National Workers party, the National Vanguard party, the Popular Liberation Front, and the National Reform party—appealed to the lower socioeconomic groups. Ambassador Boaz Long described the National Vanguard party as a collection of "starry-eyed" idealists, with a party platform that "makes some sense" in its call for wage floors, price ceilings on essential consumer goods, large-scale agricultural production, and the organization of all economic sectors in a planned effort to stimulate growth in the national economy.[14] The Popular Liberation Front and National Reform party consisted mostly of educators and students with little influence outside the capital. The leaders of the Liberal and Conservative parties, which dominated Guatemala's political scene since 1870, were believed to be hiding or in exile.

Given the makeup and support base of the new political parties, Ubico's expulsion set Guatemalan politics on a leftward drift, a direction confirmed by the presidential election of Juan José Arévalo in February 1945. Arévalo, a former teacher, returned from a lengthy exile in Argentina after Ubico's downfall. Embraced by the middle sector because of his political idealism and his appeal to the workers, Arévalo caused concern among the elites. Arévalo's "spiritual socialism" promised a new order: a Guatemala without foreign capital and with a "square deal" for the common man, an estimated 80 percent of the Guatemalan population. In application, Arévalo's rent law, housing law, social security program, labor code, and proposed income tax struck at the wealthy class and sought to improve the quality of life of the downtrodden masses. The revised electoral code prevented several of the smaller conservative political parties from participating in the 1948 congressional elections. Furthermore, the administration's $100 million in expenditures through 1947 frightened those who were accustomed to prewar national budgets of $10 million.

Such programs were a marked departure from the liberal-conservative struggle that had characterized Guatemalan politics since 1870, nor did they fall within the objectives of the middle sector. Because the appeal to the poor threatened their positions, both the elite and the middle sector labeled Arévalo and his supporters as "Communists."[15] Arévalo soon found himself increasingly isolated. Many of his original supporters, particularly professionals and business people, deserted him. Subsequently, the Social Democratic party and the Constitutional Democratic party, which represented the upper class, withdrew from the 1948 congressional elections. As the opposition intensified, so too did the charges of Communist influence. Archbishop Mariano Rossell Arellano warned Catholics that they could not vote for Communist candidates in the 1948 elections without suffering church condemnation. In July 1948, the Guatemalan Democratic League charged Arévalo with using his vaunted concern with the plight of the poor to camouflage his Communist intentions. Violence was an ever-present consideration, illustrated by a reported twenty-nine attempted coups against Arévalo. U.S. officials believed that Arévalo survived the pressure because the army, a moderating influence, convinced him to dismiss alleged "leftists" from cabinet posts.[16]

Throughout Arévalo's administration, from 1945 to 1949, American officials conceded that the ground was fertile for communism because of the disparity of wealth and land ownership patterns in Guatemala. The ambiguity of reports from the field and analysis of these reports in Washington indicated that policymakers failed to clearly define the Communist-nationalist issue. One group pointed to evidence that downplayed the Communist issue and emphasized the nationalistic character of the objectives of Arévalo and his followers. Because Ubico crushed the Communist movement during the 1930s and the 1945 constitution banned political parties with an international character, some officials argued that communism was not present in Guatemala. Ambassador Edwin Kyle often compared the Communist label pinned on Arévalo's reform program with "opinions expressed by some of [my] fellow wealthy Texans relative to President Roosevelt." Others noted that Arévalo's brand of communism was "more local" than international and that in other circumstances and countries he might be named an "advanced liberal." In 1950, the Central Intelligence Agency (CIA) concluded that Arévalo's policies were "strongly nationalistic and influenced by modern socialistic ideas" favoring the interests of the impotent laboring class but that they were not Communistic. Finally, in May 1951, the State Department concluded that the "Arévalo government cannot be said to be communist or controlled by communists." [17]

But departmental hard-liners were not persuaded. In early 1947, the assistant Secretary of State for American republics affairs, Spruille Braden, charged that the Communists had forged with Arévalo a secret agreement that expanded their participation in government and labor posts. Braden maintained that Arévalo was, not a crusading reformer, but an agent of Stalin. Later that same year, an embassy staff report indicted Arévalo and reflected the opinions of Guatemala's elite—that an estimated two hundred Communists held influential positions in labor and government circles and were allegedly linked to Moscow indirectly through Mexico City and Paris. The labor code, if fully enforced, "would facilitate the communist objective of state and worker control of industry"; the rent law was a form of confiscatory taxation; and the social security program placed an unfair burden on industry. Both the CIA in 1950 and the State Department in 1951 concluded that, while Arévalo and his spiritual socialism were not Communist, Guatemala's Communists had extensively penetrated labor and government circles. Policymakers, however, could not determine if Guatemalan communism owed its growth to design or to Arévalo's naïveté or to a mixture of both. In any case, the original revolutionary aims became distorted through their confusion with Communist jingoism in the domestic and international fields, which contributed to Arévalo's loss of his original support base.

The assassination on 18 July 1948 of Colonel Francisco Araña, a spokesman for Arévalo's opposition and a potential presidential candidate, persuaded Ambassador Richard C. Patterson and Ernest V. Siracusa, a desk officer in the State Department, that the killing was "an attempt on the part of Colonel [Jacobo] Arbenz, President Arévalo and the leftist elements . . . to eliminate the growing opposition movement." Patterson cautioned that if the opposition forces "failed to risk their resources in the near future, [they] faced the distinct possibility of not having any to risk at a later date." [18]

Jacobo Arbenz won the November 1950 presidential election by nearly 194,000 votes over his nearest competitor, General Miguel Ydígoras Fuentes. Yet, despite their concerns, U.S. officials had failed to reach a consensus about Arbenz and where he would take Guatemala's politics. The result was a series of ambiguous reports, such as that of Ambassador Patterson, who was "inclined to share" a widely held local opinion that described Arbenz as an opportunist "using labor" to get elected. "Once in office," Patterson wrote, he "will turn on the extremists," but he ominously noted that "the possibility he shares extremist ideological views may not be discounted." Throughout the campaign, Arbenz declared that he was not a Communist. Arbenz did not speak like a demagogue determined to oust foreign influence from the country. To improve his image, he instructed a wealthy Guatemalan industrialist, Jorge A. Cordero, to assure the U.S. embassy staff that "I am not a communist and that if I become President, I will deport every one who causes trouble." Yet it was clear that he had little intention of undoing what Arévalo had accomplished. More than once, Arbenz charged that the electorate was being presented with a clear choice between the goals of the 1944 revolution and "those old systems which for more than a century have tried to destroy the other social sectors by controlling the national wealth and persecuting the population." Amidst the contradictory reports, the State Department was confident that, once inaugurated, Arbenz would "steer a more nearly middle course than Arévalo" and that, with his control of the army, Arbenz possessed the means to oppose the Communists "if he so desires." But American officials clearly understood that what had begun as a nationalist movement to implement a more democratic government in Guatemala, the overthrow of Jorge Ubico in July 1944, had thereafter drifted politically to the left and taken on the characteristics of a Communist regime by 1951. They could not determine the extent of the Communist influence.[19]

Two interrelated factors contributed to the conflicting interpretations. At the beginning of Arévalo's administration, field officers and State Department analysts—Ellis O. Briggs, Andrew Donovan, Laurence Duggan, Edwin Kyle, William Cochran, Robert Newbegin, Robert Wilson, Murray Wise, and Robert Woodward—had lengthy and vast experiences in Central and South America. They understood that the middle sector desired greater political participation but that, like the elite, they were not interested in social and economic reform for the masses.

The newer officers, who began their foreign service careers in the postwar years—William Tapley Bennett, Jr., Edward Cale, John Fisher, Raymond Oakley, Richard C. Patterson, Kennedon Steins, and Milton Wells—did not have extensive Latin American experience. More important, their views were shaped by the dynamics of the cold war, which divided the world into two camps that did not allow for a middle ground. Like the Communists in Eastern and Western Europe and in the United States, Central American Communists sought to infiltrate educational, government, and labor institutions for their own objectives. American officials believed that Guatemalan Communists followed this pattern. As cold war positions hardened, a Communist came to be anyone who challenged the established order or expressed sympathy for the Soviet position in world affairs, whether or not a

direct link to Moscow was evident. Within this framework, the demands for correcting the legitimate socioeconomic grievances of the
poor received less attention than did U.S. strategic interests. U.S.
officials clearly failed to sort out the differences between the two in
Guatemala before the hard-line, myopic John Foster Dulles arrived at
the State Department.

Jacobo Arbenz, at age thirty-seven, was the youngest Guatemalan
president in the nation's history and, at the time, the youngest head
of state in the Americas. Arbenz was determined to build upon what
had begun by developing an independent economy; foreign interests,
while not excluded, would no longer be granted the special concessions that had resulted in the concentration of land in the hands of
the few and the avoidance of taxes necessary for social reforms. This
economic transformation would require social readjustment, and the
government's responsibility was to ensure that these changes did not
create massive economic chaos and discontent.[20] The implication of
what Arbenz might do was more unsettling than the specifics of his
program.

To break the *latifundio-minifundio* agricultural landowning system,
Arbenz implemented a plan that divided and distributed the idle land
of *latifundios* with more than 223 acres. The plan affected 1,059 properties averaging 4,300 acres each. Compensation was based upon the
value the landowners had assigned to them on tax declarations made
before 9 May 1952, and payment was made with 3 percent, twenty-
five-year bonds. The land distribution program was accelerated by
legislation known as decree 900, enacted on 17 June 1952. Within two
years, some 917,659 acres of idle land were expropriated and distributed to 87,659 Guatemalan peasants. The program received credit for
increasing domestic food production, with a concomitant drop in food
prices and an increase in the purchasing power of many Guatemalans.

The land distribution program understandably angered landowners, but it also provoked the church and the military. The General
Growers' Association, representing the large landowners, attacked the
government program, supported opposition parties, and conspired to
overthrow the government. Archbishop Rossell Arellano charged that

the government's Communistic reform programs would upset social stability and lead to anarchy, yet neither the landowners nor the archbishop offered alternatives. The military command, traditionally tied to the landed elite, also opposed this threat to the established order.

Foreign-owned lands were not exempt from the agrarian reform program, but the largest foreign landowner—the United Fruit Company—appeared virtually invulnerable to its application. Thanks to the 1936 contract agreement with Ubico, UFCO avoided almost the entire Guatemalan tax structure. The company was allowed to undervalue its land for taxing purposes, to leave unregulated its transportation and communications systems, and to knowingly use fictitious overseas profits to avoid domestic taxes. At best, UFCO paid 1½ cents per bunch of bananas exported from Guatemala. Such manipulations enabled the company to report a $65 million profit in 1950, while little money made its way into either the Guatemalan treasury or the Guatemalan economy.

Guatemalan workers knew that UFCO paid little in taxes, that it bribed political officials, and that it owned more land than did all the Guatemalan landholders combined. They understood the vestiges of discrimination in other ways, too. The company constructed substandard housing for its workers, who also faced limited job opportunities and lower pay scales. The condescending attitudes of company officials were augmented by other discriminatory acts, which, among other things, required workers to remove their hats while talking to company officials and forbade Indians from entering the front yards of white residents. Guatemalans, understandably, referred to UFCO as *el pulpo*, or the octopus.

When the agrarian reform law was enacted, only 15 percent of UFCO's 550,000 acres were being cultivated. Under the law's provisions, the government expropriated 400,000 acres of it, or approximately one-seventh of Guatemala's arable land. In return, the government offered to pay UFCO $1,185,000, the exact amount at which the company valued its land in the national tax records, with the twenty-five-year, guaranteed, 3 percent bonds. Both UFCO and the State

Department considered it an inadequate offer. On behalf of UFCO, the State Department, on 20 April 1954, submitted to Guatemala a bill for $15,854,849, the largest claim presented to a foreign government since the 1938 Mexican oil expropriation. Arbenz, who refused to be intimidated, did not know that the CIA was already preparing for an invasion of Guatemala.

As the Arbenz administration implemented its agrarian reform program, several forces within the United States contributed to the solidification of the perception that international communism gripped the government at Guatemala City. UFCO led the assault. As early as 1950, the company's public relations director, Edward Bernays, determined to cultivate U.S. opinion by arranging fact-finding trips for reporters from leading newspapers, including the *New York Tribune*, the *New York Times*, the *Miami Herald*, and the *Christian Science Monitor*, and popular newsmagazines, including *U.S. News and World Report*, *Time*, and *Newsweek*. All of the journalists came back to the United States reporting that communism had indeed taken control of Guatemala. Bernays also contacted congressmen on both sides of the aisle: John McCormack, a Democrat from Massachusetts; Alexander Wiley, a Republican from Wisconsin; and administration officials Walter Bedell Smith and Thomas C. Mann. Bernays also contracted with John Clements, an ex-marine who was an outspoken supporter of Senator Joseph McCarthy's anti-Communist campaign. In 1952 and 1954, for thirty-five thousand dollars, Clements Associates produced reports on the extent of communism in Guatemala. Although filled with inaccuracies and innuendo, the reports were cited in government speeches and publications, including the State Department's official explanation of the Communist penetration into Guatemala.

Furthermore, several members of the Dwight D. Eisenhower administration had links to UFCO. The Dulles brothers, John and Allen, came to the State Department and CIA, respectively, from Sullivan and Cromwell, the New York international law firm that handled UFCO's account. Others included Eisenhower's first assistant secretary for inter-American affairs, John M. Cabot; the secretary of commerce, Sinclair Weeks; the ambassador to Costa Rica, Robert Hill; an advisor, John McCloy; and Eisenhower's personal secretary, Ann Whitman.

Outside government circles, others expressed concern with the extent of communism in Guatemala. Spruille Braden, former assistant secretary of state for American republics affairs, spoke vehemently of a Communist threat. In October 1952, the prestigious Council of Foreign Relations held a series of six study groups, titled "Political Unrest in Latin America," to make recommendations to the incoming administration. John McClintock, former State Department official and then UFCO assistant vice-president, chaired the session on Guatemala. McClintock and Braden dominated the session, declaring that Communist subversion presented the United States with a dangerous situation. Their strong condemnation overshadowed the social and economic issues raised by Latin American scholars Charles Cumberland of Rutgers University and Frank Tannenbaum of Columbia University. In May 1953, Assistant Secretary John M. Cabot read to the council a paper written by one of his predecessors in his post, Adolf A. Berle. Cabot reported that "the Guatemalan situation . . . is quite simply the penetration of Central America by a frankly Russian dominated communist group," and he recommended backing the forces that would either change or oust the Communists.[21]

Also, in 1953, President Eisenhower appointed C. D. Jackson to chair a committee on international activities and to produce a cold war strategy for pushing the Russians back from their advanced position. The Central American section of the report was written by Berle after he had conferred with Salvadoran Social Democrat Miguel A. Magaña and President Figueres of Costa Rica. Both were stridently anti-Communist. Magaña feared that it was only a matter of time before Guatemalan communism, sponsored by the Soviet Union, spread throughout Central America. Figueres, it will be recalled, believed that he had saved his country from communism in 1948. The Jackson committee went on to recommend a moral condemnation of Arbenz, by both his Central American neighbors and the United States, followed by an economic embargo so that Arbenz and the Communists would be forced from government and could be replaced by a moderate administration.

The assertions about communism in Guatemala came at a time when the public was dismayed by the loss of China to the Communists, the Korean War stalemate, and the suspicion that Communists had penetrated the federal government in Washington. This frustration contributed to the election of Dwight D. Eisenhower as president in November 1952. Both Eisenhower and his secretary of state, John Foster Dulles, arrived in Washington convinced that Communists capitalized on legitimate discontent to get themselves elected and appointed to government positions from which they subverted the political structure for their own purposes. Eisenhower and Dulles saw the pattern established in Eastern Europe and believed that the Guatemalan Communists were following the same path. The reports from Guatemala and the judgments of leading figures in the United States confirmed their opinions. Under these circumstances, the new administration decided to draw the line against Communist expansion in Guatemala.

The decision to depose Arbenz was made approximately six months after Eisenhower's inauguration. Known as Operation PBSUCCESS, the plan was known only by the president, the Dulles brothers, and a few top-ranking officials at the State Department and the CIA. John Peurifoy was assigned as ambassador to direct the operations inside Guatemala. The Americans selected a former colonel in the Guatemalan army, Carlos Castillo Armas, as invasion leader over the preferred civilian Juan Cordova Cerna, who had cancer, and General Ydígoras Fuentes, who was linked to the landowning conservatives.[22]

As preparations for intervention proceeded, in March 1954 Dulles led the U.S. delegation to the tenth inter-American conference at Caracas, where he sought a multilateral blessing for a unilateral action. Speaking before the delegates, Dulles claimed that he accepted the differences in the political institutions of the hemispheric nations, but he pointed out that those serving "alien masters" needed to be changed. He denied the existence of indigenous Communist movements and asserted that every nation in the hemisphere had been penetrated by international communism under Moscow's direction. He challenged his colleagues to demand its withdrawal, to "deal with it as a situation that might endanger the peace of America," and called for decisive action, presumably under the Rio Treaty.[23] In effect, Dulles sought to Pan-Americanize the Monroe Doctrine in order to prevent what he perceived to be Soviet penetration of the Western Hemisphere.

Dulles carefully avoided mentioning Guatemala by name, but the implication was clear and understood by Guatemala's foreign minister, Guillermo Toriello. In response, he charged that Dulles was attempting to internationalize McCarthyism and to provide a pretext for intervening in Guatemala's internal affairs in order to safeguard UFCO's privileged position. He added that if the Dulles proposal were approved, Pan-Americanism would become an instrument for the service of monopolistic interests and against the forces of political and economic liberation. Toriello also asked if the administration in Washington understood that monopolistic investments stymied economic development and social improvements and that foreign investment was still welcomed in Guatemala, provided it abided by Guatemalan laws.[24] Toriello's response struck at the heart of the nationalist-Communist issue.

After a spirited debate, U.S. interests prevailed. By a seventeen-to-one vote, with Guatemala dissenting and Argentina and Mexico abstaining, the resolution passed. His objective accomplished, Dulles left the conference when attention turned to economic issues.[25] His departure fueled the anti-American sentiment already present and also reinforced Toriello's point.

Following the alleged victory at Caracas, plans for the overthrow of Arbenz were put into effect. The CIA knew that, without massive external assistance, Castillo Armas's ragtag army of about three hundred men then being trained in Honduras and Nicaragua could not win a battle, much less a war. To offset the problem, the CIA sponsored a public relations campaign that successfully deceived Arbenz into thinking that a much larger army confronted him. A shipment of Czechoslovakian small arms to the Arbenz regime on 18 June became the trigger to action. On the same day, Castillo Armas entered Guatemala from Honduras with 150 men, and the U.S. embassy in Guatemala City was turned into an operations center. From the embassy, Peurifoy directed the air assault, and the CIA jammed the Guatemalan airwaves with its own reports of a purported massive invasion by an army of liberation. Arbenz succumbed on 27 June 1954 and fled the country. An interim military junta paved the way for the September presidential election of Castillo Armas, whom the Eisenhower administration welcomed to the presidential palace. Armas's "campaign of liberation and reconstruction," after "the long period of communist influence," earned the respect of the American people, Eisenhower wrote to Armas.[26]

Once the invasion began, the United States worked to prevent interference from either the United Nations (UN) or the Organization of American States (OAS). Seeking assistance against further aggression, Guatemala appealed first to the United Nations Security Council and then to Inter-American Peace Committee of the OAS. At the UN Ambassador Henry Cabot Lodge, Jr., worked for a Security Council resolution to send the dispute to the OAS under article 51 of the organization's charter. A Soviet veto, followed by a British and French change of heart, kept the issue before the Security Council until Dulles warned the governments at London and Paris that the United States might withdraw its support of their position in the Middle East and North Africa. The threats enabled Lodge to shut off further discussion of the Guatemalan situation.

In the meantime, the State Department worked to delay the Inter-American Peace Committee's fact-finding mission from reaching Central America. By the time it departed from New York, on 28 June, Jacobo Arbenz had resigned, but Carlos Castillo Armas was not yet in the presidential palace. At the insistence of the United States, the team remained in Mexico City until the fighting ended, which obviated their mission.[27]

Both militarily and diplomatically, the United States guided events to suit its own interests. Officials insisted that it intervened in Guatemala, not to save UFCO, but to prevent the spread of international communism. As Thomas Mann succinctly stated, "This government knew that communists the world over were agents of Soviet imperialism and constituted a mortal threat to our own national existence." To a national television audience, John Foster Dulles remarked, "If the United Fruit matter were settled, if they gave a gold piece for every banana, the problem would remain just as it is today, as far as the presence of communist infiltration in Guatemala is concerned. That is the problem, not United Fruit."[28]

The Latin American nations heaped an avalanche of criticism upon the United States for its singlehanded intervention in the domestic affairs of an American republic. The governments also maintained that deep-rooted economic and social problems, not communism, threatened their political fabric.[29]

Return to Normalcy:
Central America after 1954

With the Guatemalan problem put to rest, Central American politics returned to the status quo ante. For the remainder of the decade, all five republics supported the United States in its stand against Soviet global policies, and none of them exchanged diplomats with the Soviet Union or Eastern bloc countries. In 1960, a special study authorized by the Senate Subcommittee on American Republics Affairs, confirmed that Central American contact with Communist international, student, and labor groups was minimal.[30] As the Eisenhower administration wound down, it found that Guatemala and Nicaragua were willing to serve as staging areas for the April 1961 invasion at the Bay of Pigs, an attack intended to depose Cuban dictator Fidel Castro. Washington's fear of Communist infiltration throughout Central America remained, despite the fact that a Communist organization existed only in Costa Rica, under the name of the Popular Vanguard party. In the other four countries, Communists presumably operated clandestinely and exercised influence in spite of their limited numbers.

These suspicions increased in May 1954, when a series of isolated labor protests at Tela and Puerto Cortés, Honduras, mushroomed into a sixty-six-day strike against the United Fruit Company and the Standard Fruit Company. The workers' demands for a 50 percent pay increase, fifteen days' annual paid vacation, improved hospital services and housing, better working conditions, and the right to organize and bargain collectively revealed long-standing grievances in the country. The strike spread to miners in El Mochito and to industrial workers in San Pedro Sula and Tegucigalpa. A government negotiating committee recommended a $7.5 million settlement for salary increases and social benefits, but the companies rejected it. The labor unrest came at a time when the United States was plotting against Arbenz in Guatemala, and Washington believed that Communists played a major role in orchestrating the strike. Honduran government officials and fruit company officers shared this opinion. When negotiations broke off in June, President Juan Galvéz mediated the crisis. Galvéz, a former UFCO lawyer, rejected the government committee's recommendations. He accepted instead a company offer that granted few pecuniary rewards to the workers but provided for labor's right to organize and bargain collectively, a proviso that offered the underclass the opportunity to challenge the elite.[31]

The issue of social change also lay at the base of the personal confrontation between José Figueres and Anastasio Somoza, a controversy that dated to Costa Rica's 1948 civil war, when Somoza offered military assistance to Teodoro Picado in Picado's battle against Figueres. After the war, Figueres's continued call for democracy and social reform irritated Somoza, who accused Figueres of fomenting plots against him. In response to the supposed threat, Somoza closed the San Juan River to Costa Rican merchant vessels, conducted military maneuvers along their common border, and directed a defamatory campaign in the Nicaraguan press. U.S. arms shipments to Nicaragua under the terms of the Military Assistance Act exacerbated the situation, which, following Somoza's forces' capture of Nicaraguan exile Pablo Lael, finally erupted in April 1954. Before his execution, Lael allegedly implicated Figueres in an assassination plot against Somoza. Somoza reacted with a vengeance, organizing the Authentic Anti-Communist Revolutionary Army, a five-hundred-man force that crossed the Costa Rican border on 11 July 1955. From there it conducted raids, including air attacks, on Costa Rican cities and conducted a propaganda campaign.

The United States, indebted to Somoza for his support of the overthrow of Arbenz, pursued a two-pronged course in an effort to end the conflict. It supported Costa Rica's call for action by the OAS under the terms of the 1947 Rio Treaty and then made available to Costa Rica four military aircraft to countervail Somoza's military. Somoza denounced the action and demanded that he receive an identical number of airplanes. The crisis passed in July, when Somoza's army fell into disarray and with it the necessity for OAS action. Neither leader was satisfied with American actions. Figueres believed that the U.S. ambassador in Managua, Thomas Whelan, and the CIA had provided assistance to Somoza as a measure of gratitude for his help in the overthrow of Arbenz.[32] Somoza bitterly complained about U.S. assistance to Costa Rica: "What advantage do we get for being friendly? . . . You treat us like an old wife. We would rather be treated like a young mistress."[33]

The continued fear of communism prompted Vice-President Richard Nixon, during his February 1955 goodwill visit, to caution Central American leaders about Communist inroads gained through intellectual, labor, and student organizations. The same fear contributed to a four-month delay of Milton Eisenhower's trip to Central America in 1958, although the trip went smoothly, with only a small demonstration in San Salvador. Despite the purported Communist influence, the National Security Council concluded in January 1959 that none of the five republics faced the threat of an immediate Communist takeover and that there was no need for the Central American governments to expend a great deal of their energy and resources on internal security.[34]

After the turmoil ended in 1955, Washington policymakers gave minimal attention to Central America. However, given their varied assessments of the region's heads of state, they also failed to appreciate fully the region's political dynamics. Despite the unsuccessful efforts by a U.S. medical team in the Panama Canal Zone to save Somoza's life following his shooting in 1956, an effort that gave credence to the allegation of a close bond between Washington and Managua, the United

States actually favored the political liberalization of Nicaragua's family regime. The Somozas, but not the public, understood this. In Guatemala, the Castillo Armas government was described as "middle of the road," despite the country's rightward drift, as evidenced by the 1956 constitution. Castillo Armas's successor, Ydígoras Fuentes, was portrayed as a strongman who drew support from all social classes because "he represents strong government, which so many Guatemalans seem to want."[35] Salvadoran presidents Oscar Osorio and José Lemus received cool treatment, largely because of Osorio's unwillingness to support the 1954 Guatemalan invasion and Lemus's supposed leftist policies, which included the establishment of the Institute of Urban Housing, the legalization of labor unions, the implementation of a social security system, and the completion of the Lempa River hydroelectric project. Neither, however, disturbed the privileged position of the so-called families that dominated the Salvadoran economy. Washington officials perceived the Honduran military as the stabilizing political influence during the presidencies of Julio Lozano and Ramón Villeda Morales. Finally, Costa Rican president José Figueres's anti-American attitude and his newly found friendship with local Communist leader Manuel Mora were not appreciated in Washington, but his socialist programs were accepted. The Eisenhower administration was more content with his successor, Mario Enchandi, whose election in 1958 was viewed a victory for free enterprise.[36]

While the United States appeared satisfied with Central America's political tranquility after 1955 and the absence of a Communist threat in the region, the underlying social and economic disparities continued. Still, there was nothing to indicate that policymakers had heeded the advice of Henry Holland, the former assistant secretary for Latin American affairs, who had cautioned, "Distinctions between extreme leftist parties and the communists are often fluid. [Therefore,] we should caution against [labeling] leaders as communists."[37]

8　From False Hope to Entrenchment of the Old Order, 1960–1976

On 30 August 1960, Theodore Sorenson, political advisor to the Democratic presidential candidate, John F. Kennedy, accused the Eisenhower administration of squandering Latin American goodwill by its close association with dictators and its assumption that what was good for American big business was automatically good for Latin America as well. If elected, Kennedy promised, he would forge a new direction in Latin American policy.[1] Shortly after his election, Kennedy signaled that change when he expressed a willingness to accept moderately leftist governments that were meeting the needs of the "generation of rising expectations" by sponsoring constructive change. He promised to use U.S. leverage to keep liberal governments in power, and he warned local oligarchies, the major obstacle to the modernization of Latin American society, that they could no longer expect the support of the U.S. government.[2]

Despite such rhetoric, Kennedy and his advisors also believed that many Latin Americans used communism not only as an outlet for anti-American resentments but also as the most expedient means to achieving social modernization. This provided the Soviet Union and Cuba with an opportunity for exploiting the hemisphere's adverse economic and social conditions, and to do so at the expense of the United States. Within a few years, U.S. strategic interests largely voided the social and economic commitments of Kennedy's pledge.

New Directions?: The Kennedy Years

At the White House on 13 March 1961, the same week that, 139 years earlier, President James Monroe had urged U.S. recognition of the Latin American republics, President John F. Kennedy announced the Alliance for Progress, an ambitious ten-year program to bring political reform as well as social and economic progress to the southern hemisphere. Admitting to the policy failures of the past, Kennedy asked for a new beginning "to satisfy the basic needs of the American people for homes, work and land, health and schools—*techo, trabajo y tierra, salud y escuela.*"[3]

The impetus for the alliance had begun late in the Eisenhower administration and represented a departure from earlier U.S. policies. Its general goals found expression in the Declaration of the Peoples of America and the Charter of Punte del Este in August 1961. The documents committed the American nations to working toward a number of goals: improving and strengthening democratic institutions; accelerating economic and social development; implementing urban and rural housing programs; encouraging agrarian reform; eliminating illiteracy; and initiating health and sanitation programs. The nations also pledged to work toward assuring fair wages and satisfactory working conditions for all workers; instituting tax reform laws; developing monetary and fiscal policies to check inflation; stimulating private enterprise; finding a solution to the problems created by excessive price fluctuations in the basic exports of Latin America; and finally, accelerating the economic integration of Latin America.[4]

Envisioned as a ten-year, $100 billion program, it required a U.S. commitment of $20 billion. The remainder, it was thought, would come from Western Europe, from Japan, and from a return of Latin America's flight capital. In addition, Latin Americans were expected to devote an increasing share of their own resources to economic and social development and to make the appropriate reforms to ensure that all people shared fully in the program's benefits. In agreeing to these changes, the participants believed that a bloodless social revolution would result, obviating a Communist revolution.[5]

During its ten-year life, the Alliance for Progress and related programs provided the five Central American nations with $644 million, including assistance to the Central American Common Market (CACM). National planning agencies were established to guide the development and implementation in six categories of assistance: industry, agriculture, infrastructure, taxation, health and sanitation, and housing and education.[6] Industrial development funds went for the improvement of banking, management, and commodity marketing and for training technical staffs. Manpower training programs emphasized study abroad for persons working or planning to work in business administration, economics, and public administration. Loans were used to help owners of small businesses finance their industrial enterprises and those organizing capital investment projects by the private sector. Labor leaders received training in the United States.

Agricultural programs included funds for increasing domestic foodstuff production and for crop diversification to cooperatives and small farmers not involved in the export of coffee and bananas. Land distribution programs sought to provide landless families with small plots of land. In addition, agricultural research, college training and extension services, cooperative projects, and planning policies for marginal farmers were developed. Infrastructure projects included the expansion of electricity to rural areas and road construction into regions considered to have the greatest economic potential. Major hydroelectric projects financed with alliance funds included Nicaragua's Rio Tuma River fifty-megawatt plant and the Honduran Rio Lindo plant, both of which were essential for industrial development.

To improve the collection of government revenues, U.S. advisors assisted with the implementation of a modern property-tax system, budgeting and accounting procedures, and the training of tax technicians and office managers at both the national and the local level throughout Central America.

Health and sanitation projects included the construction of hospitals and water treatment and sanitation plants. Mobile medical units were established to reach isolated villages that had previously received no medical attention; they conducted self-help educational programs and taught basic sanitary procedures. Family planning programs were introduced in an effort to cut the region's high birth rate.

In the education field, alliance financing provided for textbooks, more training programs for teachers in primary schools and vocational schools, and, in El Salvador, a nationwide educational television network to reach the rural areas. Teacher training centers, faculty development programs, and demonstration schools were established.

Housing projects sought to improve the quality of life for the poor, but political considerations often influenced decisions, as happened with those undertaken at La Lima and El Progreso, Honduras, where the Tela railroad workers were considered strongly pro-American.

The Kennedy administration also encouraged the development of the Central American Common Market, whose origins can be traced to the 1951 meeting of the Central American foreign ministers, when they established the Organization of Central American States (ODECA). It became a major influence in the drive for regional economic cooperation that culminated with Costa Rica's ratification of a 1960 treaty providing for economic integration through liberal trade policies, elimination of quota restrictions, reduction or abolition of tariffs, and creation of integrated industries. ODECA appeared to be a modern-day fulfillment of Central America's historic desire for integration. The United States gave no indication of supporting the economic integration movement until late 1958, when the Eisenhower administration determined that economic development served as an important countermeasure to communism. At a meeting of Central American heads of state in San José, Costa Rica, in March 1963, Kennedy, who shared Eisenhower's opinion, pledged the United States' cooperation with the project.[7] As in the past, the United States favored Central American union when it served Washington's interests. Subsequently, the Regional Office of Central America and Panama (ROCAP) was established as a "special mission" of the Agency for International Development (AID) to assist CACM with economic planning and development and with fiscal, monetary, investment, and trade policies and to help foster free movement of goods, people, and capital within the region.

The U.S. government also advanced funds to the Central American Bank for Economic Integration (CABEI), established in 1961 as the principal intermediate credit institution in Central America. Resources came from AID, the Inter-American Development Bank, and subsequently from several European banks and Mexico. By 1967, CABEI had approved 187 individual subloans totaling $120.7 million, mostly for infrastructure and industrial projects.[8]

In addition to the assistance programs, Central America received increased visibility during Kennedy's administration. Visits by presidential advisor Arthur M. Schlesinger, Jr., the vice-president, Lyndon B. Johnson, and the president's brother, Edward M. (Ted) Kennedy. The high point came on 19 and 20 March 1963, when Kennedy met with the Central American heads of state at San José, Costa Rica. Kennedy's reception indicated not only his personal popularity but also the hopes he had raised across the isthmus with the United States' commitment to improving the impoverished's quality of life. The Declaration of San José reasserted Central America's commitment to continued social reform and economic integration.[9]

Kennedy demonstrated his support for social-minded governments in 1963, when the Honduran defense minister, Colonel Oswaldo López Arellano, ousted President Ramón Villeda Morales, whose program since 1957 had included domestic tax relief, investment guarantees for both domestic and foreign capital, social security legislation, a labor code, and, in 1962, an agrarian reform law. During Villeda Morales's administration, the church revitalized its rural bases through literacy programs, religious revivals, and community development projects. In response, the Honduran landed oligarchy labeled these programs Communistic and, with the foreign-owned fruit companies, fought against their implementation. In the face of the growing opposition, Villeda Morales reorganized his security forces. He dissolved the national police and replaced it with a two-thousand-man civil guard, one more loyal to the president. The move did not sit well with the military, which viewed the civil guard as a threat to its own position.

The political atmosphere intensified, as elements on both the left and the right increased their pressure on Villeda Morales. The left charged that he failed to do enough for the peasant and the worker, while the right asserted that Communists had made their way into the government's inner circles. At the same time, the military and civil guard clashed in their own power struggle. Distrust and anxiety spread across Honduras, contributing to a pessimistic outlook for the general elections scheduled for 1963, which never came off. On 3 October, ten days before the elections, Colonel López Arellano directed a bloody military coup against Villeda Morales, for reasons not yet fully clear. In response, Kennedy withheld recognition, halted economic aid, and withdrew military advisors from Honduras until the López Arellano regime pledged not to dismantle the reform programs already in place.[10]

More important to the United States than Honduran politics were the small bands of guerrillas that conducted terrorist campaigns from Central America's inaccessible mountains and jungles. In order to meet the new challenge, the United States altered its military assistance to Central America. During the 1950s, regional defense policy emphasized the security of the Panama Canal, Mexican and Venezuelan oil, and Caribbean trade. The Eisenhower administration indiscriminately granted military assistance to governments that demonstrated a favorable attitude toward the United States and expressed opposition to communism. Such actions contributed to the charge that the United States continued to support right-wing dictatorships, an assertion made by both Milton Eisenhower and Richard Nixon following their trips to Central and South America in 1958.

In contrast to the Eisenhower policy, the 1961 Military Assistance Program (MAP) shifted the emphasis from preparation against an external attack to preparation for internal security. This meant replacing heavy equipment with mobile lightweight equipment and training of Central American troops in the art of counterinsurgency warfare. Counterinsurgency included a wide range of economic, political, social, psychological, and military activities utilizing several U.S. government agencies. AID was charged with the responsibility for economic programs and its Office of Public Safety, for the training of police forces in interrogation and riot-control techniques. The United States Information Agency (USIA) worked with governments to improve their image both at home and abroad, while the Central Intelligence Agency engaged in intelligence gathering and in covert and paramilitary activities. U.S. military missions in each target country provided training, advice, and supplies to the local armed forces and were assisted by Mobile Training Units (MTUs). These varied activities were directed by the U.S. ambassador to each country.

The newly established Commander in Chief of the Southern Command (SOUTHCOM), headquartered at the Panama Canal Zone, was responsible for training Central America's military forces. The training programs called military civil action programs were intended to carry out counterinsurgency activities and to stimulate nation building and economic development, in the latter case by improving the image of the local military through actively participating in the construction of bridges, hospitals, and schools, serving as medics for rural civilians, and clearing jungle terrain for the establishment of small farms. In Central America, SOUTHCOM was aided by the Consejo Defensa Centroamericano (CONDECA), created in 1963 and headquartered in Guatemala City. CONDECA provided the regional structure for sharing intelligence, setting up communications networks, holding multilateral military exercises, and providing a forum for United States–Central American military exchanges.[11] The five Central American presidents agreed to "reinforce the measures [needed] to meet subversive aggression originating in the focal points of communist agitation which Soviet imperialism may maintain in Cuba or in any other place in America."[12]

By 1963, however, evidence indicated that the armed forces trained in the United States in counterinsurgency did not act as Kennedy intended. They often moved against the non-Communist left and, occasionally, as in Guatemala, the soldiers themselves became insurgents. Rather than becoming an instrument of constructive change, the military remained a defender of the status quo.

Return to the Hard Line: Lyndon B. Johnson

"Let us continue," asserted Lyndon B. Johnson on 27 November 1963, five days after assuming the presidency. It proved to be an assertion only. In a two-week period, from 14 December to 27 December 1963, Johnson replaced Kennedy's Latin American appointments. Shortly thereafter, Thomas C. Mann, a cold warrior who had served in the State Department under John Foster Dulles, emerged as the single most important person directing Johnson's Latin American policy. He believed that private investment was the key to the hemisphere's development and that the United States should assume a neutral stance on economic and social reform while at the same time championing economic development and protection of U.S. private investment.[13]

Johnson altered the American policy toward Latin America. He deemphasized economic and social reform programs and reduced pressure upon military governments when that pressure interfered in the political process. The change was signaled in January 1964 with the recognition of the López Arellano administration in Honduras. Two months later, Thomas Mann reaffirmed the administration's cold war mentality when he announced that the United States would give greater attention to its own security interests by thwarting communism in Latin America rather than attempting to impose democracy.[14] The Mann Doctrine meant that there would no longer be a differentiation between good guys and bad guys. Subsequent promises to promote constitutional government became empty rhetoric.

To combat communism in the hemisphere, Johnson continued Kennedy's military assistance programs, which emphasized the purchase of small, lightweight weapons and mobile equipment, and U.S. supervision of military training in counterinsurgency warfare. By 1967, however, with the escalating costs of the Vietnam War, Congress scrutinized the Latin American military assistance programs and concluded that the governments were purchasing equipment beyond their needs and financial capabilities and that, in some instances, the aid was used to maintain military dictatorships. As a result, Congress restricted the value of defense material that the United States furnished annually to Latin American countries to $10 million or less and limited the amount of arms sold to Latin America to $75 million. Only when the president foresaw a threat to U.S. security interests could he raise the amount of sales without congressional approval.[15] The loophole became an important factor in providing subsequent assistance to Guatemala.

At the beginning of the Johnson administration, the CIA reported that the Central American republics were staunchly pro-American in their foreign policy and appeared committed to the goals of the Alliance for Progress. The Communist party remained illegal across the isthmus, and no Central American government had diplomatic relations with the Soviet Union or Eastern bloc countries. The CIA concluded that the Guatemalan and Honduran political rivalries remained a struggle among the elite, with minimal impact upon the masses. The agency also concluded that the local militaries were capable of suppressing any insurgent movement, a threat not believed to be on the horizon, except perhaps in Guatemala. With only about 125 members, the guerrilla forces had been active in the mountains for over three years, and they appeared capable of mounting urban terrorist attacks. Still, the CIA was confident that Guatemala's four-thousand-man security force could meet any challenge that the guerrillas might offer.[16]

In 1968, when Johnson flew to San Salvador to attend a meeting of the Central American Defense Council, the State Department repeated the description of political tranquility in the region. Johnson was advised that Guatemalan president Mario Méndez Montenegro "has the upper hand on the guerrillas and [has] reasserted civilian authority over military elements indulging in excessive counter-terrorism"; that Somoza "turned out to be a far better President than anyone anticipated, . . . giving strong, enlightened leadership"; that Costa Rican president José Joaquin Trejos was "providing adequate if not dynamic leadership"; and that there were no great issues separating the United States and El Salvador, but that economic and social development should be accelerated to blunt the appeal of international communism. Only Honduran president López Arellano received poor marks.[17]

His policies mired by the war in Vietnam and the congressional emasculation of the Great Society, Johnson had already removed himself as a 1968 presidential candidate when he visited El Salvador. While his trip was nothing more than window dressing, Johnson used the occasion to applaud the Central American Common Market as a model for the entire hemisphere, to announce a new loan package worth $65 million for the region, and turned on the Salvadoran nationwide educational television station, an AID project. Only a small group of egg- and paint-throwing students marred the visit, and they stood in sharp contrast to the tens of thousands of enthusiastic Salvadorans who turned out to greet Johnson.[18]

Although the United States disinterested itself in Central America in the late 1960s, events on the isthmus signaled that a new and more violent era was at hand. In Guatemala, a guerrilla movement seized upon the plight of the peasants. The 1969 Soccer War between El Salvador and Honduras not only destroyed the Central American Common Market but also revealed the depth of the economic and social deprivation in both countries.

The roots of the Guatemalan insurgency can be traced to a military coup attempted in 1960 against President Miguel Ydígoras Fuentes. Charging that the coup attempt was supported by Cuba's Fidel Castro and that Cuban arms and troops could be expected, Ydígoras Fuentes declared a state of siege. The Eisenhower administration, without hard evidence, apparently accepted Ydígoras's claims that Castro intended to interfere. In order to protect Guatemalan security and the Cuban exiles training there for the eventual invasion at Bay of Pigs in 1961, Eisenhower ordered a naval flotilla to the Central American waters. In retrospect, Eisenhower overreacted to protect the exiled Cuban military brigade. The coup was doomed before it began. The revolt was an internal affair prompted by grievances within the military, particularly among the young officers who opposed the dominance of U.S. influence in Guatemalan military affairs since the overthrow of Jacobo Arbenz in 1954. The aborted rebellion became a high-water mark in Guatemalan history, because the country soon entered a long phase of guerrilla warfare.

Among the officers who took part in the rebellion were Lieutenants Marco Aurelio Yon Sosa, age twenty-two, and Augusto Turcos Lima, age nineteen. After the failed coup attempt, they came into contact with the peasants, developed a sympathy for their plight, and concluded that the only means to correct the situation was to overthrow the Ydígoras regime. They accepted support from Guatemala's Communist Partido Guatemalteco del Trabajo (PGT) and launched a guerrilla offensive in February 1962. Turcos Lima and Yon Sosa eventually visited Cuba and received instruction from Ernesto "Che" Guevara, which led to an alliance known as the Fuerzas Armadas Rebeldes (FAR). It included Turcos Lima and Yon Sosa's Movimiento Revolucionario 13 de Novembre (MR-13) and the PGT's Frente Unido de Resistencia (FUR). FAR provided the military arm and FUR the political arm of the struggle against Ydígoras. Loosely following the "foco" theories of Guevara and Regis Debray, the movement concentrated on a long-term strategy of creating revolutionary conditions in the countryside.

The rebellion in Guatemala appeared tailor-made for testing the United States' counterinsurgency policy. Under the direction of American advisors, the Guatemalan military conducted civic action programs to offset the guerrilla movement. These included school lunch programs; well digging, road building, and other construction projects; medical care; youth camp and community development experiments; and literacy and education programs. The advisors kept a low profile, as the Guatemalan military met or exceeded the initial goals. After 1964, the program diminished with decreases in U.S. funding, shortages of trained personnel, and Guatemala's bureaucratic inertia and traditional mistrust of the military.

As the guerrilla movement began in the early 1960s, the Guatemalan armed forces consisted of understrength brigades, battalions, and companies scattered throughout the country without central direction, deficiencies that were addressed by the Military Assistance Program. MAP's accomplishments, however, were offset by the latitude given brigade commanders, which militated against centralized control. For example, the failure to coordinate intelligence and police operations hindered cooperative efforts against the guerrillas. The lack of dedication by the senior officer corps prevented many field actions. Colonel Enrique Peralta Azurdia's decisions to use U.S. aid to expand the country's internal security system without informing U.S. advisors proved most disturbing.

Shortly after Mario Méndez Montenegro won the "relatively honest" presidential election in July 1966, the guerrillas increased their activity in the countryside, expanded their attacks in the urban areas, and targeted wealthy Guatemalans for kidnapping and ransom. To counter the increased guerrilla activity, Méndez Montenegro permitted the United States Green Berets to come into the country and accepted $6 million in new military assistance and $11 million in equipment. President Johnson, who favored a military solution over economic and social reforms, capitalized upon the loophole in the 1967 legislation that had limited military aid to Latin America: he declared that U.S. security interests were at stake in Guatemala.

As the violence increased, particularly in the urban areas, some army officers and national policemen combined with right-wing zealots to organize the MANO BLANCO, a death squad that attacked anyone suspected of sympathizing with the guerrillas. The terrorist activities—kidnapping, torture, and summary executions—continued well into the 1970s. Although Méndez Montenegro failed to, or could not, contain the urban terrorism, he ordered a military campaign against the guerrilla stronghold in the rural areas of Oriente Department. Government troops destroyed both the guerrilla armies and their supporting infrastructure, resulting in the death of an estimated four thousand innocent peasants. By early 1968, the guerrilla forces in Zacapa and Izabal were destroyed. Yon Sosa took refuge in Mexico, and the remainder of his forces scattered.

Several factors other than U.S. military assistance contributed to the guerrillas' demise by 1968. Not only was there a debilitating schism in their ranks, but they failed to increase the number of their fighting forces because they operated in areas that had few inhabitants. The guerrillas also failed to gain the support of the Guatemalan middle sector, which was interested in political, not economic and social, reform. When the guerrillas turned to urban violence, their tactic served to further distance them from the middle sector. On the battlefield, the guerrillas proved incapable of defeating the army's well-conceived plan.[19]

The rebels who did escape into the countryside after 1968 later joined urban guerrilla forces that extended their attacks to U.S. personnel, including the assassination of Colonel John Webber, chief of the U.S. military mission, his aide, Lieutenant Colonel Ernest Munro, and Ambassador John G. Mein. Following the 1970 presidential election of Carlos Arana Osorío, the government instituted draconian measures against the urban left. The Guatemalan experience demonstrated the dilemma that confronted MAP during the 1960s. The original emphasis on economic and social reform became lost in the pursuit of prompt military solutions. Whatever accomplishments the civic action programs achieved, they were offset by the unwarranted violence used to suppress the guerrilla bands.

However, Guatemala's experience was but one symptom of the impending crisis. Contradictions characterized the development of the Central American Common Market in the 1960s. By 1969, the CACM had achieved numerous successes. Intraregional trade had grown by over 700 percent, and 1,195 products had received free trade status. New industrial pursuits included chemicals, fertilizers, insecticides, and rubber tires and tubes. Bilateral arrangements in food processing stimulated agricultural production sufficiently to meet the demands of annual population growth rates that approached 3.8 percent. The CACM had nearly achieved its goal of complete common market status. Unfortunately, a number of negative factors hampered the development process. By the late 1960s, world prices for Central America's key agricultural exports—sugar, coffee, and cotton—were declining. This, combined with the cost of importing machinery, spare parts, and semiprocessed goods for industrial development, worsened the region's already unfavorable trade balance. Foreign capital fueled the industrial development within the CACM, but it focused on transfer production, which meant that profits went to companies based abroad. U.S. companies, particularly those in textiles and electronics, took advantage of the situation. These were capital, not labor-intensive, industries, so they created few employment opportunities for Central America's excessive unskilled labor force.[20] In effect, the goal of import substitution was not realized.

These economic adversities were most evident in Honduras, the least developed Central American country. Honduras blamed the CACM, and particularly El Salvador, for its trade imbalance. In the 1960s, the Honduran economy was further weakened by a depression in its banana industry. Both factors contributed to the xenophobic character of Honduran nationalism late in the decade and to the 1969 Soccer War with El Salvador. The underlying causes of the conflict date to the 1920s, when Salvadoran landowners consolidated their coffee holdings and thus displaced thousands of workers, many of whom made their way into Honduras to work for the labor-intensive banana plantations on the northern coast. During the depression of the 1930s, uncounted thousands more came. Estimates place the total number of immigrants at anywhere from seventy thousand to three hundred thousand. The workers' plight was compounded by Honduran landownership patterns. In 1960, 67 percent of the farming population occupied only 12 percent of the farmland, an imbalance that contributed to the development of one of Central America's most militant peasant organizations, the National Association of Honduran Peasants (ANACH). By the late 1960s, ANACH demanded that the provisions of the 1962 agrarian reform law be strictly applied, which meant the replacement of *latifundias* and *minifundias* with a "fair system of land ownership, tenure and use" along with necessary support and assistance for the farmer. The law specified, however, that one had to be a Honduran citizen to be a land recipient.

Salvadoran immigrants and their descendants, who never became Honduran citizens, immediately suffered. Both ANACH and the National Federation of Farmers and Ranchers (an association of large landowners founded in 1966) charged the Salvadoran immigrants with usurping rural properties. The United Fruit Company, determined to protect its own interests, promoted the Honduran cause and advised Hondurans to place Soviet weapons in the hands of dead Salvadorans in order to influence U.S. public opinion.[21]

Emotions in El Salvador also ran high. By the end of the 1960s, the decline in demand for coffee, cotton, and sugar contributed to government deficits that brought public works projects to a standstill and restricted social welfare programs at a time of rising unemployment. The economic adversity and decrease in government social programs increased labor militancy, which in turn prompted the military to take over the administration of the Labor Ministry and quickly denounce the demonstrators as Communists. The situation worsened in June 1969 with the return of Salvadorans expelled from Honduras as a result of the application of the 1962 agrarian reform law. El Salvador severed diplomatic relations with Honduras and filed a petition with the Inter-American Commission on Human Rights, accusing Honduras of gross violations against the resident Salvadorans.

The situation became critical in early June 1969, when the two national soccer teams competed, first in Tegucigalpa and then in San Salvador. In both capitals there was violence against each visiting team and its fans. Nicaraguan, Costa Rican, and Guatemalan efforts to mediate the situation failed, largely due to Salvadoran recalcitrance. Provocations continued on both sides until 14 July, when Salvadoran troops invaded Honduras to seize and hold territory as a bargaining chip for future negotiations. The Honduran army and particularly its air force responded in unexpected fashion and defeated the invaders, which forced El Salvador to accept the OAS's offer to mediate the dispute. Honduras used the Soccer War as its reason for cutting ties with the CACM.[22] Matters rested there until the Nicaraguan revolution in 1979, which facilitated an agreement to officially end the war and to commit the belligerents to a revitalization of the Common Market. The United States supported the treaty, seeing it as an opportunity to prevent the contagion of Central American violence.

After June 1969 segments of the oligarchies in both countries strengthened their positions. The Salvadoran government increased its budgetary support for the modernization of the military and gave it a greater voice in national politics at a time when the Salvadorans returning from Honduras further strained the nation's economy and social structure. The Honduran military was profoundly divided by the war. Older officers retained their links to the nation's traditional conservative elite; younger officers were now more disposed toward social reform. Honduran industrialists, freed from their unfavorable ties to the CACM, improved their productivity during the 1970s; at the same time, they resisted labor's demands and reintegration into the CACM.

Benign Neglect: Nixon and Ford

The Soccer War took place during Richard Nixon's first year in office, a time of doubt about the U.S. commitment in Vietnam, the effects of large-scale aid programs to Latin America, and the urgency of social issues in hemispheric policy. The Alliance for Progress had diminished in estimation among both Americans and Latin Americans. In an effort to replace it as a source of information, Nixon commissioned Nelson Rockefeller to a fact-finding tour of Latin America and formulated the Nixon Doctrine, which called for a decrease in U.S. military presence in certain areas of the world, with the allies assuming a greater degree of self-responsibility. But there were conflicting signals regarding Latin America. The Senate Subcommittee on Western Hemisphere Affairs heard testimony that criticized U.S. military assistance programs on the grounds that Latin America's military was more entrenched in politics now than at any time in recent history. In contrast, the Rockefeller report declared that U.S. military assistance was vital to countervail the Communist threat in Latin America and recommended the continued training of Latin American troops in counterinsurgency and ideological education.[23]

In this context, the Alliance for Progress in Central America received a somber evaluation. In 1973 AID, which administered most of the programs, reported that Costa Rica remained the most advanced of the five republics, with the highest literacy rate, highest per capita income ($540 annually) in the region, ample natural resources, and a democratic tradition. But elsewhere in Central America, the masses of people had made little progress during the preceding decade. The most privileged of 1960 remained the most privileged of 1970.

The benefits anticipated from agricultural growth did not materialize. Costa Rica's small and medium-sized farmers failed to qualify for government loans because they did not meet the government's precondition of land ownership. Despite AID's efforts, El Salvador's small farmers did not reach a commercial level of operation by 1972 and had few prospects for doing so in the near future. Nor did Guatemala's landholding patterns change. Plantations geared to export crops, largely cotton and coffee, continued to exist side by side with subsistence farms. Nicaragua's agricultural sector remained plagued by low productivity, insufficient marketing, and reliance on cotton and coffee exports. Low productivity, underutilization of manpower, and uncertain land titles hampered agricultural development in Honduras.

Continued high rates of population growth strained all levels of education, even in Costa Rica, where the government emphasized education. In Guatemala, where 40 percent of the population spoke Mayan dialects rather than Spanish, the illiteracy rate was estimated in 1972 at 62 percent. In Nicaragua, less than 20 percent of the children completed the sixth grade, despite a mandatory school law, increased national expenditures on education, increased classroom construction, and teacher training programs. In Honduras, primary education reform continued, but the training of competent administrators and technical support staff lagged behind projections. Only in El Salvador had there been a degree of accomplishment. Primary education improved with the introduction of a national educational television system to reach rural regions and adult education programs to contribute to progress in health, sanitation, nutrition, and home economics.

Family planning measures met with limited success only in Costa Rica, where the rate of annual population growth dropped from 4 percent in 1960 to 2.8 percent in 1971–72. In the other four countries, population growth remained a serious problem, one exacerbated by the migration of illiterate and unskilled rural workers to the urban centers, where they compounded an already difficult employment situation and increased the pressure for food support, housing, and maternal and child health care.[24] The burgeoning urban population created long-term political difficulties across the isthmus. Central American governments became hard-pressed to meet the cost of replacing alliance-sponsored social programs, because the middle and upper sectors resisted higher taxes. Neglected by the established political parties, the urban poor became more receptive to leftist political spokesmen.

Nixon finally enunciated his Latin American policy on 31 October 1969. He indicated that political tranquility should take precedence over social, economic, and political reform. Two years later, when he obtained congressional approval to increase the annual ceiling on arms sales to Latin America from $75 million to $150 million, the motivation was profit, not security, but the action gave credence to the charge that Nixon followed in Lyndon Johnson's footsteps in supporting and maintaining Latin American military dictatorships.[25] After Nixon's resignation, President Gerald R. Ford continued the military assistance programs, despite contrary recommendations from a twenty-three-member Latin American commission. The commission foresaw the impending political crisis and strongly urged the United States to deemphasize hemispheric security as an issue of primary consideration "in the narrow military sense" and to emphasize the goal of "mutually satisfactory political and economic relations."[26]

During the Nixon-Ford years, the continued war in Southeast Asia, the 1973 Middle East conflict, followed by the world's first oil shock, and detente with the Soviet Union dominated international issues, which, along with the Watergate scandal, contributed to a policy of benign neglect for the hemisphere. Trade, not aid, became the guideline of hemispheric policy. Only the 1976 energy crisis brought a renewed interest in Latin America from Secretary of State Henry Kissinger.[27]

Despite the variance in the administration of hemispheric policies from Kennedy to Ford, there was consistency in the military assistance programs. Although the amount of military aid to all of Latin America declined after 1966, the amount to Central America increased. The United States rationalized that its assistance had a greater impact on the smaller countries of Central America than on the larger ones of South America. Furthermore, Washington policymakers continued to

Table 8.1

United States Military Grants to Central America 1953–1976
(in millions of dollars)

Years	Costa Rica	El Salvador	Guatemala	Honduras	Nicaragua
1953–1961	0.1	0.1	1.4	1.1	1.9
1962–1969	1.8	5.5	12.8	5.9	10.9
1970–1976	0.1	6.2	11.2	5.2	11.3

Source: Special Report Prepared for the House Foreign Affairs Committee, *U.S. Overseas Loans and Grants*, 1 July 1945 to 30 June 1970, and 1 July 1945 to 30 September 1977. Published annually by the Agency for International Development, Washington, D.C.

maintain, Central America's geographic importance to national security interests in the Caribbean meant that the Communist effort to capitalize upon regional poverty had to be stopped.

The Southern Command at the Panama Canal Zone administered the military assistance program for Central America and, in so doing, gave considerable attention to internal security measures rather than to the impact of military assistance upon the region's political dynamics. The personnel in the U.S. military missions in Central America closely associated with the officers and other top military personnel in each country; their relationships attracted wide publicity in Central America, particularly in Honduras and Guatemala, and contributed to the impression that the United States was involved in the political repression. On balance, however, the impact of the U.S. military training of Central American officers and rank personnel proved difficult to analyze, although some conclusions were made about the programs in Guatemala, where the exposure of its military to the lifestyle of their American counterparts (officers' clubs, golf, swimming, and so on) influenced them to aspire to a higher standard of living. Thereafter, the Guatemalan soldiers often sought and acquired government positions, made private investments, and bought estates in land colonization programs, which brought protest from the affected private sectors.[28]

Between 1950 and 1972, more than fourteen thousand Central American soldiers received military instruction from the U.S. officers, which was a substantial number given the size of military and civil forces throughout the region. After Panama, Nicaragua ranked first in the number of trainees. By 1969, 70 percent of the courses offered at the School of the Americas in the Panama Canal Zone dealt with various aspects of counterinsurgency, including military and paramilitary operations and political, sociological, and psychological warfare techniques. Also, 2–4 percent of the enlisted trainees' course time and 15–20 percent of the officers' course time focused upon anti-Communist and pro-American indoctrination. Typical of the anti-Communist literature read at the SOUTHCOM training center in Panama was this definition of communism:

> It means government by a small group of men who acquired power by violent revolution. They contend that they govern in the name of the peasants and the laborers, but in reality they use force and deceit to keep that power. Their government is the only owner of and administrator of all estates. These dictators talk of an ideal society, but they do not allow the people to take part in the decision-making society. The Communist dictators promise freedom, yet they destroy freedom of speech and freedom of the press, as well as many other personal freedoms.[29]

Such indoctrination probably contributed to the increase in the Central American military's fears of political groups advocating reforms and to the consequent increased use of repression to restrict the activities of civilian political parties, populist politicians, newspapers, radio stations, university students and professors, and any citizen or entity advocating radical change. Labor unions and peasant organizations in particular were singled out because they allegedly were Communist-inspired.

Civic action programs were designed to teach the military about construction and medical techniques, but in practice these programs ranked second to internal security. Throughout the 1960s civic action remained a small part of the Military Assistance Programs. For example, in 1966, the peak year of U.S. military assistance to Latin

America, only 15.8 percent of the total expenditure was for civic action programs, while 56.6 percent went for internal security and 15.8 percent for maritime defense. Critics charged that civic action programs curtailed civilian employment and, in Guatemala, Nicaragua, and Honduras, became a means of institutional (and dynastic, in the case of Nicaragua) self-preservation, rather than an attempt to get at the region's fundamental economic and social problems. By 1976, programs for military assistance to Central America solidified the relationship between the military and the landed elite (except in Costa Rica, which had no army). Committed to the old order, the military and landed elite refused to accept the legitimacy of the demands made by the lower socioeconomic groups. In these polarized conditions, those who held power should have recalled Kennedy's 1961 warning: "Those who make peaceful revolution impossible, make violent revolution inevitable."[30]

9 Crisis of the Old Order: Carter, Reagan, and Central America

Shortly after becoming president, Jimmy Carter directed a review of U.S. policy toward Latin America by every agency that dealt with the region. With two exceptions, the agencies concurred with the concluding observation of the Linowitz Commission: the American presumption that "Latin America is somehow our sphere of influence is no longer appropriate in an increasingly interdependent world in which the Latin American nations seek to be active and independent participants."[1] Only the State Department's American Republics Affairs Division remained committed to the special relationship. And the Joint Chiefs of Staff noted that no administration took seriously the 1933 pronouncement of nonintervention whenever U.S. security had been threatened. Otherwise, all were committed to a new approach. After adding human rights to the agenda, Carter indicated that, during his administration, the U.S. policy toward Latin America would fit within a consistent framework of global economic patterns. Carter's concern for human rights stemmed from his deep convictions and his awareness of the massive human rights violations in Latin America. Carter found Congress sympathetic because of earlier legislation that withheld foreign aid from nations violating human rights. He also saw the need to restore faith in the executive branch at home, and the pursuance of lofty goals abroad was considered a step in that direction. Carter announced the new course in a speech before the Organization of American States on 14 April 1977.[2]

Carter's most demonstrable effort at ending the special relationship came with the administration's commitment to the Panama Canal treaties. Throughout the century, the canal had been a focal point for anti-American sentiment. The 1903 canal treaty, although modified in 1936 and 1955, permitted the United States to act as if it were sovereign in the canal zone, limiting Panama's foreign policy options and intervening in its internal affairs. The U.S. operation of auxiliary canal services—from commissaries to dry dock facilities—restricted the republic's economic development and the employment opportunities for Panamanians in the zone. The 1977 treaties promised to remove these vestiges of control by turning the canal and its auxiliary services over to Panama by the year 2000.

Removing the American colony from Panama clearly signaled the beginning of a new relationship with Latin America. National security advisor Zbigniew Brzezinski, who accompanied Carter to Panama for the signing ceremony in June 1978, observed that the new treaties set in motion "a different pattern of relations with Latin America" and that their ratification was a "necessary pre-condition for a more mature and . . . just relationship with Central America, a region which we had never understood too well and which we occasionally dominated the way that the Soviets have dominated Eastern Europe." Furthermore, if the canal issue was not resolved, Panamanian nationalism might erupt into violence and spill over into Central America, and Brzezinski therefore concluded that an agreement with Panama had a significant and positive impact upon Central America.[3] Although the roles of Panama and Central America were now reversed, Brzezinski's logic demonstrated the continuity of U.S. foreign policy since 1900 toward the entire isthmus.

Shattering the Policy of Idealism, 1976–1980

In January 1977, shortly after Carter's inauguration, the State Department hosted a group of academics in Washington for two days of discussions on Central American affairs. The academicians agreed that El Salvador's socioeconomic problems were more important than its guerrilla movement and that, in Nicaragua, Somoza could effectively deal with the insignificant guerrilla movement that confronted him. In fact, the symposium concluded that nothing in Central America threatened U.S. interests or demanded its immediate attention, a situation that warranted a reduction in U.S. involvement in the region. A young State Department officer assigned to the Nicaraguan desk reportedly requested a transfer to a post that promised more excitement and greater opportunity for advancement.[4]

The situation in Central America belied the assessment in Washington. Since the Soccer War in 1969, Central America's economies had declined, and the concomitant social debilities had inspired renewed demands for political change. The Costa Rican economy suffered under the weight of falling world prices for bananas and coffee at a time when the Arab oil embargo caused oil to skyrocket, another disaster for a country dependent on foreign oil. Relations with the United States were strained by a coffee agreement with the Soviet Union that was designed to replace funds lost when aid from Alliance for Progress ran out. The political reputation of José Figueres had suffered by his association with Robert Vesco, a financial speculator wanted in the United States for his alleged participation in a $224 million business scam but safe from deportation because of the lack of an extradition agreement.

In Honduras, Guatemala, and El Salvador the military remained entrenched in power. In Honduras, Oswaldo López Arellano, who returned to the presidential palace via a coup in 1972, initiated a new land reform program that touched off violence between the landed elite and organized peasant groups. That same year, a scandal involving Honduran government officials and United Brands, the conglomerate that took over UFCO in 1972, resulted in the suicide of United Brands' chairman, Eli Black, and the overthrow of López Arellano by General Juan Alberto Melgar Castro. Although United Brands survived the subsequent threats of nationalization, peasant violence against landowners continued.

In Guatemala, successive presidents Colonel Carlos Arana Osorío and General Kjell Eugenio Laugerud García, both of whom had gained office in fraudulent elections in 1970 and 1974, faced increased violence, particularly in the urban areas. According to the Committee of Relatives of Disappeared Persons, an estimated fifteen thousand Guatemalans disappeared during Arana's administration. General Laugerud tried to reduce the urban unrest by easing government restrictions so that unions, student groups, professional societies, *campesino* organizations, and moderate political parties could organize and conduct public demonstrations, but he offset these gestures with a program of selective assassination, beginning with the killing of labor leader Mario López Lavare in June 1977. Public protest brought further repression, which, in turn, brought condemnation from human rights groups and a suspension of U.S. aid.

Opposition to the Salvadoran oligarchy had emerged during the 1960s, mostly from the Christian Democratic party, headed by José Napoleón Duarte; the Revolutionary National Movement, led by Guillermo Manuel Ungo; and the National Democratic Union, composed mostly of young military officers. In 1972 the three groups united under the banner of the National Opposition Union (FAO) and nominated Duarte for the presidency, but the military denied Duarte his apparent victory and instead placed a conservative, Colonel Arturo Armando Molina, in the presidential palace. Molina promptly exiled Duarte to Venezuela. However, the military's subsequent repressive measures failed to silence the middle sector's demand for constitutional government and peasant organizations' cry for social and economic improvements.[5]

In Nicaragua, the old order was under attack, and the crisis quickly put Carter's Latin American policy to the test. Since the assassination of Anastasio Somoza García in 1956, opposition to the family dynasty intensified in the traditional conservative groups and in the middle sector. Nicaragua's peasants remained outside the political process except as a tool manipulated by the landowners. The Sandinista National Liberation Front (FSLN), founded in 1962, was not yet considered an important political actor, nor did their sporadic attacks on government outposts threaten the Somoza regime.[6] Throughout the 1960s, Somoza continued to demonstrate his apparent close ties to the United States.

All of this began to change after December 1972, when an earthquake devastated Nicaragua and left an estimated ten thousand people dead and another three hundred thousand homeless. In the . immediate aftermath, many national guardsmen, rather than maintaining the civil order, left their posts to tend to their family needs, while others took to looting and pillaging. Afterward, Somoza and his friends reportedly grafted about half of the $32 million of American relief assistance. Somoza also used the occasion to secure his own political position. As the 1974 elections approached, he outlawed several opposition groups, jailed others, and controlled the press. Somoza declared that he received 748,000 of the 815,000 votes cast in that election, but few believed him.

Somoza's actions prompted the opposition forces to coalesce. Several of the upper- and middle-sector groups formed the Democratic Liberation Union (UDEL), which sought reform achieved through the existing political system, but more important was the emergence of the FSLN as a vibrant force in the countryside and several outlying cities. To control the urban opposition, Somoza declared a state of siege, and in the countryside he formed counterinsurgency military units, which, along with the National Guard, attacked northern villages suspected of being FSLN strongholds. The brutality of these attacks brought condemnation from observers both within and outside Nicaragua.[7]

At the time Carter became president, Somoza's dynasty began to unravel. The crisis presented Carter with an opportunity to demonstrate his commitment to human rights and nondictatorial governments. In an effort to force Somoza to alter his policy, Carter first chose to restrict military and economic assistance to Managua in the spring of 1977.[8] Despite the cutback in aid and the international community's vociferous condemnations of his human rights violations, Somoza did not budge, and the situation in Nicaragua continued to deteriorate. By January 1978 "the crisis in Nicaragua . . . [began] to preoccupy and absorb us," Brzezinski later recalled.[9] The pressure against Somoza intensified following the assassination of the editor of *La Prensa*, Pedro Joaquín Chamorro, on 10 January 1978. Street violence was followed by a UDEL-sponsored general strike that shut down an estimated 80 percent of Nicaragua's businesses for up to two weeks. Beyond this, the moderate factions had no plans, but the FSLN used the occasion to increase its activities against the government. Foreign political figures also exhorted Somoza to resign. Shortly after Chamorro's assassination, the U.S. ambassador to Nicaragua, Mauricio Solaun, acting without instructions, advised Somoza to announce his retirement from national politics at the end of his six-year term in 1981. Somoza was also encouraged to resign by the Venezuelan president, Carlos Andrés Pérez, and the Panamanian head of state, Omar Torrijos, both of whom warned Somoza of Carter's determination to oust him.[10]

Somoza did not resign, but on 19 June 1978, in response to Carter's pressure for an improved record in human rights, he declared an amnesty for some political prisoners, permitted the *tercerista* faction of the FSLN to return home from Costa Rica, promised electoral reform, and invited the Human Rights Commission of the Organization of American States to inspect the country. Shortly thereafter, he visited the United States, hoping to reach Carter through people connected to the Democratic party. One of those contacts, former defense secretary Clark Clifford, advised Somoza that his efforts were futile. Somoza was more successful at home. He rekindled the facade of friendship with the United States with a letter sent by Carter to Somoza on 30 June 1978. The letter was intended to encourage the dictator to further improve human rights, but when it was leaked to the Nicaraguan press, its congratulatory tone stunned the moderates. Carter's letter, along with the release of $12 million in economic aid to Somoza, prompted the newly formed Broad Opposition Front (FAO) to conclude that the dictator still had a friend in Washington. In reality he did not.

In the summer of 1978, the administration was still without a long-term strategy, but Carter's advisors understood that because the FAO had no plans beyond ousting Somoza and that because the FSLN was the most organized opposition group in the country, the United States might soon have "to deal with a real possibility of a strong leftist revolutionary movement and an evaporating political middle."[11] Nicaragua now became a political security crisis, pushing the human rights agenda to the side. Convinced that Somoza would never regain total control of the country but wary of a possible FSLN victory, the United States sought a middle ground. In November 1978, the Carter administration decided to work for a plebiscite and a negotiated settlement that included Somoza's promise to depart, a provision initially accepted by both the FAO and Somoza. Only the Sandinista leadership hesitated until the completion of a secret strategy meeting in Cuba, after which the FSLN factions (excluding Edén Pastora, who had led a daring assault on the national assembly) rejected the proposed plebiscite as a "trap that leads to compromise and treason" and then demanded the removal of Somoza and the dismantling of the National Guard as "the indispensable conditions for a true democracy."[12] The FSLN declaration prompted Somoza to also reject the proposed plebiscite and strengthened Washington's conviction that the FSLN leadership was Marxist-Leninist and that it considered Cuba and the Soviet Union as its allies and the United States as its enemy. Still, Carter remained determined to force Somoza's resignation.

On 29 December 1978, after Somoza had rejected the proposed plebiscite, Carter approved the implementation of phased sanctions that he hoped would pressure Somoza out of office. The sanctions began in February 1979 with cuts in both new military and economic assistance and embassy and military staffs in Managua. Although the sanctions weakened the Nicaraguan economy and contributed to the demise of the FAO, Somoza found military supplies for his National Guard elsewhere. Also, in early 1979, the FSLN formed the National Government of Reconciliation (GRN). Nicaraguan politics were now polarized.

In the spring of 1979, following a few months of relative military calm, the FSLN struck again, this time at major cities. Despite a ferocious response from the National Guard, the FSLN did not fold, because it had a secure flow of arms from Cuba through Panama and Costa Rica. In June, the Sandinistas began what became their final battlefield offensive. At the same time, the FSLN took its case to the OAS, demanding Somoza's removal and a legitimate transfer of power to them.

In Washington, the question now became, not whether Somoza

would leave, but what would follow his departure. Carter wanted to prevent the emergence of an extremist government, but the GRN, confident of victory, rejected his proposals for an OAS peacekeeping force and a coalition government that included representatives of the National Guard and Somoza's Liberal party, but not Somoza himself. Nicaragua's moderate factions also rejected Carter's proposals, because neither an OAS force nor a coalition government promised to strengthen their already weakened position. Politically isolated and without a source of arms, Somoza finally surrendered on 17 July 1979 and left for Miami. Two days later, the GRN marched triumphantly into Managua. Nicaragua's old order had crumbled and, along with it, the victors were determined, U.S. interference.

The junta that formed Nicaragua's new provisional government inherited a prostrate nation. Somoza left behind a wrecked economy and a $1.6 million national debt. The political elite and most of the mid-level government bureaucrats had left the country, effectively paralyzing the nation's administrative machinery. Despite these obstacles, the provisional government announced its intention to create a new Nicaragua that included a reconstructed national economy, a society with less class inequality, an improved standard of living, increased economic opportunity for the lower classes, and the establishment of a democratic government. The last goal, democracy, soon became the focal point of the Sandinista image both at home and abroad, because the Sandinistas intended to form, rather than a western-style representative government, a more corporatist government, with elections postponed until the national institutions were capable of defending the revolution. At the same time, the Sandinistas' promise of economic pluralism appeared jeopardized by the increased government participation in the economy. These actions contributed to moderates Violetta Chamorro's and Adolfo Calero's resignation from the junta, leaving it with only Marxist members. Suspicious of the United States because of its record of interference in Central America in general and Nicaragua in particular, the Sandinistas announced that they would pursue an independent foreign policy and that economic assistance would be welcomed from all sources and markets sought everywhere.

In order "to maintain our ties with Nicaragua, to keep it from turning to Cuba and the Soviet Union,"[13] Carter wanted to aid Nicaragua's
war-torn economy. The U.S. government almost immediately advanced $8 million in reconstruction assistance, but Congress debated
the administration's request for $80 million in long-term economic
assistance. When the resolution passed, Congress imposed several
restrictions, among them the designation of monies for Nicaragua's
private sector.

During the last two years of Carter's tenure, the situation elsewhere
in Central America also worsened. Costa Rica suffered another drop
in world coffee prices and another rise in OPEC oil prices. The concomitant loss of government revenues dramatically slowed its social
programs, which in turn raised the possibility of violent protest among
the usually tranquil Ticos. Despite the suspension of military aid to
Guatemala in 1977, human rights violations increased, most mark-
edly after the presidential election of General Fernando Romeo Lucas
García in 1978. While the violence further frustrated the Carter administration, it further alienated Guatemala's political moderates.[14]

Revolution came, not in Costa Rica or Guatemala, but in El Salvador.
Its immediate causes lay in the 1960s, when U.S. aid programs designed to modernize the economy had only exacerbated the disparity
of wealth. Improved technology and the use of fertilizers had increased agricultural productivity but simultaneously displaced laborers. The industrial boom was capital-intensive, not labor-intensive,
effectively increasing unemployment in the urban sector. While the
Christian Democrats had responded to the urban middle-sector Salvadorans' demand for constitutional government, other groups came
forward to represent the needs of the poor. Among the most important was the Roman Catholic church, which emerged as an advocate
of social reform following the 1968 bishops' conference at Medellín,
Colombia, and the emergence of liberation theology, which called for
grass-roots organizations to help the poor. In El Salvador, some fifteen
thousand lay leaders in Christian Base Communities (CEBs) preached
that the poor had a right to organize and to press the government
for reform. Church advocacy of reform accelerated with the appoint-

ment of Monsignor Oscar Romero as archbishop of El Salvador in 1977.

Also, several Marxist popular organizations emerged, including the United Popular Action Front (FAPU), the Popular Revolutionary Bloc (BRP), and the Twenty-eighth of February Popular League (LP-28). These groups reached out to the rural and urban poor. Two umbrella groups formed, the largest and most significant being the Farabundo Martí National Liberation Front (FMLN), named after the leader of the 1932 insurrection; it was committed to the violent overthrow of the government. The second organization, the Democratic Revolutionary Front (FDR), became the political partner of the FMLN.

In opposition to these organizations stood government and right-wing death squads. Representing the landowners, they became increasingly repressive of anyone advocating a change in the existing order, including clerics. From 1977 to 1979, the violence increased, despite U.S. suspension of military aid and the presence in San Salvador of a proreform ambassador, Frank Devine.

In October 1979, a group of young officers in the Salvadoran military installed a reformist junta and declared that ORDEN (the dreaded right-wing death squad) would be abolished, inflation controlled, and a land reform program implemented. They intended to prevent a bloody civil war similar to that in Nicaragua. The Carter administration cautiously viewed this development as a window of opportunity. Resisting advice that unconditional support be given to the junta, Carter conditioned U.S. aid on the junta's ability to keep its promises for ending repression and implementing land reform. In the months following the October coup, the junta introduced agrarian, trade, and banking reforms; disbanded ORDEN; and dismissed from service hundreds of military officers associated with the repression. However, it failed to control its own security forces. Even so, Carter was encouraged, and by the end of his presidency advanced $56 million for agrarian reform and another $5.6 million in military aid to help the government achieve civil stability.

But the violence did not recede. In March 1980 a gunman assassinated Archbishop Romero as he was saying mass in San Salvador's cathedral. By the year's end, about nine thousand people had been killed. "They don't have anybody in jails; they're all dead. It's their way of enforcing the so-called law," Carter was told on 11 December 1980. The killing of six highly respected leaders of the FDR and four American churchwomen in November and December caused Carter to put the full weight of his office behind the Christian Democratic party, the group headed by José Napoleón Duarte, whom Carter determined to be the only viable alternative to the two extremes, the right-wing landowners and the left-wing guerrillas.[15]

While the events in Nicaragua, Costa Rica, Guatemala, and El Salvador may have appeared to be indigenous to the region, other events in the Caribbean during 1979 caused the administration to place Central America within the context of the East-West struggle. Left-leaning leaders Maurice Bishop in Grenada and Michael Manley in Jamaica publicly denounced the United States and praised Castro and the Soviet Union. Sandinista leader Daniel Ortega visited Cuba at the same time that a Soviet military brigade was discovered on the island. Brzezinski counseled the president to counter the Soviet probe in the Caribbean, including the Cuban military potential in Central America. Carter signaled the change in a speech before the OAS on 1 October 1979, when he called for the expansion of U.S. security presence in the Caribbean region.[16]

Carter's subsequent actions set the tone for the new U.S. policy in Central America, which made Honduras the linchpin for regional defense against the potential spread of the Sandinista revolution across the isthmus. Toward that end, the Carter administration worked for an agreement that officially ended the Soccer War, permitted Honduras to resume its relationship with the moribund CONDECA, advanced five hundred thousand dollars in military aid prior to the April 1980 election of a constituent assembly, and signed a military agreement that provided Honduras with a loan of ten helicopters and a training mission. The Honduran government expressed its appreciation by speaking out against the spread of the Sandinista revolution and applauding the Salvadoran government efforts against the guerrillas.[17]

Meanwhile, Carter became increasingly concerned with Nicaragua's apparent drift toward the Soviet camp. The Sandinistas' failure to implement a western-style democracy paled in comparison to the increased Soviet presence in the country. Among the Soviet personnel who began arriving in Nicaragua one month after the Sandinista victory were five generals and vice-generals sent to advise the Sandinista army chief of staff, Joaquín Cuadra. Soviet embassy personnel, including officials sent to organize planning and trade missions, began arriving in January 1980. Humberto Ortega and Tomás Borge headed a Sandinista delegation to Moscow in March 1980, when they signed economic and technical assistance agreements.[18] In light of these events, Carter approved the CIA's support of opposition groups that protested the one-party rule of the Sandinistas and the agency's effort to develop "alternatives to parties and people thought to be close to the Soviet Union." Two days before leaving the White House, Carter received a CIA recommendation calling for an end to economic aid to the Sandinista government.[19] The president, however, did not pull the string.

End of U.S. Dominance?: Since 1980

If Jimmy Carter appeared hesitant, Ronald Reagan did not. Convinced that the malaise of the Carter administration had tarnished America's image around the globe and that Carter's indecisiveness and weakness had permitted the forces of communism to make advances, Reagan determined to restore the image and to strengthen the global forces of freedom. In bold rhetoric, Reagan portrayed the United States as a strong nation and pursued tough-talking bilateral relations with the Soviets. Critics charged, however, that the operational policy did not match the rhetoric and that, in reality, the containment policies of the past continued.[20]

The Reagan administration placed its Latin American policy within the East-West context, which meant that military, not economic, solutions received first consideration and that human rights would be promoted through quiet diplomacy, not through public denunciations and aid cutoffs. Reagan's first foreign policy team—Secretary of State Alexander Haig, Assistant Secretary for Latin American Affairs Thomas O. Enders and United Nations Ambassador Jeane Kirkpatrick—reflected these views. By the time George Shultz and Elliot Abrams replaced Haig and Enders, the policy was well entrenched.

If Reagan's actions failed to match his bold words elsewhere, Central America was an exception. Here, Reagan concluded that U.S. power and prestige had dwindled in the face of Soviet-Cuban expansion. He accepted the contentions of both the Department of Defense and the intelligence community that failure to act close to home would only encourage the Soviets to become aggressive elsewhere.

Two intertwined considerations guided Reagan's Central American policy. The first, best espoused by Jeane Kirkpatrick, sharply distinguished between right-wing authoritarian dictators and left-wing totalitarian regimes. Kirkpatrick admitted that right-wing dictators were undemocratic, committed human rights violations, and maintained the established social and economic patterns of the countries over which they presided. Like Anastasio Somoza in Nicaragua, however, these dictators were strong anti-Communists who supported the United States in global affairs and, with proper encouragement, could be persuaded to evolve into leaders of democracies. Kirkpatrick considered totalitarian regimes to be the worse of the two, for they were more brutal in their administration of government and more abusive in their attacks upon U.S. interests, while at the same time demonstrating Communist leanings.[21] For Central America, Kirkpatrick's logic meant maintenance of the old order, except in Nicaragua, where it meant its restoration.

The second, and more important, geopolitical consideration dated to 1823, when the United States first looked upon the circum-Caribbean area as a border region where foreign encroachments would not be tolerated. The Reagan administration, 158 years later, was convinced that the Soviets were violating that foreign policy principle by capitalizing upon Carter's weakness and utilizing their Cuban proxies to expand Soviet influence throughout the Caribbean and to threaten U.S. interests. The bulk of the raw materials shipped to the United

States passed through the Caribbean's thirteen maritime routes. Also, the Panama Canal remained an important factor in defense consider-ations because only 13 of the United States Navy's 475 ships were unable to use the passageway. Finally, it was thought that the con-struction of any Soviet naval and air facilities in the Caribbean would threaten U.S. coastal military installations.

In Central America, Reagan was convinced that Castro served as the Soviet proxy because of Castro's role in unifying the diverse factions of the Sandinista movement in December 1978 and the subsequent presence of Cuban advisors during the final offensive in 1979. Accord-ing to Reagan's foreign policy team, the Soviet-Cuban plan targeted El Salvador and Guatemala as the next dominoes to fall, with Hon-duras used as the transit route for supplying the guerrilla forces. Just as the Eisenhower team had reasoned thirty years earlier, the Rea-gan group anticipated that the Communists would seize control of the revolutionary movement and, once in power, steer the country into the Soviet camp.[22] To check the Soviet-sponsored expansion, Reagan determined to follow Kirkpatrick's logic: to strengthen the old order, except in Nicaragua, where it was to be restored.

Reagan's policy had its critics. Those against the administration ar-gued that the causes of the isthmian violence were indigenous. They pointed to the long history of oligarchical rule in the region, the mis-treatment of the peasants, and the failure of the middle sector to achieve its political ambitions. The critics accepted the Marxist orienta-tion of the revolutionary groups, but dismissed their link to the Soviet-Cuban orbit. Rather, like policymakers of thirty-five years before, Rea-gan's critics described Marxism across the isthmus as peculiar to the area and that constructive assistance would nurture these movements in the proper direction. Reagan's determination to seek a military solution, they argued, only entrenched the oligarchy and forced the opposition groups to rely upon Soviet-Cuban support. The analogy with Vietnam reinforced concerns that the United States might be drawn into another quagmire from which withdrawal would be both painful and expensive. Further, the belligerents' continued violations of civil and human rights raised questions about the moral righteousness of U.S. involvement. Like the antiwar movement of the 1960s, the human rights groups represented a wide cross section of American society. Academicians published reports and conducted workshops and seminars that offered alternatives to Reagan's policies. Student and church groups demonstrated against the human costs of warfare in Central America. Representatives of the underprivileged charged that military expenditures in Central America could be better spent on social ills at home. The problem of illegal Central American immigrants was most taxing, particularly for Costa Rica, Mexico, and in the sunbelt sector of the United States, where existing social services were severely strained and social tensions exacerbated. Because southern Mexico served as a haven for Guatemalan Indian exiles and because those coming to the United States traversed that country, relations worsened between Washington and Mexico City.[23] Despite the extent of the opposition, the Reagan administration remained committed to its objective of a military solution, adjusting its tactics when congressional opposition proved too strong and rejecting a negotiated settlement when its objectives were not ensured.

Just as Reagan came into office in January 1981, the FMLN's final offensive collapsed in El Salvador, thanks largely to the reinstitution of U.S. military assistance to the Salvadoran government in the waning days of the Carter presidency. However, Reagan asserted that the setback did not mean total defeat of the guerrillas, because this was a textbook case of indirect armed aggression by the Communist powers operating through Cuba. To illustrate the point, the State Department issued a paper entitled "Communist Interference in El Salvador," which presented evidence of Communist-bloc military aid flowing to the FMLN through Nicaragua. The paper's flimsy proof was indicative of the shallow case made by the administration and contributed to the congressional rejection of Reagan's request for additional military aid and advisors for El Salvador, but the rejection did not stop the president from doing the same by executive order: Reagan dispatched fifty-six military advisors and $25 million in military aid to the Salvadoran government.

In an effort to defuse domestic opposition to the military assistance, the Reagan administration persuaded El Salvador to hold elections for a national assembly in March 1982. The elections, although free, did not go Washington's way. Leftists refused to participate, and the rightist parties, led by the National Republican Alliance, won control of the national assembly over the center-left Christian Democrats led by Duarte, Washington's choice.

After the March 1982 elections, the war intensified. Despite the training of Salvadoran government troops in the United States and Panama and an increased supply of new weaponry from Washington, the war went poorly for government forces. The FMLN launched an offensive in October 1982 and won major victories in Morozan and Usulutan provinces. More impressive was the FMLN's four-day seizure of Berlin, in the nation's second largest province, in January. By the summer of 1983, the FMLN controlled much of Chalatenago and La Union provinces. At this juncture, both France and Mexico offered to mediate for an end to the conflict, but Reagan rejected the offer.

The increase in terrorism after March 1982 prompted the U.S. Senate to approve a resolution that required the president to certify human rights progress every six months as a precondition for additional aid to the Salvadoran government. Reagan skirted the issue in the summer of 1983 by using the "pocket veto" rather than submitting a human rights report to Congress. Only after a visit by Vice-President George Bush and pressure by Ambassador Thomas Pickering did the violence momentarily recede.

In the midst of the turmoil, a presidential campaign and election were held in El Salvador in March 1984. With a reported $1.4 million in campaign assistance from the CIA, Christian Democrat José Napoleón Duarte captured the presidency, becoming the country's first civilian president in nearly twenty years. For a short time thereafter, Duarte fared well. At home, several treasury police officers, allegedly responsible for directing state-sponsored terrorism, were reassigned, and five national guardsmen were found guilty and sentenced for the 1980 murder of four American churchwomen. Outside El Salvador, Duarte received warm receptions in France, West Germany, and the

United States. In Washington he garnered promises of additional military and economic assistance. At home, Duarte fulfilled a promise made before the United Nations General Assembly when he met with FMLN spokesmen Rubén Zamora and Guillermo Ungo on 15 October 1984 at La Palma, a small town near the Honduran border. The initial euphoria over a negotiated settlement quickly faded when each side failed to move from its starting point. Duarte wanted to discuss only the opposition's participation in future elections, while Zamora and Ungo wanted to discuss broader political and structural issues.

The diplomatic impasse was exacerbated by renewed terrorist violence magnified by the assassination of Archbishop Arturo Rivera y Damas in early 1985 and four off-duty U.S. marines that June. Also in mid-1985, the FMLN pursued a new strategy, one designed to destroy the country's infrastructure. It resulted in an estimated $1 million in damages. Amidst the ongoing crisis, Duarte's government became increasingly dependent upon U.S. economic and military assistance and the Salvadoran military for its own survival.[24]

As the Reagan administration sought the defeat of the FMLN in El Salvador, it attempted to unify Honduras, Costa Rica, and Guatemala against the Sandinista government in Nicaragua. As so often happened in the past, Honduras was exploited by a larger power. By 1983, U.S. military assistance climbed to $31 million, the number of embassy staff in Tegucigalpa reached 110, and about 300 military advisors arrived in the country. The American military presence escalated with troop training exercises along the Nicaraguan border and with the establishment of a camp for the Green Berets at Trujillo. In 1983, General Gustavo Alvarez Martínez, chief of the Honduran armed forces, proposed that CONDECA be used to form a common military front against Nicaragua.[25] These actions pleased the Reagan administration.

Washington's efforts to bring Guatemala and Costa Rica into line with its anti-Sandinista policy met with less success, but for different reasons. Plagued with a repressive military government and a widening disparity in the quality of life between rich and poor, Guatemala seemed a likely place for a Communist-led guerrilla insurrection.

Hope for improved conditions following a March 1982 coup directed by General Efrain Rios Montt soon faded. In early August, Oscar Humberto Mejía Victores met upon the USS *Ranger* with high-ranking Honduran, Salvadoran, and American officials; the meeting gave credence to the charge that the United States had approved in advance Mejía's overthrow of Montt later that month. Subsequently, Mejía declared his support of Reagan's Central American policy, lifted the state of siege, and took other measures to alleviate human rights abuses. The U.S. Congress, however, remained hesitant about supplying assistance until the election of a constituent assembly in October 1985. Only then did Congress approve $300,000 for military training. But continued human rights violations caused Congress to resist Reagan's request for an additional $35 million in military assistance.[26]

Before Somoza's fall, Costa Rica was an ardent supporter of the Sandinista cause. Afterward, it became a haven for political exiles from its northern neighbors, served as a ferrying point for the shipment of arms to anti-Sandinista forces inside Nicaragua, became the training center and headquarters for Edén Pastora following his desertion from the Sandinista government in Managua, and experienced confrontations along its common border with Nicaragua. With Reagan's election, Costa Rica was drawn into Washington's anti-Sandinista political orbit. U.S. assistance, President Rodrigo Carazo learned, depended on Costa Rican support for the United States' policy in Central America. Carazo resisted, but his successor, Luis Alberto Monge, who was elected to the presidency in 1982, did not. He agreed to professionalize the civil guard so that it could better deal with the violence brought about by the presence of exiles and with the border incidents. By late 1984, Monge assented to the construction of roads capable of handling heavy military equipment and an airstrip capable of handling military aircraft. In return, Monge won Reagan's approval for increased economic assistance, including Costa Rica's designation as one of the first countries to receive aid under the Caribbean Basin Initiative (CBI).[27]

As Reagan sought to weave Central America into his policy against Nicaragua, many of the Sandinistas' political actions substantiated Reagan's description of a leftist, totalitarian government linked to

Soviet-Cuban designs upon the region. The resignations of Adolfo Calero, Violetta Chamorro, and Edén Pastora demonstrated the unfilled promise of a pluralistic society. Government intervention in the economy, press censorship, a neighborhood spy system, establishment of the people's courts, increased taxation, military conscription, land distribution programs, and the announced postponement of elections sent middle- and upper-sector Nicaraguans into exile. When elections were finally held in 1984, the opposition was not fully represented. The continued increase in Eastern-bloc military supplies and the presence of their advisors, sent to help with the development of the largest army in Central America, confirmed Washington's belief that Nicaragua would serve as a Soviet base for expansion in the region. More direct threats to the United States included a 1982 agreement that permitted the Soviet fishing fleet, which often included radar vessels, to use San Juan del Sur on Nicaragua's Pacific coast. Following surveys by Soviet engineers, Bulgarian crews constructed a port facility at El Bluff, near Bluefields on the Caribbean Coast, capable of handling ships up to twenty-five thousand tons, which included Soviet guided-missile cruisers. Cuban technicians planned a ten-year railroad project to connect the Atlantic and Pacific coasts of Nicaragua, and in the spring of 1983, both Jeane Kirkpatrick and Fernando Volio Jiménez, the Costa Rican foreign minister, reported that the Soviets had concluded a secret agreement to construct a sea-level canal across Nicaragua.[28]

To stem the leftward drift of the Sandinistas and the expansion of Soviet influence, the Reagan administration designed a policy that it believed would lead to a new government in Managua. On the economic front, Reagan suspended the remaining $15 million in reconstruction aid appropriated during the Carter administration. He also canceled $9.6 million in credits for the purchase of Nicaraguan wheat, $15 million in economic aid, and $11 million in rural-development, health, and education loans. The United States used its leverage to block loans from the Inter-American Development Bank and World Bank and dissuaded private American banks from participating in any international financial agreements with Nicaragua. In May 1983, Reagan cut the Nicaraguan sugar quota by 90 percent. Two years later, he placed a total embargo on United States–Nicaraguan trade. While the impact contributed to severe economic dislocations, the Sandinista regime did not collapse.

Military pressure commenced in March 1981, when Reagan informed Congress that U.S. security requirements in Central America necessitated the implementation of CIA-directed covert operations in the region. At first, some 150 Contras were trained in Honduras, allegedly to interdict arms supplies flowing from Nicaragua to El Salvador. By December 1981, the National Security Council approved a much broader operation, calling for a 500-man Contra unit to fight the Sandinista-Cuban infrastructure. The force slowly expanded to an estimated 2,000 men under the direction of an ex-*Somicista*, Colonel Enrique Bermudez. By late 1983, the Contra cover was lost, and the public became aware of their mining of harbors, violating of human rights, and destruction of bridges, electric towers, oil storage facilities, and crops. The Contras never gained popular support within Nicaragua, largely because of their *Somicista* connection. On the battle front, they did not carry the fight to the cities or gain hold of territory within Nicaragua. A 1982 assessment by the Pentagon's Defense Intelligence Agency, one repeated by the CIA in 1987, doubted the Contras' ability to gain popular support or to overthrow the Sandinista regime.

With time's passage, Congress became increasingly skeptical of Reagan's policies, but, immersed in the debate over the extent of Soviet-Cuban influence and the question of a local indigenous movement, Congress wavered on cutting off the operation. Its first restrictive action came in December 1982 with the passage of the Boland Amendment, which forbade the administration from providing military equipment, training, advice, or other support for military activities designed to overthrow the government of Nicaragua or to provoke an exchange between Nicaragua and Honduras. From August 1984 until June 1985, Reagan failed to convince Congress to loosen the purse strings. Still, the Contras found support from other sources: Israel, Argentina, Taiwan, and private interests in the United States. After Nicaraguan president Daniel Ortega visited Moscow in June

1985, Congress appropriated $27 million to the Contras but limited its use to "nonlethal" material. A year later, influenced by the increased Soviet connection with Nicaragua, Congress approved $100 million for the Contras, the bulk of it going for military supplies.[29]

In an effort to short-circuit congressional and public discontent over the support given the Contras, Reagan pursued three other paths, two diplomatic and one economic. In June 1983, former Democratic senator Richard Stone was appointed special envoy to Central America with the mission of bringing together the various factions to work for regional peace. After making several unsuccessful trips to Central America, Stone resigned in January 1984 because of personal differences with Assistant Secretary of State Langhorne H. Motley.[30] Reagan's second diplomatic initiative came in July 1983 with the appointment of former secretary of state Henry Kissinger as chairman of a high-level commission to recommend long-range policy options for Central America. The commission, however, did not include any known administration critics. With its task completed in January 1984, the commission concluded, not surprisingly, that U.S. interests were at stake in the region. The commission recognized the historic roots of the contemporary regional conflict and the need for economic, political, and social reform, but, because of the Soviet-Cuban connection, recommended continued military support of the Contras and the Salvadoran government. Ominously, it did not rule out U.S. military intervention in Nicaragua.[31]

Reagan's economic initiative had begun with the Caribbean Basin Initiative (CBI) proposed to Congress in February 1982 and passed by the end of its 1983 session. Excluding Nicaragua, the CBI was designed to encourage industrial development through private investment, trade through American tariff relief, and development through American financial assistance. Despite some restrictive features, the CBI registered some positive gains by 1986. In addition to changing many Central American producers' focus from domestic to export marketing, several extrahemispheric businesses capitalized upon CBI provisions that permitted them to assemble goods in the region for transshipment to the United States.[32]

If Reagan's diplomatic and economic initiatives were intended to silence the critics of his policy, the attitude toward the Contadora peace process did not. In January 1983 representatives from Panama, Mexico, Colombia, and Venezuela met on Contadora Island, off Panama's Pacific coast, to explore ways to a possible negotiated settlement of the crisis. In September 1983, the Contadora nations persuaded the Central American governments to accept a twenty-one-point regional peace program that included a negotiated settlement of the war in El Salvador and removal of all foreign troops from the region. Reagan issued verbal assurances of support. A year later, the Contadora group completed a draft treaty based on the original twenty-one points, but, unfortunately, it was open to various interpretations. Although the Sandinistas announced that they would sign the agreement, the Reagan administration now moved from its lukewarm endorsement to outright criticism. The administration refused to accept the Sandinistas' promises to hold free elections and charged that the verification provisions did not ensure Nicaraguan compliance with the provisions for arms reductions and foreign troop withdrawal. Secretary of State George Shultz was quickly dispatched to Central America, where he persuaded the governments at San José, San Salvador, Guatemala City, and Tegucigalpa to call for modifications in the proposed treaty, which effectively stalled the Contadora peace process. What the administration really sought was to preserve U.S. prominence in Central America. If fully implemented, the Contadora peace plan would have required the United States to cut off all military aid to Central America and end its support of the Salvadoran and Honduran militaries and the Contras.[33]

Reagan's policy ignited criticism, not only at home but also in Costa Rica, Honduras, and Guatemala. Despite previous signs of support, Costa Rican president Monge resisted U.S. pressure to send civil guardsmen to Honduras for military training, instructed the Costa Rican United Nations delegation to support the General Assembly's censure of the United States for its 1983 invasion of Grenada, and openly criticized the efforts of Ambassador Curtin Winsor to have Costa Rica take a stronger stand against Nicaragua. Finally, in December 1983, Monge declared his country's neutrality in international affairs.³⁴

Honduras paid a heavy price for its close link to the United States. Despite its civilian president, Roberto Suazo Córdova, the real power rested with General Gustavo Alvarez Martínez, who maintained a close association with the U.S. ambassador, John Negropronte, and allegedly siphoned off U.S. assistance for personal gain. As a proponent of the American Contra policy, local critics charged that Honduras had become an American colony and that it might be drawn into a war with Nicaragua. When the U.S. Congress began cutting aid to the Contras in 1984, Honduran officials pondered their country's fate in the case of a total U.S. withdrawal. The rising tide of opposition contributed to the ouster of Alvarez in late 1984. He was replaced by General Walter López Reyes, who did not enjoy good relations with Ambassador Negropronte. In 1985, the Honduran foreign minister, Edgardo Paz Barnica, sought to deemphasize the country's military relationship with the United States. He directed the government's confiscation of $27 million in aid destined for the Contras and subsequently denied the existence of Contra forces inside Honduran borders. In 1986, newly elected president José Azcona Hoyo pursued a policy more independent of the United States.³⁵

In October 1986, the Guatemalans elected their first civilian president in fifteen years, Christian Democrat Vinicio Cerezo. While receptive to badly needed economic aid, Cerezo did not want to be swept into the U.S. policy vacuum. He preferred to deal with domestic issues, such as human rights violations and the military's political presence.³⁶

By 1986, amidst these crosscurrents, the Central American crisis reached a stalemate. The Contras had yet to control any territory or gain any friends. The guerrilla war in El Salvador continued at a slow pace. The Contadora peace process lost its luster.

The tenuous environment exploded late that same year, when revelations in Washington indicated that, because of restrictions on the CIA's covert operations in Central America, their supervision passed to the National Security Council, where Lieutenant Colonel Oliver

North circumvented the Boland Amendment by soliciting money from leaders of oil-rich nations and diverting funds to the Contra operation from missile sales to Iran. Subsequent congressional hearings on the Iran arms sales brought further criticism of Reagan's Central American policy and contributed to a peace proposal worked out between the White House chief of staff, Howard Baker, and the house majority leader, Jim Wright, in midsummer 1987.[37] The six-point plan called for an immediate, verifiable cease-fire, cessation of military aid to all belligerents, and restoration of civil rights in Nicaragua. Once in place, regional negotiations on total arms reduction would begin. Controversy immediately surfaced. Critics charged that the proposal was a ploy to force Nicaraguan rejection and gain an additional $140 million in aid for the Contras.

However, Reagan's proposal was pushed aside when the five Central American presidents, meeting in Guatemala City, agreed on 7 August to a peace proposal initiated by Costa Rican president Oscar Arías. The plan, in the works since February 1987, provided for a cease-fire within ninety days (5 November); a cutoff of arms to insurgent groups; amnesty for combatants who laid down their arms; restoration of civil rights; and formation of national reconciliation groups in each country. Each Central American government saw its own survival in the Arías peace plan.[38] For Costa Rica, an end to the crisis would halt the stream of immigrants, which in turn would alleviate the pressure upon the national welfare system and reduce the potential for it to be drawn into the quagmire. President Cerezo of Guatemala viewed a general peace as an opportunity to further curtail the political presence of the military. Honduras viewed the peace treaty as a means of reducing the possibility of Nicaraguan vengeance should Washington abandon the Contras. For the Sandinistas, an end to the Contra war meant solidification of its position in Managua. President Duarte believed that the Arías peace plan would end outside military support for the FMLN guerrillas. Underlying these individual objectives was the common desire to end U.S. dominance of isthmian affairs.

Although the Arías plan satisfied Reagan's demand that the Sandinistas negotiate directly with the Contras, grant political amnesty, provide for unfettered elections, and guarantee that no Soviet bases be constructed in Nicaragua, the administration remained critical. "What the president wants is a peace process that either sees the Sandinistas out of power by the time his term ends or that at least sets in motion an irreversible process in that direction," one official remarked.[39] Reagan remained committed to the same objective he had outlined in 1981.

Following an initial euphoria, by the spring of 1988 the peace process had stagnated. The Sandinistas strengthened their position at home and appeared unwilling to concede anything to the Contras, now abandoned by the United States Congress. Violence increased in El Salvador, where the government became more dependent upon the military. A failed military coup against Cerezo put the civilian government on notice in Guatemala. Anxiety increased in Honduras as it feared the prospects of a U.S. withdrawal and the abandoned Contras' increased presence.

In the United States, as the 1988 presidential election approached, the debate focused upon the continued support of the Contras and the concomitant issue of American security interests in the region. At the same time, the American people appeared weary of a near decade-long crisis that offered no immediate solution. The weariness was exacerbated by the continued human rights violations that were linked to the administration's insistence on a military solution. As was the case in Central America, in the United States, little attention was given to the economic, political, and social structural problems that plagued the isthmus.

Epilogue

What eight years of warfare failed to accomplish, the ballot box did. In February 1990, the Sandinistas were ousted from political power. Violetta Chamorro, whose husband's assassination twelve years earlier set in motion events that ended the Somoza dynasty, led the United National Opposition, a broad-based coalition, to a resounding victory over Daniel Ortega's Sandinistas. The road to the Nicaraguan elections began a year earlier at Tesoro Beach, El Salvador, where the Central American presidents extracted a pledge from Nicaragua's Sandinista government to implement democratic changes and hold national elections in return for a pledge that the Contras would disband.

The peace process crossed its next milestone in August 1989 at Tela, Honduras, where the five Central American presidents (Oscar Arías, Costa Rica; Alfredo Cristiani, El Salvador; Vinicio Cerezo, Guatemala; José Azcona, Honduras; and Daniel Ortega, Nicaragua) gathered in a Caribbean seaside compound once owned by the United Fruit Company. There they reached an agreement calling for the disbandment of the Contras before the year's end. Just as UFCO represented the long-standing arrogance of U.S. economic imperialism in the region, the Contras represented Washington's determination to dominate Central America's political affairs. The symbolism escaped no one.

Subsequently, the Sandinistas agreed to concessions that their domestic and international opponents had long demanded: a liberalization of the national electoral law, a guarantee of free expression for all political parties in the press and the electronic media, a promise to release an estimated three thousand political prisoners, and a setting of 25 February 1990 as the date for national elections. On the economic front, the Sandinista government ended its nationalization measures and provided incentives for private investments. These actions prompted the Sandinistas' internal political opponents to endorse the Tela accords.

Other regional events favored a solution to the isthmian crisis. In El Salvador, right-wing president-elect Alfredo Cristiani offered to negotiate an end to that nation's civil war with the Farabundo Martí National Liberation Front. Honduran president Azcona warned that his country was flirting with economic and social disaster because of the presence of an estimated 180,000 Nicaraguan refugees. In Guatemala, President Cerezo survived two coup attempts and an eleven-week teacher and postal-worker strike for increased wages to offset mounting inflation. Central American foreign ministry and military officials obtained approval from representatives of the OAS and the United Nations to police regional borders and supervise the disbandment of the Contras.

As the U.S. role declined, other hemispheric leaders moved to direct Washington's attention to larger concerns. Taking advantage of the attendance by Latin American heads of state at his inauguration in February 1989, Venezuelan president Carlos Andrés Pérez forged a consensus that resulted in a message to Washington. The communication asked for a reorientation of U.S. hemispheric policy away from Nicaragua and toward other issues, most importantly the $400 billion international debt that threatened Latin America's economic, political, and social structures. In return, Pérez's group promised to work for supporting and broadening the Sandinista government's efforts to institute meaningful multiparty democracy in Nicaragua, allegedly the primary reason for U.S. intervention in 1981.

The Soviet presence also diminished. In the Soviet Union there was a sense of outrage when it was learned that Moscow averaged $5 billion annually to keep Fidel Castro's Cuba afloat at a time when the Soviet economy appeared near collapse. Given these conditions, Soviet President Mikhail Gorbachev indicated that his nation could not be expected to rescue the failed Nicaraguan economy. He also announced a cessation of arms deliveries to Managua, allegedly the second reason for U.S. intervention in 1981.

By the time of the Tesoro Beach agreement in February 1989, President George Bush had abandoned his immediate postelection pledge to provide military assistance to the Contras but had yet to define a policy course. While Bush publicly endorsed the Central American initiative, he continued the economic embargo against Nicaragua. These conflicting signals represented contradictory advice from the National Security Council, which favored acceptance of the Central American peace initiative, and the State Department, which opposed the demobilization of the Contras. Congress had a similar split. In March, Secretary of State James Baker bridged the gap between the two factions when he forged an agreement that provided for a ten-month, $45 million humanitarian aid package for the Contras, with the administration reserving the right to seek military assistance if conditions deteriorated in Central America.

Despite the altered conditions in Central America, the new pressures from external actors, and the apparent abandonment of former president Ronald Reagan's policy, Washington exerted intense pressure upon the conferees at Tela in August 1989—they were not to abandon the Contras. Two visits from Bernard Aronson, the assistant secretary of state for inter-American affairs, and telephone calls from Secretary Baker and President Bush went unheeded. At home, the Democratic Congressional party indicated that it would not extend humanitarian aid to the Contras beyond the 30 November 1989 deadline.

Bush was not the only loser. In registering his displeasure at the Tela accords and the congressional abandonment, Contra leader Adolfo Calero lambasted the signatories at Tela and the legislators in Washington for selling out his "freedom fighters." He warned that Central America faced the same future that Cuba did thirty years earlier when Fidel Castro marched into Havana.

Ironically, as the Central American peace initiative took root, the Agency for International Development began a classroom program, deep inside the mountains of southern Honduras, to teach the rudiments of democracy to the freedom fighters should they choose to return home to Nicaragua to participate in the political process—the same goal that they had supposedly sought in eight years of fighting that cost nearly 100,000 lives.

As Chamorro prepared to move into the presidential palace and UNO representatives into the national legislature, supporters of Ronald Reagan and George Bush claimed that their aggressive policies of the 1980s brought democracy to Nicaragua in 1990. In contrast, congressional critics asserted that their cutoff of aid to the Contras forced an end to the civil war. Supporters of former president Jimmy Carter, whose statesmanlike image grew after he left Washington, led a group of international observers that provided a stamp of legitimacy to the elections.

While the North Americans stumbled over each other to claim credit for the cessation of hostilities in Nicaragua, they overlooked the fact that the peace effort was truly an *American* undertaking. The patient persistence of Costa Rican president Oscar Arías cannot be dismissed lightly. In 1986, Costa Rica, wedged between Panama to the south and Nicaragua to the north, appeared on the verge of becoming another Lebanon. In the face of that possibility, Arías determined to find a solution. Reasoning that U.S. political institutions could not sustain a long-term, low-intensity conflict, while the Sandinistas and their supporters in Havana and Moscow, lacking accountability, could continue to fight indefinitely, Arías set out to find the path to the ballot box. From Esquipulus to Tesoro Beach to Tela, Arías forged ahead. Tribute to Arías came with a Nobel Peace Prize and with recognition from his hemispheric counterparts when he hosted a conference of the heads of state in 1989. Throughout the process, the other Central American leaders, including Daniel Ortega, also came to agree that continued warfare was not in their nations' best interest.

Other Latin American nations also played a role in the peace process. Prompted by larger hemispheric issues, the Contadora nations— Colombia, Mexico, Panama, and Venezuela—and its support group— Argentina, Brazil, Peru, and Uruguay—worked for a solution to the crisis. The presence of an OAS observer team in Nicaragua for the February 1990 elections further indicated the hemisphere's concern with the Central American crisis. In both instances, the Latin Americans demonstrated their desire to end U.S. domination of isthmian affairs.

Despite the euphoria over the success of the peace process, Nicaragua still faced immediate political and economic difficulties and deep-rooted structural disparities that illustrate the complexity of Central America's internal problems. President Violetta Chamorro must satisfy the interests of UNO's fourteen-party coalition, which represents the political spectrum from the Communists on the left to the Conservatives on the right. She must also come to grips with the potential political power of the Sandinistas, the largest opposition party, and their efficiently trained, Marxist army and internal security force. Among the populace, the bitterness between winner and loser threatens the political climate. The integration of an estimated 8,000 to 12,000 Contras and their families (totaling an estimated 50,000 people) presents a difficult problem, because nearly 70 percent of the Contra group is illiterate and has no employable skills. Finally, Chamorro badly needs to lure back to Nicaragua the middle sector—managers, technicians, small businessmen, skilled labor, and professionals— which escaped the violence and hardship of civil war to make a new life elsewhere in the region, Mexico, and the United States. Will they return to start over again in a volatile political atmosphere and in an economy that needs $300 to $600 million for war reconstruction alone?

UNO's victory did not solve related problems across the isthmus. The possible repatriation of Nicaraguan exiles among its neighbors will only saddle government social services already incapable of meeting existing conditions, particularly in Honduras. Peace in Nicaragua may contribute to a negotiated settlement in El Salvador, but it will also strengthen the rightist position there and in Guatemala and Honduras, further stifling inclination toward reform. That will leave Costa Rica as a safety valve for those seeking to escape socioeconomic impoverishment and civil and political rights restrictions. Their presence will further tax Costa Rica's economy and social structure. A possible return to the old order will test the Tela accords. The promises to institute democracy across the region and not to harbor revolutionaries in neighboring countries stand as stark reminders of previous U.S. efforts to impose constitutional order upon Central America.

Isthmian peace also provides the United States with an opportunity to take a leadership role in addressing issues that have long plagued Central America—social injustice, restricted political participation, land distribution, monoagriculture, and flight capital. Should Washington be willing to pursue far-reaching social and economic programs, such as those suggested by the Kissinger Commission, it will assist in advancing modernity across the isthmus. But Washington may not seize the opportunity, because, as in the past, the threat of foreign intervention has receded. The vast political and economic changes sweeping the Soviet Union and Eastern Europe curtail their interest and ability to support leftist forces in the Western Hemisphere. This scenario provides Washington with an opening to retreat.

Notes

1. A Hesitant Beginning

1. Joseph B. Lockey, "Diplomatic Futility," *Hispanic American Historical Review* 10 (August 1930): 265–94.
2. John Quincy Adams, *Memoirs of John Quincy Adams*, ed. Charles Francis Adams, 12 vols. (Philadelphia, 1874–77), 7:325–26.
3. Franklin D. Parker, *Travels in Central America, 1821–1840* (Gainesville, Fla., 1970), 1–13.
4. Charles L. Stansifer, "United States–Central American Relations, 1824–1850," in *United States–Latin American Relations, 1800–1850: The Formative Generations*, ed. T. Ray Shurbutt (Tuscaloosa, Ala., 1991).
5. José Milla and Augustíne Goméz Carillo, *Historía de America Central desde 1502 hasta 1821*, 5 vols. (Guatemala, 1879–1905); Murdo J. MacLeod, *Spanish Central America: A Socioeconomic History, 1520–1720* (Berkeley, 1973); and Miles Wortman, *Government and Society in Central America, 1680–1840* (New York, 1982).
6. The University of San Carlos was founded in Antigua in 1676 and moved to Guatemala City after the 1773 earthquake. The university had some notable thinkers on its faculty, including José Felipe Flores and José Antonio Liendo y Goicoechea. Other Central Americans influenced by the U.S. model were the Honduran José Celicio del Valle and Salvadoran Juan Bautista Irisarri. Constantino Lascaris, *Historia de las ideas en Centroamérica* (San José, 1970); John T. Lanning, *The Eighteenth-Century Enlightenment in the University of San Carlos de Guatemala* (Ithaca, N.Y., 1956); John T. Reid, *Spanish American Images of the United States* (Gainesville, Fla., 1977), 3–36; and José de Onís, *The United States as Seen by Spanish American Writers* (New York, 1952).
7. David Howarth, *Four Hundred Years of Dreams and Cruelties* (New York, 1966), 3–153.
8. For example, of the $48.2 million in exports to the Spanish Caribbean in 1799–1800, only $291,717, or 4 percent, went to Central America.
9. John Hale, quoted in Ricardo Fernandez Guardia, *Costa Rica en el siglo XIX*

(San José, 1929), 29, 27; Dorothy B. Goebel, "British Trade to the Spanish Colonies, 1796–1823," *American Historical Review* 43 (January 1938): 288–320.

10. Thomas Jefferson, *The Writings of Thomas Jefferson*, comp. Richard Holland Johnson (Washington, D.C., 1903), 12:187.

11. Samuel Flagg Bemis, *The Latin American Policy of the United States: A Historical Interpretation* (New York, 1943), 16–59.

12. James D. Richardson, ed., *A Compilation of the Messages and Papers of the Presidents* (New York, 1897), 2:785–89.

13. Troy S. Floyd, *The Anglo-Spanish Struggle for Mosquitia* (Albuquerque, 1967), and R. A. Humphries, *The Diplomatic History of British Honduras, 1638–1901* (London, 1961), 1–9.

14. Mario Rodríguez, *The Cádiz Experiment* (Berkeley, 1978).

15. Until the reorganization of the Foreign Service in 1921, the State Department assigned two types of consuls abroad: career consuls, who were appointed by the government and not permitted to engage in business of any kind, and commercial consuls, who were either U.S. or foreign nationals who engaged in business. Most of the U.S. consuls in Central America during the nineteenth century were private businessmen. See Graham H. Stuart, *American Diplomatic and Consular Practice* (New York, 1936), 340–44.

16. Andrés Townsend Ezcurira, *Las Provincias Unidas de Centroamérica: Fundación de la republica* (San José, 1973).

17. John Williams to Henry Clay, 23 August 1826, Despatches from U.S. Ministers in Central America, 1824–1842, National Archives, Washington, D.C. (hereafter cited as Ministers' Despatches); and Charles Savage to Martin Van Buren, 2 March 1829, Despatches from U.S. Consuls in Guatemala, 1824–1849, National Archives, Washington, D.C. (hereafter cited as Consular Despatches).

18. Charles DeWitt to Louis McLane, 25 December, 4 January, 17 January, 10 April, 10 May, and 26 May 1834, Ministers' Despatches.

19. David Chandler, "Juan José Aycinena, Nineteenth-Century Guatemalan Conservative: An Historical Survey of His Political, Religious, Educational, and Commercial Careers" (master's thesis, Tulane University, 1965), 34. See also Mario Rodríguez, *The Livingston Codes in the Guatemalan Crisis of 1837–1838* (New Orleans, 1955).

20. George P. Connick, "The United States and Central America, 1823–1850" (Ph.D. diss., University of Colorado, 1969), 157–69. Cañas's suggestion

in 1824 prompted every secretary of state to instruct every diplomat assigned to Central America during the confederative period to study the route's feasibility, to provide a cost estimate, and to determine the extent of Central America's commitment to the project and the possible economic benefits to the United States.

21. William M. Malloy, comp., *Treaties, Conventions, International Acts, Protocols, and Agreements between the United States of America and Other Powers, 1776–1904* (Washington, D.C., 1910), 1:160–69; Williams to Clay, 26 August 1825, Ministers' Despatches; and Savage to Livingston, 22 August 1832, Consular Despatches; and Thomas Schoonover, "Compilation of Statistics on United States–Central American Trade" (used with Schoonover's permission).

22. Juan Galindo, quoted in DeWitt to Forsyth, 7 November 1934, Diplomatic Despatches, National Archives, Washington, D.C. See also William J. Griffith, "Juan Galindo: Central American Chauvinist," *Hispanic American Historical Review* 80 (February 1980): 25–52.

23. Charles DeWitt to John Forsyth, 24 March 1835, Ministers' Despatches.

24. Wortman, *Government and Society*, 215–68; Ralph Lee Woodward, Jr., "Social Revolution in Guatemala: The Carrera Revolt," *Applied Enlightenment: Nineteenth-Century Liberalism* (New Orleans, 1972), 45–70; and Manuel Montúfar, *Reseña historia de Centra-América* (Guatemala, 1878–79), 3:76–79.

25. José Aycinena, quoted in Chandler, "Aycinena," 25. See also Hubert Howe Bancroft, *History of Central America* (San Francisco, 1887), 3:186–326; Louis Beltrana Sinibaldi, *Fundación de la republica de Guatemala* (Guatemala City, 1971).

26. *Gaceta de Guatemala*, 29 December 1849, 21 February 1850, and 26 July 1850.

27. John L. Stephens, *Incidents of Travel in Central America, Chiapas, and Yucatán*, 2 vols. (New York, 1841; New York, 1969.)

28. Robert A. Naylor, "The British Role in Central America Prior to the Clayton-Bulwer Treaty," *Hispanic American Historical Review* 43 (November 1963): 361–70.

29. Robert A. Naylor, "The Mahogany Trade as a Factor in the British Return to the Mosquito Shore in the Second Quarter of the Nineteenth Century," *Jamaican Historical Review* 7 (1967): 40–67.

30. William R. Manning, ed., *Diplomatic Correspondence of the United States, Inter-American Affairs* (Washington, D.C., 1933), 3:152–60, 161–80, 183–93, 225–27, 231–33, 249–53, 255–61, and 265–68.

2. The Outside World Comes to Central America, 1845–1865

1. John O'Sullivan, "Annexation," *United States Magazine and Democratic Review*, July–August 1845, 5–10.

2. Albert Weinberg, *Manifest Destiny* (Chicago, 1963), 160–89.

3. Manning, *Diplomatic Correspondence* 3:259–87. Great Britain also feared other European competitors. The Nicaraguan government first sought out Louis Phillipe in France and then some Belgian promoters before turning to Louis Napoleon Bonaparte in May 1846. See E. W. Richards, "Louis Napoleon and Central America," *Journal of Modern History* 34 (June 1962): 178–84.

4. The Nicaraguan treaty was never submitted to the Senate. The Guatemalan treaty was ratified by the U.S. Senate on 24 September 1850, and ratifications were exchanged on 13 May 1852. See Malloy, *Treaties* 1:861.

5. John M. Clayton, quoted in Manning, *Diplomatic Correspondence* 3:36–41.

6. Ibid.

7. Mary W. Williams, ed., "Letters of E. George Squier to John M. Clayton," *Hispanic American Historical Review* 1 (November 1918): 427.

8. Charles L. Stansifer, "The Central American Career of E. George Squier" (Ph.D. diss., Tulane University, 1959), 1–84.

9. Mary W. Williams, *Anglo-American Isthmian Diplomacy, 1815–1915* (Washington, D.C., 1916), 62–109; see also Malloy, *Treaties* 1:660.

10. Roger S. Baldwin, "Tarrying in Nicaragua: Pleasures and Perils of the California Trip in 1849," *Century Magazine*, October 1891, 911–31.

11. Ephraim George Squier, "San Juan de Nicaragua," *Harper's New Monthly Magazine*, December 1854, 50–61.

12. Mario Rodríguez, "The *Prometheus* and the Clayton-Bulwer Treaty," *Journal of Modern History* 36 (September 1964): 260–78.

13. Richard Van Alstyne, "British Diplomacy and the Clayton-Bulwer Treaty, 1850–1860," *Journal of Modern History* 11 (June 1939): 149–83; and Dean Kortge, "The Central American Policy of Lord Palmerston" (Ph.D. diss., University of Kansas, 1973).

14. David Wadell, "Great Britain and the Bay Islands, 1821–1861," *Historical Journal* 2 (1959): 59–77.

15. U.S. Congress, Senate, *Establishment of a New British Colony in Central America*, 32d Cong., 2d sess., serial 671, Senate doc. 407; and James

Buchanan, *The Works of James Buchanan: Comprising His Speeches, State Papers, and Private Correspondence*, ed. John B. Moore (Philadelphia, 1911), 9:1–10, 88–97, 215–41.

16. "The Career of Solon Borland in Central America, 1853–1854," *Americas* 40 (January 1980): 399–416; and U.S. Congress, Senate, *Presidential Message Transmitting Reports on the Destruction of San Juan de Nicaragua*, 33d Cong., 1st sess., serial 734, Senate miscellaneous document 126, 19–25.

17. "Colonel Kinney Defends His Plan," *New York Times*, 15 December 1854.

18. William O. Scroggs, *Filibusters and Financiers* (New York, 1916), 93–107; and José Ramirez M., *José de Marcoleta, padre de la diplomacia nicaraguesne* (Managua, 1975).

19. For a discussion of Walker's life, see Charles Brown, *Agents of Manifest Destiny: The Lives and Times of the Filibusters* (Chapel Hill, N.C., 1980); and Albert Carr, *The World of William Walker* (New York, 1963).

20. Nicaragua, Ministry of Foreign Relations and Home Office, *Contracto de canalización: Celebrado entre el gobierno de Nicaragua y una compañía de ciudadanos de los Estados Unidos de Norte América* (León, 1849).

21. David I. Folkman, Jr., "Westward via Nicaragua: The United States and the Nicaragua Route, 1826–1869" (Ph.D. diss., University of Utah, 1966), 119–48.

22. Thomas H. McKee, *National Conventions and Platforms of All Political Parties* (Baltimore, 1906), 93.

23. John J. TePaske, "Appleton Oaksmith, Filibuster Agent," *North Carolina Historical Review* 35 (October 1958): 427–47.

24. Robert E. May, *Southern Dream of a Caribbean Empire* (Baton Rouge, La., 1963). The actual number of persons Walker attracted to Nicaragua is unknown. Estimates range from a low of 1,300 to a high of 11,000, but, for sure, Walker did not attract the quality of people he anticipated. Only a few farmers and artisans came to Nicaragua. Most émigrés were discontented intellectuals, mechanics, and small businessmen seeking personal advancement.

25. Randall O. Hodson, "The Filibuster Minister: The Career of John Hill Wheeler as United States Minister to Nicaragua," *North Carolina Historical Review* 49 (July 1972): 280–97.

26. Scroggs, *Filibusters and Financiers*, 9–17, 31–70.

27. The Costa Ricans also believed that, with Walker in power, all hopes of settling the San Juan River boundary dispute with Nicaragua appeared

gone. See Mary Z. Froncek, "Diplomatic Relations between the United States and Costa Rica, 1823–1882" (Ph.D. diss., Fordham University, 1959), 95–105.

28. These actions and the continued occupation of the Bay Islands were also intended to force the United States to budge from its uncompromising position regarding the Clayton-Bulwer Treaty. See Manning, *Diplomatic Correspondence* 4:81–84.

29. Miguel Angel Alvarez, *Los filíbusteros en Nicaragua, 1855, 1856, 1857* (Managua, 1944); and Rafael Obregón Loría, *Costa Rica y la guerra del 56 (La campaña del transito, 1856–1857)* (San José, 1976).

30. Quoted in William H. Patterson, "United States Aggrandizement, 1850–1860: The Walker Expeditions as an Illustrative Case," *South Carolina Historical Association Proceedings 1947*, 9–20.

31. V. Cáares Lara, "La aventura posrera de William Walker en Honduras," *Executive* 1 (September 1965): 27–44.

32. Quoted in United States, *Congressional Globe*, 35th Cong., 1st sess., part 1, 216–17.

33. Decree, 27 June 1856, in Commission for the Historical Investigation of the Campaign of 1856–1857, *Documentos relativos a la guerra contra los filibusteros* (San José, 1956), 64.

34. Clarendon quoted in Williams, *Anglo-American Isthmian Diplomacy*, 217.

35. Kortge, "Central American Policy," 130–49.

36. Dade Sparks, "Central America and Its Relations with the United States, 1860–1893" (Ph.D. diss., Duke University, 1934), 34–39.

37. U.S. Department of State, *Papers Relating to the Foreign Relations of the United States*, 1862 (Washington, D.C., 1863), 881 (hereafter referred to as *FRUS*, followed by the year).

38. Quoted in Charles Albro Barker, ed., *Memoirs of Elisha Oscar Crosby: Reminiscences of California and Guatemala from 1849 to 1864* (San Marino, Calif., 1945), 90.

39. Quoted in Thomas Schoonover, "Misconstrued Mission: Expansionism and Black Colonization in Mexico and Central America during the Civil War," *Pacific Historical Review* 49 (November 1980): 607–20. See also Warren A. Beck, "Lincoln and Negro Colonization in Central America," *Abraham Lincoln Quarterly* 6 (1950–51): 162–83.

3. Relationships Established, 1865–1903

1. John A. Kasson, "The Monroe Doctrine in 1881," *North American Review*, December 1881, 527–33.
2. Quoted in Victor Miguel Díaz, *Barrios ante la posteridad* (Guatemala, 1935), 474.
3. Charles N. Riotte to Secretary of State William H. Seward, 29 August 1861, Ministers' Despatches, Costa Rica.
4. Riotte to Seward, 24 September 1865, ibid.
5. Froncek, "United States and Costa Rica," 194–99.
6. Alberto Herrarte, *La unión de Centro America* (Guatemala, 1964), 154–64.
7. *FRUS*, 1885, 73–144.
8. R. Ogden, "The Proposed Central American Union," *The Nation*, 27 July 1887, 47–53.
9. Imports from Central America included food products of relatively high bulk and low unit value: sugar, hides, wool, cocoa, fruits, rubber, quinine (chinchona bark), and other tropical and subtropical products. U.S. exports to Central America ranged from unprocessed agricultural items to semimanufactured products: tools of all descriptions (especially for agriculture and mining), arms and ammunitions, locomotives, hardware, petroleum and kerosene, flour, lard, and cheap cotton cloth (*FRUS*, 1870, 260–61, 274–75).
10. George Williamson to Hamilton Fish, 16 October 1873, Ministers' Despatches, Central America.
11. Despatches Received from the Commission to Central and South America, 1884–1885, Record Group 59, National Archives.
12. Malloy, *Treaties* 2:1279–87. Nicaragua denounced the treaty in October 1902.
13. Ulysses S. Grant, "The Nicaraguan Canal," *North American Review*, February 1881, 71–80.
14. Jackson Crowell, "The United States and a Central American Canal, 1869–1877," *Hispanic American Historical Review* 49 (February 1869): 29–49.
15. U.S. Congress, House of Representatives, *Report of Historical and Technical Information Relating to the Problem of Interoceanic Communication by Way of the American Isthmus*, 47th Cong., 2d sess., serial 2112, H. Exec. Doc. 107.
16. For a discussion of the de Lesseps project, see David McCullough, *The*

Path between the Seas: The Creation of the Panama Canal, 1876–1914 (New York, 1977), 17–242.

17. Richardson, *Messages and Papers* 10:4537–38.

18. J. Fred Rippy, "Justo Rufino Barrios and the Nicaraguan Canal," *Hispanic American Historical Review* 20 (May 1940): 190–92.

19. "U.S. and Nicaragua Conclude Treaty," *New York Times,* 16 December 1884.

20. Roscoe D. Hill, "Nicaraguan Canal Idea to 1913," *Hispanic American Historical Review* 28 (February 1948): 201–4.

21. Herrarte, *La unión,* 165–74.

22. Nicaragua, *Gaceta Oficial* 25 (1887).

23. Gerstle Mack, *The Land Divided: A History of the Panama Canal and Other Isthmian Canal Projects* (New York, 1944), 213–23; and Craig L. Dozier, *Nicaragua's Mosquito Shore: The Years of American and British Presence* (Tuscaloosa, Ala., 1985), 123–40.

24. Quoted in Díaz, *Barrios,* 471–74.

25. For a discussion of liberalism, see Ralph Lee Woodward, Jr., ed., *Positivism in Latin America, 1850–1890* (Lexington, Ky., 1971).

26. David McCreery, *Development and the State in Reforma Guatemala, 1871–1885* (Athens, Ohio, 1983); and Sanford Mosk, "Coffee Economy of Guatemala, 1850–1918," *Inter-American Economic Affairs* 9 (Winter 1984): 6–20.

27. John E. Findling, "The United States and Zelaya: A Study in the Diplomacy of Expediency" (Ph.D. diss., University of Texas at Austin, 1971), 57–58.

28. Kenneth V. Finney, "Precious Metal Mining and Modernization of Honduras: In Quest of El Dorado (1880–1900)" (Ph.D. diss., Tulane University, 1973), 1–78.

29. Kenneth V. Finney, "Our Man in Honduras: Washington S. Valentine," *West Georgia College in the Social Sciences* 17 (June 1978): 13–20, and Finney, "Rosario and the Election of 1887: The Political Economy of Mining in Honduras," *Hispanic American Historical Review* 59 (February 1979): 81–106.

30. J. Fred Rippy, "United States and Costa Rica during the Guardia Era," *Bulletin of the Pan American Union* 77 (1943): 61–68; and Watt Stewart, *Keith of Costa Rica* (Albuquerque, N.M., 1964).

31. Findling, "United States and Zelaya," 58–59; and Wayne F. Anderson, "The Development of Export Transportation in Liberal Guatemala, 1871–1920" (Ph.D. diss., Tulane University, 1986).

32. Dozier, *Nicaragua's Mosquito Shore,* 141–62; and John E. Findling, "La

diplomacia norteamericana y la reincor poración Mosquitia," *Boletin Nica-raguense de Bibliografía y Documentación* 26 (November–December 1978): 15–24.

33. Quoted in R. L. Morrow, "A Conflict between the Commercial Interests of the United States and Its Foreign Policy," *Hispanic American Historical Review* 10 (February 1930): 8.

34. Quoted in Julius W. Pratt, "The Large Policy of 1898," *Mississippi Valley Historical Review* 19 (September 1932): 219.

35. Paul F. Scheips, "United States Commercial Pressures for a Nicaraguan Canal in the 1890s," *Americas* 20 (April 1964): 333–58.

36. Herrarte, *La unión*, 165–74.

37. Frederick U. Adams, *Conquest of the Tropics* (Garden City, N.Y., 1914), 54.

38. Ibid., 54–97.

39. Quoted in Findling, "United States and Zelaya," 60–61.

40. J. Fred Rippy, *British Investments in Latin America, 1822–1949* (Minneapolis, Minn., 1959), 105–9.

41. William E. Curtis, "Central America: Its Resources and Commerce," *Forum* 25 (April 1898): 166–67.

42. Quoted in *Report on United States Relations with Panama*, 86th Cong., 2d sess., H. Rept. 2218, 5.

43. McCullough, *Path between the Seas*, 243–615; and Dwight C. Miner, *The Fight for the Panama Route: The Story of the Spooner Act and the Hay-Herran Treaty* (New York, 1971), 75–156.

44. Joseph L. Arbena, "The Panama Problem in Colombian History" (Ph.D. diss., University of Virginia, 1970); Richard L. Lael, *U.S. Policy toward Colombia, 1903–1922* (Wilmington, Del., 1987), 1–24.

45. *Public Opinion*, 19 November 1903, 643.

46. John Patterson, "Latin American Reactions to the Panama Revolution of 1903," *Hispanic American Historical Review* 24 (November 1944): 342–51.

4. The Search for Stability, 1903–1920

1. U.S. Congress, Senate, *Message from the President of the United States Transmitting a Report with Accompanying Papers, of the Delegates of the United States, Held at Mexico City from October 22, 1901, to January 22, 1902*, Second International Congress, S. Doc. 330, 31–32.

2. Richardson, *Messages and Papers* 16:6923–24.

3. For a discussion of the U.S. intervention in the Dominican Republic, see Lester D. Langley, *The Banana Wars: An Inner History of American Empire, 1900–1934* (Lexington, Ky., 1983), 117–65.

4. Ministry of Foreign Relations, *Memoría de relaciones exteriores, 1907* (Managua, 1907), xxi; Findling, "United States and Zelaya," 136–43.

5. *FRUS, 1907,* 2:601–728; and A. Martínez Moreno, *La conferencia de Washington de 1907 y la corte de justicia centroamericana* (San Salvador, 1957).

6. *FRUS,* 1912, 1091.

7. Taft, quoted in Dana G. Munro, *Intervention and Dollar Diplomacy in the Caribbean, 1900–1921* (Princeton, N.J., 1964), 227.

8. Findling, "United States and Zelaya," 148–58; and Charles L. Stansifer, "José Santos Zelaya: A New Look at a Liberal Dictator," *Interamericana/Interamerican Review* 7 (Fall 1977): 468–85.

9. Dana G. Munro, "Dollar Diplomacy in Nicaragua, 1909–1913," *Hispanic American Historical Review* 38 (May 1938): 208–34.

10. Whitney T. Perkins, *Constraint of Empire: The United States and Caribbean Interventions* (Westport, Conn., 1981), 21–39; and Langley, *Banana Wars,* 63–76.

11. Warren Kneer, *Great Britain and the Caribbean, 1901–1917* (East Lansing, Mich., 1975), 134–63.

12. Lester D. Langley, "Lee Christmas and the Banana Man" (Paper delivered at the Southern Historical Association Meeting, New Orleans, La., November 1987).

13. William Bayard Hale, "With the Knox Mission to Central America," *World's Week* 24 (May 1912): 320–27.

14. All quoted in David Dinwoodie, "Expedient Diplomacy: The United States and Guatemala, 1898–1920" (Ph.D. diss., University of Colorado, 1966), 103, 108; see also 87–120; Peter Calvert, "The Last Occasion on Which Britain Used Coercion to Settle a Dispute with a Non-Colonial Territory in the Caribbean: Guatemala and the Powers, 1909–1913," *Inter-American Economic Affairs* 26 (Winter 1971): 57–75; and George W. Baker, Jr., "The Woodrow Wilson Administration and Guatemalan Relations," *The Historian* 27 (February 1963): 159–61.

15. "Central America Offers Big Problem for U.S. to Solve," *New York Times Magazine,* 18 May 1913, 3.

16. Huntington Wilson, "The Relation of Government to Foreign Investment," *Annals of the American Academy of Political and Social Sciences* 68 (November 1916): 298–311.

17. Mark T. Gilderhus, "Pan-American Initiatives: The Wilson Presidency and Regional Integration, 1914–1917," *Diplomatic History* 4 (Fall 1980): 409–23.

18. Woodrow Wilson, *The Papers of Woodrow Wilson*, ed. Arthur S. Link (Princeton, N.J., 1978), 27:169–70.

19. Quoted in Dexter Perkins, *Hands Off: A History of the Monroe Doctrine* (Boston, 1941), 263–64.

20. Karl Bermann, *Under the Big Stick: Nicaragua and the United States since 1848* (Boston, 1986), 172–81.

21. Quoted in John K. Turner, "Nicaragua," *The Nation*, 31 May 1922, 468.

22. Thomas A. Bailey, "Interest in a Nicaraguan Canal, 1903–1931," *Hispanic American Historical Review* 16 (February 1936): 1–4.

23. Boaz Long to William Jennings Bryan, 10 February 1914, Decimal File 815.77/259.

24. George W. Baker, Jr., "Ideals and Realities in the Wilson Administration's Relations with Honduras," *The Americas* 21 (July 1964): 3–6.

25. *Demanda de la república de Costa Rica contra la de Nicaragua, ante corte de justica centroamericana, con motivo de una convención firmada por la segunda con la república de los Estados Unidos de América par la venta del río San Juan, y otros objetos* (San Juan, 1916); and Rodríguez Gonzalez, *El Golfo de Fonseca y el tratado Bryan-Chamorro, celebrado entre los Estados Unidos de Norte América y Nicaragua: Doctrina Melélendez* (San Salvador, 1917).

26. Manley O. Hudson, "The Central American Court of Justice," *American Journal of International Law* 26 (October 1932): 759–86.

27. Chester Lloyd Jones, *Costa Rica and Civilization in the Caribbean* (New York, 1935), 103–5.

28. Quoted in Hugo Murillo-Jiménez, "Wilson and Tinoco: The United States and the Policy of Nonrecognition in Costa Rica, 1917–1919" (Ph.D. diss., University of California at San Diego, 1978), 87.

29. Ibid.

30. Baker, "Wilson Administration," 162–63.

31. *FRUS*, 1917, Supplement 1, 237–38, 259, 290–91; *FRUS*, 1918, Supplement 2, 89, 379; and Baker, "Wilson Administration," 160–63.

32. Juan C. Zamora, "Honduras, the Monroe Doctrine, and the League of Nations," *Cuba Contempránea* 20 (May–August 1919): 541–42; and Warren H. Kelchner, *Latin American Relations with the League of Nations* (Boston, 1930), 128–29.

33. Munro Memorandum, 21 April 1922, Decimal File 813.00/Tacoma 8.

5. Abandoning Intervention, 1920–1940

1. *Report of the Delegates of the United States of America to the Seventh Inter-national Conference of American States, Montevideo, Uruguay, 3–26 December 1933* (Washington, D.C., 1934), 18–19; and Decimal File JA 710.G/123; 710.11/1876; and 710.G International Law/6.
2. Herrarte, *La unión*, 187–203; and Kenneth J. Grieb, "The United States and the Central American Federation," *The Americas* 24 (October 1967): 107–121.
3. *FRUS*, 1922, 1:417–33.
4. Thomas M. Leonard, "U.S. Policy and Arms Limitation in Central America: The Washington Conference of 1923," *Occasional Paper Series*, Center for the Study of Armament and Disarmament, California State University at Los Angeles, 1982. The United States signed the inquiry commissions and court agreements in order to maintain its influence in Central America's political affairs, but avoided the other pacts—the General Treaty of Peace and Amity, the agreement on electoral commis-sions, and arms limitation pact—because they promised more direct and visible involvement and because of U.S. disinterestedness. However, the United States did not sign the seven agreements dealing with Central American cooperation—agreements on customs, currency and banking reforms, agricultural development, transportation and communication, mutual licensing of professionals, student exchanges, and extradition and protection of laborers.
5. Papers of Charles Evans Hughes, Period of International Activity, "Latin American Conferences, 1922–1927," 1–4, Library of Congress.
6. Department of State, Decimal File 813.00/Washington 238 to 343, 10 March 1923 to 27 November 1926, National Archives, Washington, D.C.
7. Stokeley W. Morgan, "American Policy and Problems in Central America" (Lecture delivered at the Foreign Service School, Department of State, 29 January 1926), 1–4.
8. *FRUS*, 1924, 2:216–324; *FRUS*, 1925, 2:317–25; Charles Hackett, "The Background of the Revolution in Honduras," *Review of Reviews* 69 (April 1924): 390–96; Dana G. Munro, *The United States and the Caribbean Republics, 1921–1933* (Princeton, N.J., 1974), 132–45; and Thomas L. Karnes, *Tropical Enterprise: The Standard Fruit and Steamship Company in Latin America* (Baton Rouge, La., 1978), 81–87.
9. William Kamman, *A Search for Stability: United States Diplomacy toward Nicaragua* (Notre Dame, Ind., 1968), 1–68.

10. Richard V. Salisbury, *Anti-Imperialism and International Competition in Central America, 1920–1929* (Wilmington, Del., 1989), 67–98.

11. Richard V. Salisbury, "United States Intervention in Nicaragua: The Costa Rican Role," *Prologue* 9 (Winter 1977): 209–17; Perkins, *Constraint of Empire*, 114; and Thomas J. Dodd, Jr., "United States in Nicaraguan Politics: Supervised Elections, 1927–1932," *Revisita del Pensamiento Centroamericano* 30 (July–September 1975): 5–102.

12. Coolidge, as quoted in Berman, *Under the Big Stick*, 189.

13. Olds, Department of State Decimal File, 817.00/5854, January (?) 1927.

14. Moncada, as quoted in Perkins, *Constraint of Empire*, 148.

15. Neill Macaulay, *The Sandino Affair* (Durham, N.C., 1985), 54–185.

16. Ibid., 54.

17. Ibid., 55, 59.

18. Ibid., 61.

19. All quoted in Berman, *Under the Big Stick*, 199–201.

20. Carlton Beals, "Sandino: Bandit or Patriot?" *The Nation*, 28 March 1928, 341.

21. Kamman, *Search for Stability*, 193–216; Kenneth V. Finney, "The Central American Reaction to Herbert Hoover's Policy" (master's thesis, Tulane University, 1969), 16–32; *Report of the Delegates of the United States to the Sixth International Conference of American States* (Washington, D.C., 1928); and Charles A. Thomson, "The Caribbean Situation: Nicaragua and El Salvador," *Foreign Policy Reports* 9 (August 1933): 145–46.

22. "Una grave problema social," *El Diario Nicaraguense*, 2 September 1930.

23. Quoted in Macaulay, *Sandino*, 147.

24. Kenneth J. Grieb, "American Involvement in the Rise of Jorge Ubico," *Caribbean Studies* 10 (April 1970): 5–21.

25. Kenneth J. Grieb, "The United States and the Rise of General Maximiliano Hernández Martínez," *Journal of Latin American Studies* 3 (November 1971): 151–72.

26. Martí, as quoted in Jorge Arias Goméz, "Augustín Farabundo Martí," *La Universidad* 4 (July–August 1971): 188.

27. Thomas P. Anderson, *Matánza* (Lincoln, Neb., 1971).

28. Quoted in Carmelo Francisco Esmeralda Astilla, "The Martínez Era: Salvadoran-American Relations, 1931–1944" (Ph.D. diss., Louisiana State University, 1976), 73.

29. For a sampling of the press treatment, see C. W. Hackett, "Death of Sandino," *Current History* 40 (April 1934): 78–80; Editorial, *Newsweek*, 3 March 1934, 14; "Sandino," *Nation*, 15 February 1933, 161; "Crushing

Communism," *Literary Digest*, 2 February 1932, 15; "Taps for Sandino: Patriot, Bandit, or Both?" *Literary Digest*, 3 March 1934, 7; and C. W. Hackett, "Communist Uprising in El Salvador," *Current History* 35 (March 1932): 843.

30. Leonard, "U.S. Policy and Arms Limitation," 30–40.

31. "Los pactos Washington son la llave," *La Prensa*, 8 November 1932.

32. Skinner-Klee, as quoted in *FRUS*, 1934 4:429.

33. *Documentación relativa a la tratados centroamericanos firmados en Guatemala el 12 de abril de 1934* (San José, 1934); and Astilla, "Martínez Era," 72–73.

34. Kenneth J. Grieb, *The Latin American Policy of Warren G. Harding* (Fort Worth, Tex., 1977); Joseph S. Tulchin, *The Aftermath of War: World War I and U.S. Policy toward Latin America* (New York, 1971); Franklin D. Roosevelt, "Our Foreign Policy: A Democratic View," *Foreign Affairs* 6 (July 1928): 573–96; and J. Reuben Clark, *Memorandum on the Monroe Doctrine* (Washington, D.C., 1930).

35. Munro Memorandum, 2 June 1926, Stokeley Morgan, Decimal File 810.00/24; Henry L. Stimson, *Diary*, Historical Manuscripts and Archives, Yale University Library; and Lawrence Dennis, "Revolution, Recognition, and Intervention," *Foreign Affairs* 9 (January 1931): 207–8.

36. As quoted in *Report of the Delegates of the United States of America to the Seventh International Conference of American States, Montevideo, Uruguay, December 3–26, 1933* (Washington, D.C., 1934), 18–19.

37. For a discussion of the Good Neighbor policy, see Irwin F. Gellman, *Good Neighbor Diplomacy: United States Policies in Latin America* (Baltimore, 1979).

38. Thomas M. Leonard, *The Decline of the Recognition Policy in United States–Central American Relations, 1933–1949*, Occasional Paper Series (Miami, 1985).

39. Lane, as quoted in Department of State Decimal File 817.00/7935, 14 February 1934.

40. Macaulay, *Sandino*, 242–56.

41. William Kamman, "The United States Recognition Policy and the Rise of Anastasio Somoza" (Paper delivered at the Southern Historical Association Meeting, Memphis, Tenn., November 1982).

42. Leonard, *Recognition*, 13.

6. Incorporating Central America into Global Strategies, 1933–1948

1. Lloyd Gardner, *Economic Aspects of New Deal Diplomacy* (Madison, Wis., 1964), 26–39.
2. J. M. Letiche, *Reciprocal Trade Agreement Acts in the World Economy* (New York, 1948), 22–28.
3. Victor Bulmer-Thomas, *The Political Economy of Central America since 1920* (New York, 1987), 48–67.
4. Ibid., 68–86; Thomas P. McCann, *An American Company: The Tragedy of United Fruit* (New York, 1976), 18–24.
5. Except as noted, the discussion of trade reciprocity with Central America is based upon Dick Steward, *Trade and Hemisphere: The Good Neighbor Policy and Reciprocal Trade* (Columbia, Mo., 1975), 219–33, 270–71.
6. Charles I. Bevans, comp., *Treaties and Other International Agreements of the United States, 1776–1949* (Washington, D.C., 1971), 8:517–24.
7. Ibid., 8:919–26.
8. Ibid., 10:395–405.
9. Ibid., 11:536–44.
10. Ibid., 6:1048–57.
11. Laurence Duggan, *The Americas: The Search for Hemispheric Security* (New York, 1947), 212.
12. David G. Haglund, *Latin America and the Transformation of U.S. Strategic Thought* (Albuquerque, N.M., 1984).
13. R. A. Humphries, *Latin America and the Second World War* (London, 1981), 1:13, 2:11–12.
14. Kenneth J. Grieb, *Guatemalan Caudillo: The Regime of Jorge Ubico in Guatemala, 1931–1934* (Athens, Ohio, 1979), 248–63.
15. Report of Colonel Joseph Pate, 27 October 1940, Decimal File 817.00/MID/50.
16. Astilla, "The Martínez Era," 146–70.
17. Richard Millett, *Guardians of the Dynasty* (Maryknoll, N.Y., 1977), 191–200; and J. Fred Rippy, "State Department Operations: The Rama Road," *Inter-American Economic Affairs* 9 (Summer 1955): 17–32.
18. Report of Colonel Joseph Pate, 27 October 1939, Decimal File 817.00/MID/50.
19. Humphries, *Latin America* 2:7–10.
20. Stetson Conn, Rose C. Engleman, and Byron Fairchild, *Guarding the United*

States and Its Outposts: The United States Army in World War II (Washington, D.C., 1964), 423–24.

21. *FRUS*, 1942, 6:228–52, 428–59, 566–76; *FRUS*, 1943, 5:90–98, 231–34; *FRUS*, 1944, 7:1037–1113, 1132–68, 1391–1424; and *FRUS*, 1945, 9:334–37.

22. U.S. Congress, House, *Message of the President, 16th Report to Congress on Lend-Lease Operations for Period Ending July 30, 1944,* 77th Cong., 2d sess., serial 10884, H. Doc. 674, 36.

23. Grieb, *Guatemalan Caudillo,* 248–63; Astilla, "Martínez Era," 172–91; Carlos Calvo Gamboa, *Costa Rica en la segunda guerra mundial, 1939–1945* (San José, 1985), 73–78; and Humphries, *Latin America* 1:10–12, 97–98.

24. *FRUS*, 1943, 6:309–10; and "CF Justice, Lend-Lease and State," Franklin D. Roosevelt Papers, Confidential Folder, 76–20, Franklin D. Roosevelt Presidential Library, Hyde Park, New York.

25. Astilla, "Martínez Era," 176–91; Gamboa, *Costa Rica,* 115–66; Grieb, *Guatemalan Caudillo,* 248–63; Humphries, *Latin America* 2:75–76, 215–16; and Juan Suárez Rojas, *Costa Rica en la segunda guerra mundial* (San José, 1943), 273–74.

26. U.S. Department of State, Office of Inter-American Affairs, *History of the Office of the Coordinator of Inter-American Affairs* (Washington, D.C., 1947).

27. For a discussion of the generation of rising expectations in Central America, see Ralph Lee Woodward, Jr., *Central America: A Nation Divided* (New York, 1976), 203–69.

28. Thomas M. Leonard, *United States and Central America, 1944–1949: Perceptions of Political Dynamics* (Tuscaloosa, Ala., 1984).

29. Antonio Gómez Robledo, *La seguridad colectiva en el continente americano* (Mexico, 1960); and Louis A. Pérez, "International Dimensions of Inter-American Relations, 1944–1960," *Inter-American Economic Affairs* 27 (Winter 1973): 47–68.

30. George C. Marshall, "Public Speeches, 1947–1949," George C. Marshall Research Foundation, Lexington, Virginia; Dean Acheson, "Waging Peace in the Americas," *United States Department of State Bulletin,* 26 September 1949, 462–66 (hereafter referred to as *Bulletin*); and Edward G. Miller, Jr., "Inter-American Relations in Perspective," *Bulletin,* 3 April 1950, 521–23.

31. Leonard, *Recognition,* 14–24.

7. Nationalism or Communism: Costa Rica and Guatemala

1. Papers of Harry Hopkins, Federal Bureau of Investigation Reports, "Totalitarian Activities: Costa Rica Today," 114, Franklin D. Roosevelt Presidential Library, Hyde Park, New York.
2. Ibid., 12–24, 53–58, 113–17.
3. For a discussion of the Calderón administration, see Oscar Aguilar Bulgarelli, *Costa Rica y sus hechos políticos de 1948* (San José, 1970), 22–121.
4. Decimal File 818.00/2–1246.
5. Burt H. English, *Liberación nacional in Costa Rica: The Development of a Political Party System in a Transitional Society* (Gainesville, Fla., 1971), 15–129; and Thomas M. Leonard, "Costa Rica: The U.S. Perception of the Church and Communism, 1931–1948," in *The Church and Society in Latin America*, ed. Jeffrey A. Cole (New Orleans, La., 1984), 305–20.
6. Johnson and Murray A. Wise memoranda, Decimal File 818.00/12–1045.
7. Leonard, *United States and Central America*, 15–46.
8. John P. Bell, *Crisis in Costa Rica: The 1948 Revolution* (Austin, Tex., 1971), 3–130; and Aguilar Bulgarelli, *Costa Rica*, 197–397.
9. Papers of Nathaniel P. Davis, Diary Extracts, March–April 1948, Harry S. Truman Presidential Library, Independence, Mo.
10. Bell, *Crisis in Costa Rica*, 131–62.
11. "U.S. Expresses Satisfaction with New Costa Rican Government," *Bulletin*, 28 November 1949, 883.
12. Richard M. Nixon, Prepresidential Papers, ser. 361, vice-president, Central American Trip, 1955, box 1, "Briefing for Central American Trip"; Declassified Documents, Office of Intelligence Research Reports, 7154.3, 7154.4, 7154.5, and "Calendar of Soviet Bloc–Latin American Relations," June–December 1956, all in National Archives Center, Los Angeles, Calif. See also Memorandum for the President, 27 March 1958, Eisenhower Library, Abilene, Kan., International Series, Ann Whitman File, box 1.
13. "Totalitarianism Activities: Guatemala, July 1944," 10–14, Hopkins Papers, Federal Bureau of Investigation Reports.
14. Long, quoted in Leonard, *United States and Central America*, 81.
15. For a discussion of Arévalo's administration, see Jim Handy, *Gift of the Devil: A History of Guatemala* (Toronto, 1984), 103–22; Marco Antonio Villamar Contreras, "El pensamiento político de la generación revolucionaría de 1944," *Economía* 21 (July–September 1969):55–61; Luis Cardoza y

Aragón, *La revolución guatemalteca* (Montevideo, 1956); Grieb, *Guatemalan Caudillo;* and Leonard, *United States and Central America*, 75–106.

16. A discussion of the Communist influence in Arévalo's administration can be found in Ronald M. Schneider, *Communism in Guatemala, 1944–1954* (New York, 1968).

17. Quoted in Thomas M. Leonard, "Nationalism or Communism?: The Truman Administration and Guatemala, 1945–1952," *Journal of Third World Studies* 8 (Spring 1990): 178, 180.

18. Ibid., 182.

19. Ibid., 182, 183, 184.

20. *Informe del presidente Jacobo Arbenz Guzmán al congresso nacional en su primer períodode sesiones ordinarias del año 1953* (Guatemala City, 1953).

21. Richard H. Immerman, *The CIA in Guatemala: The Foreign Policy of Intervention* (Austin, Tex., 1982), 128.

22. Ibid., 3–133. See also Stephen Schlesinger and Stephen Kinzer, *Bitter Fruit: The Untold Story of the American Coup in Guatemala* (Garden City, N.Y., 1982), 79–95.

23. "Statement by Secretary Dulles at Caracas, March 8, 1954," *Bulletin*, 22 March 1954, 422–23.

24. Guillermo Toriello Garido, "A Pretext for Intervening in Our Affairs," in *Intervention in Latin America*, ed. C. Neale Ronning (New York, 1970), 72–77.

25. Phillip B. Taylor, Jr., "The Guatemalan Affair: A Critique of United States Foreign Policy," *American Political Science Review* 50 (September 1956): 787–806.

26. Eisenhower Papers, Official File, Box 873, Guatemala, 185, 1 February 1955, Dwight D. Eisenhower Library, Abilene, Kan.

27. Immerman, *CIA in Guatemala*, 133–72.

28. Ibid., 82.

29. Stephen G. Rabe, *Eisenhower and Latin America: The Foreign Politics of Anticommunism* (Chapel Hill, N.C., 1988), 57–61.

30. U.S. Congress, Senate Committee on Foreign Relations, Subcommittee on American Republics, *Soviet-Bloc Activities and Their Implications for United States Foreign Policy*, 86th Cong., 2d sess., 25 February 1960.

31. Lonigino Becerra, *Evolución de Honduras* (Tegucigalpa, 1983), 151–67.

32. J. Lloyd Mecham, *The United States and Inter-American Security, 1889–1960* (Austin, Tex., 1963), 403–6.

33. Quoted in John D. Martz, *Central America: The Crisis and the Challenge* (Chapel Hill, N.C., 1959), 199.

34. Richard Nixon, Central American Trip, 1955; Eisenhower Library, Office of the Special Assistant for National Security Affairs, Records 1952–1961, Box 12, U.S. Policy toward Latin America; Declassified Documents, 1980–318 B, Naval Intelligence Memorandum, 3 March 1958.

35. Thomas M. Leonard, "The United States and Central America, 1955–1960," *Valley Forge Journal* 3 (June 1986): 59.

36. Ibid., 56–72.

37. Henry F. Holland, "U.S. Relations with the American Republics," *Bulletin* 41 (11 April 1955): 598–604.

8. From False Hope to Entrenchment of the Old Order, 1960–1976

1. Papers of Theodore Sorenson, Subject Files 1961–64, Latin America, Memorandum on Latin America, 30 August 1960, John F. Kennedy Presidential Library, Boston, Mass.

2. De Lesseps Morrison, "The U.S. Position on OAS Consideration of Coups d'Etat," *Bulletin*, 8 October 1962, 539–41.

3. *Public Papers of the Presidents of the United States: John F. Kennedy, 1961* (Washington, D.C., 1962), 170–75.

4. *Official Documents Emanating from the Special Meeting of the Inter-American Economic and Social Council at the Ministerial Level, Held in Punte del Este, Uruguay, from 5 August to 17 August 1961* (Washington, D.C., 1961).

5. For a discussion of the Kennedy administration's goals for the Alliance for Progress, see Arthur Schlesinger, Jr., "The Alliance for Progress: A Retrospective," in *Latin America: The Search for an International Role*, ed. Ronald G. Hellman and H. John Rosenbaum (New York, 1975), 57–92.

6. The summary of the Alliance for Progress programs is based upon Agency for International Development, Congressional Presentations, Fiscal Years 1962–72, Annex, Latin America, and the Caribbean; the presentations are available in the AID Library, Reston, Va.

7. James L. Busey, "Central American Union: The Latest Attempt," *Western Political Quarterly* 14 (March 1961): 49–63; and James D. Cochrane, "U.S.

Attitudes toward Central American Integration," *Inter-American Economic Affairs* 18 (Autumn 1964): 73–91.

8. AID Congressional Presentations, 1964–70.

9. "Victoria contra la probeza y injusticia busca Kennedy," *El Imparcial* (Guatemala City), 18 March 1963; "Reforma y Defensa," *La Prensa* (Managua), 20 March 1963; "Saludo a John F. Kennedy," *La Republica* (San Salvador), 21 March 1963; *Kennedy en Centro America* (San José, 1963); Karl Holbik and Philip Swan, *Trade and Industrialization in the Central American Common Market: The First Decade* (Austin, Tex., 1972). The Central American presidents included Miguel Ydígoras Fuentes, Guatemala; Ramón Villeda Morales, Honduras; Louis Somoza DeBayle and President-elect René Schick Gutíerrez, Nicaragua; Francisco Orlich, Costa Rica; and Julio Adelberto Rivera, El Salvador.

10. James A. Morris, *Honduras: Caudillo Politics and Military Rulers* (Boulder, Colo., 1984), 35–43.

11. Willard Barber and C. Neale Ronning, *Internal Security and Military Power: Counterinsurgency and Civic Action in Latin America* (Athens, Ohio, 1966).

12. "Six Nations and U.S. Avoid Cuba Showdown," *New York Times*, 20 March 1963.

13. Thomas Mann, "Democratic Ideal in Our Policy toward Latin America," *Department of State Bulletin* 50 (29 June 1964): 995–1000.

14. Ibid.

15. U.S. Congress, House Committee on Foreign Affairs, *Inter-American Relations*, 92d Cong., 2d sess., 475.

16. National Security Council Files, National Security Council Report 1063/64, Survey of Latin America, 1 April 1964, Lyndon Baines Johnson Presidential Library, Austin, Tex.

17. Lyndon Baines Johnson Papers, Back-Up Diary, Appointment File, Box 105, 8 July 1968, Johnson Library.

18. "Central American Leaders Deplore Curbs on Exports," *New York Times*, 6 July 1968; "Johnson Arrives in San Salvador," *New York Times*, 7 July 1968; and "President Johnson Meets with Central American Presidents," *Department of State Bulletin* 59 (20 July 1968): 109–20.

19. For a discussion of the Guatemalan guerrilla movement during the 1960s, see Milton Henry Jamail, "Guatemala, 1944–1972: The Politics of Aborted Revolution" (Ph.D. diss., University of Arizona, 1972). U.S. policy is discussed by Lawrence A. Yates, "The United States and Rural Insurgency in Guatemala, 1960–1970," in *Central America: Historical Perspectives on the*

Contemporary Crisis, ed. Ralph Lee Woodward, Jr. (Westport, Conn., 1988), 47–66. Yon Sosa's corevolutionary, Turcos Lima, was killed in an automobile accident in 1966.

20. Karl Holbik and Philip L. Swan, *Trade and Industrialization in the Central American Common Market: The First Decade* (Austin, Tex., 1972); and Robert G. Williams, *Export Agriculture and the Crisis in Central America* (Chapel Hill, N.C., 1986).

21. William H. Durham, *Scarcity and Survival in Central America: Ecological Origins of the Soccer War* (Stanford, Calif., 1979).

22. Thomas P. Anderson, *The War of the Dispossessed: Honduras and El Salvador* (Lincoln, Neb., 1983).

23. U.S. Congress, Senate Committee on Foreign Relations, *United States Military Policies and Programs in Latin America: Hearings before the Subcommittee on Western Hemisphere Affairs,* 91st Cong., 1st sess.; and Nelson A. Rockefeller, *The Rockefeller Report on the Americas: The Official Report of a United States Presidential Mission for the Western Hemisphere* (Chicago, 1969).

24. AID, Congressional Presentation, 1973; and Jerome Levision and Juan de Onís, *The Alliance That Lost Its Way: A Critical Report on the Alliance for Progress* (Chicago, 1972).

25. *Public Papers of the Presidents, Richard M. Nixon, 1969,* 893–901; and Robert S. Litwack, *Détente and the Nixon Doctrine: American Foreign Policy and the Pursuit of Stability, 1969–1976* (Cambridge, Eng., 1984).

26. "Latin Policy Change: It's Got a Chance," *Miami Herald,* 4 November 1974.

27. Ben S. Stephansky, "New Dialogue with Latin America: The Cost of Political Neglect," in *The Search for a New International Order,* ed. Ronald G. Hellman and H. Jon Rosenbaum (New York, 1975).

28. For a fuller discussion, see Don L. Etchison, *The United States and Militarism in Central America* (New York, 1975).

29. Quoted in ibid., 122.

30. Kennedy, *Presidential Papers, 1961,* 173.

9. Crisis of the Old Order: Carter, Reagan, and Central America

1. *The Americas in a Changing World: A Report of the Commission on United States–Latin American Relations* (New York, 1975).

2. Robert A. Pastor, "The Carter Administration and Latin America: A Test

of Principle," in *U.S. Policy toward Latin America: Quarter Century of Crisis and Challenge*, ed. John D. Martz (Lincoln, Neb., 1988), 61–97; and *Public Papers of the Presidents: Jimmy Carter, 1977* 1:611–16.

3. Zbigniew Brzezinski, *Power and Principle: Memoirs of the National Security Advisor, 1977–1981* (New York, 1983), 51, 139.

4. Shirley Christian, *Nicaragua: Revolution in the Family* (New York, 1985), 34–35.

5. Findling, *Close Neighbors, Distant Friends*, 124–37, 143–46.

6. Raymond Estept, *Guerrilla Warfare in Latin America, 1963–1975* (Maxwell Air Force Base, Ala., 1975), 92–95.

7. John Booth, *The End and the Beginning: The Nicaraguan Revolution* (Boulder, Colo., 1982).

8. Unless otherwise noted, the discussion of Carter's policy is based upon Robert A. Pastor, *Condemned to Repetition: The United States and Nicaragua* (Princeton, N.J., 1987), 49–187. Pastor was director of Latin American and Caribbean affairs in the National Security Council during Carter's administration.

9. Brzezinski, *Power and Principle*, 358.

10. Christian, *Nicaragua*, 50–55.

11. Pastor, *Repetition*, 70.

12. John Bartlow Martin, *U.S. Policy in the Caribbean* (Boulder, Colo., 1978), 225–26.

13. Jimmy Carter, *Keeping Faith: Memoirs of a President* (New York, 1982), 585.

14. S. W. Sanders, "Carter Lights a Fuse under Guatemala's Tinderbox," *Businessweek*, 4 August 1980, 33.

15. Tommie Sue Montgomery, *Revolution in El Salvador: Origins and Evolution* (Boulder, Colo., 1982).

16. *Public Papers, Carter, 1979* 2:1802–6.

17. Findling, *Close Neighbors, Distant Friends*, 171.

18. Department of State and Defense, "The Sandinista Military Buildup," Department of State Publication 9432, May 1985.

19. U.S. Congress, House, Senate, *Report of the Congressional Committee Investigating the Iran-Contra Affair*, 100th Cong., 1st sess., H. Rept. 100–433, S. Rept. 100–216, 27.

20. Henry Grunwald, "Foreign Policy under Reagan II," *Foreign Affairs* 63 (Winter 1984–85): 219–39.

21. Jeane Kirkpatrick, "Dictatorships and Double Standards," *Commentary*, November 1979, 34–45.

22. Timothy Ashby, *The Bear in the Back Yard* (Lexington, Ky., 1987).

23. Policy Alternatives for the Caribbean and Central America, *Changing Course: Blueprint for Peace in Central America and the Caribbean* (Austin, Tex., 1984); and Echeveria Zuno, *Centroamérica: La guerre de Reagan* (Mexico, 1983).

24. Martin Diskin, *The Impact of U.S. Policy in El Salvador, 1979–1985* (Berkeley, Calif., 1986).

25. James A. Morris, "Honduras: The Burden of Survival in Central America," in *Central America: Crisis and Adaptation,* ed. Steve C. Ropp and James A. Morris (Albuquerque, N.M., 1984), 189–286.

26. Richard Millett, "Guatemala: Progress and Paralysis," *Current History* 84 (March 1985): 109–13, 136.

27. Thomas M. Leonard, "The United States, Costa Rica, and the Nicaraguan Revolution," in *The Foreign and Domestic Dimensions of Modern Warfare: Vietnam, Central America, and Nuclear Strategy,* ed. Howard Jones (Tuscaloosa, Ala., 1988), 124–34.

28. Department of State, "Revolution beyond Our Borders: Sandinista Intervention in Central America," Special Report no. 132, September 1985.

29. Forrest Colburn, "Nicaragua under Siege," *Current History* 84 (March 1985): 105–8, 131–32.

30. "The Mission That Failed," *Newsweek,* 25 July 1983, 85.

31. Henry A. Kissinger, chairman, National Bipartisan Commission on Central America, *Report of the President's National Bipartisan Commission, Central America, 10 January 1984* (Washington, D.C., 1984).

32. "The Caribbean Basin Initiative," *Foreign Policy* 47 (Summer 1982): 114–38.

33. Nina M. Serafino, "The Contadora Initiative: Implications for Congress," Congressional Research Service, *Issue Brief,* 2 February 1986.

34. Leonard, "Costa Rica and Nicaragua."

35. Morris, "Burden of Survival."

36. Millett, "Guatemala."

37. *Report of the President's Special Review Board,* 26 February 1987 (popularly known as the Tower Commission Report); and U.S. Congress, Senate and House, *Report of the Congressional Committees Investigating the Iran-Contra Affair,* 100th Cong., 1st sess., S. Rep. 100–216, H. Rep. 100–433, November 1987.

38. "Regional Leaders Take a Giant Step toward Peace," *Central America Report,* 14 August 1987, 241–42.

39. "U.S. Seen Stalling on Peace," *Miami Herald,* 4 September 1987.

Bibliographical Essay

Three factors characterize the study of United States–Central American relations: a reliance upon primary materials in the United States, an emphasis on topical or period studies, and the availability of British studies.

Scholarly studies focusing on U.S. policy dominate the literature on the United States' relations with Central America, while the study of Central America's foreign policy remains largely unexplored, even by Central American scholars themselves. This can be partly explained by the differences in availability of primary source materials. The United States National Archives are rich in materials that are open for research, but Central America does not have an equivalent institution. With the exception of Costa Rica, fire, flood, and government restrictions have prevented researchers from examining the diplomatic record. For these reasons, only a few scholars have been able to tap foreign ministry records. The works by Kenneth Grieb, Richard Salisbury, and Hugo Murillo, noted below, are the exception rather than the rule in their utilization of Central American Foreign Ministry records. More recent studies, such as those by José Ramirez and Carlos Gamboa, point to the lack of availability of archival material. Both works, however, illustrate that Central America's foreign policy can be analyzed from other source material and that it is an area awaiting serious study. Mario Argueta also illustrates the dearth of Central American sources. He utilizes extensively the holdings in the United States National Archives for his *Tiburcio Carías: Anatomía de uno época, 1923–1948* (Tegucigalpa, 1989).

Literature on United States–Central American relations is generally either topical or broken into small time periods, although a few biographies and memoirs can also be found. The current popular interest in Central America has produced a few survey studies, two of which provide analysis dating to the 1820s: Walter LaFeber, *Inevitable Revolutions: The United States in Central America* (New York, 1983), and John E. Findling, *Close Neighbors, Distant Friends: United States–Central American Relations* (Westport, Conn., 1987). LaFeber's "New Left" approach places the responsibility for the contemporary problems on U.S. economic imperialism, while Findling uses a straightforward geopolitical approach. With the exception of Karl Berman's *Under the Big*

Stick: Nicaragua and the United States since 1848 (Boston, 1986), which is critical of United States policy, relations between one of the five Central American nations and the United States remain an unexamined area.

Finally, because of the nineteenth-century British interests in Central America, several studies regarding London's Central American policy are based upon British Foreign Office records. These works are indispensable to those wanting to understand issues and events from 1820 to 1903.

Generally, U.S. relations with Central America are treated as part of U.S. relations with Latin America. Three standard texts are J. Lloyd Mecham, *A Survey of United States–Latin American Relations* (Boston, 1965), Gordon Connell-Smith, *The United States and Latin America* (London, 1974), and Graham H. Stuart and James L. Tigner, *Latin America and the United States* (New York, 1975). Three recent studies that focus on the contemporary in an effort to explain U.S. national security interests in Latin America are Margaret Daly Hayes, *Latin America and the U.S. National Interest: A Basis for U.S. Policy* (Boulder, Colo., 1984), Harold Molineu, *U.S. Policy toward Latin America: From Regionalism to Globalism* (Boulder, Colo., 1986), and Lars Schoultz, *National Security and United States Policy toward Latin America* (Princeton, N.J., 1987).

A more focused approach is the treatment of Central America as part of the circum-Caribbean region, as illustrated by Lester D. Langley in his two volumes, *Struggle for the American Mediterranean: United States–European Rivalry in the Gulf Caribbean, 1776–1904* (Athens, Ga., 1976) and *The United States and the Caribbean, 1900–1970*, rev. ed. (Athens, Ga., 1984).

To understand United States–Central American relations, one must also grasp the contours of Central American history. Ralph Lee Woodward, Jr.'s *Central America: A Divided Nation* (New York, 1985) best describes the dominance of the landed elite and the challenge to it. Other surveys include Franklin D. Parker, *The Central American Republics* (London, 1964), and Mario Rodríguez, *Central America* (Englewood Cliffs, N.J., 1965). Two recent works by Costa Rican historians illustrate the need to understand isthmian internal dynamics: Hector Perez-Brignoli, *A Brief History of Central America*, translated by Ricardo B. Sawrey A. and Susana Stettri de Sawrey (Berkeley, Calif., 1989), and Edelberto Torres-Rivas, *Repression and Resistance in Central America* (Boulder, Colo., 1989). Because the question of Central American unity permeates the region's history, one should consult Thomas L. Karnes, *The Failure of Union: Central America, 1824–1975* (Tempe, Ariz., 1976), and Alberto Herrarte, *La unión de Central America* (Guatemala, 1964).

The Nineteenth Century

Throughout the nineteenth century, the United States and Great Britain contended for influence in Central America. Mary W. Williams, in *Anglo-American Isthmian Diplomacy, 1815–1915* (Washington, D.C., 1916), argues that the U.S. concern with security anchored its decision to eliminate the British from the region. Her study, along with Craig L. Dozier's *Nicaragua's Mosquito Shore: The Years of British and American Presence* (Tuscaloosa, Ala., 1985), demonstrate Washington's inclination to deal directly with a European power when it perceived a threat to Central America. Dana G. Munro's *The Five Republics of Central America* (New York, 1918) is an important study of the nineteenth century because it illustrates the United States' perception that Central America was an underdeveloped area.

Diplomatic documents for the period from 1831 to 1860 are found in William R. Manning, compiler, *Diplomatic Correspondence of the United States: Inter-American Affairs, 1831–1860* (Washington, D.C., 1933). Volumes 3 and 4 cover Central American relations.

Two works that place Central America within larger hemispheric issues in the early nineteenth century are John J. Johnson's *A Hemisphere Apart: The Foundations of United States Policy toward Latin America* (Baltimore, 1990), and Peggy K. Liss, *Atlantic Empires: The Network of Trade and Revolution, 1713–1826* (Baltimore, 1983).

For accounts of relations during Central America's confederative period, from 1823 to 1839, one should start with Joseph B. Lockey's "Diplomatic Futility," *Hispanic American Historical Review* 10 (1930): 265–94, and Charles L. Stansifer's "United States–Central American Relations, 1824–1850," in *United States–Latin American Relations, 1800–1850: The Formative Generations,* edited by T. Ray Shurbutt (Tuscaloosa, Ala., 1990). Lockey's contention that nothing significant materialized during this time period is countered by Stansifer. The argument that the United States did not perceive a foreign threat to the region during this time is illustrated by William J. Griffith, "Juan Galindo, Central American Chauvinist," *Hispanic American Historical Review* 40 (1980): 25–52.

The influence of foreign political ideas upon Central America is discussed by Mario Rodríguez in *The Cadíz Experiment* (Berkeley, Calif., 1978) for the early confederation period and in *The Livingston Codes in the Guatemalan Crisis of 1837–1838* (New Orleans, La., 1955) for the late confederation period. David M. Chandler's master's thesis at Tulane University, "Juan José Aycinena, Nineteenth-Century Guatemalan Conservative: An Historical Survey of

His Political, Religious, Educational, and Commercial Careers" (1965), illustrates the ongoing conflict between liberals and conservatives regarding the importation of Western ideas to Central America.

British influence in Central America reawakened the United States' interest in the isthmus in the late 1840s. Robert A. Naylor's *Influencia durante las primeras décadas de la independencia (1821–1851)* (Antigua, 1988) examines the British goals and objectives on the isthmus. Mario Rodríguez considers the implementation of British policy in his *A Palmerstonian Diplomat in Central America: Frederick A. Chatfield, Esq.* (Tucson, Ariz., 1964). The place of Central America in British relations with the United States is examined by Wilbur D. Jones, *The American Problem in British Diplomacy, 1841–1861* (Athens, Ga., 1974). The initial chapters of Charles L. Stansifer's "The Central American Career of E. George Squier," his Ph.D. dissertation (Tulane University, 1959), illustrates the growing U.S. response to the British presence in Central America.

The controversy surrounding the interpretation of the Clayton-Bulwer Treaty is examined from the British perspective by G. E. Hickson, "Palmerston and the Clayton-Bulwer Treaty," *Cambridge Historical Journal* 3 (1931): 295–303. In contrast is Kenneth Bourne, "The Clayton-Bulwer Treaty and the Decline of the British Opposition to the Territorial Expansion of the United States, 1857–1860," *Journal of Modern History* 33 (1961): 287–91. Bourne argues that the United States' resentment of the treaty led the British to withdraw by 1860. One should also consult James Buchanan, *The Works of James Buchanan: Comprising His Speeches, State Papers, and Private Correspondence,* edited by John B. Moore (Philadelphia, 1911), volume 10, and George M. Dallas, *Diary of George M. Dallas While Minister to Russia, 1837 to 1839, and to England, 1856 to 1861* (Philadelphia, 1897) for discussions of the U.S. determination to remove British influence from Central America in the 1850s.

Charles H. Brown's *Agents of Manifest Destiny: The Lives and Times of the Filibusters* (Chapel Hill, N.C., 1980) is a well-written account of the filibusters of the 1850s. The relationship between the desire to expand slavery and William Walker's expedition to Nicaragua is described by Robert E. May in *Southern Dream of a Caribbean Empire, 1854–1861* (Baton Rouge, La., 1973). William Walker has received much attention. The standard account of his career is William O. Scroggs, *Filibusters and Financiers* (New York, 1916). Dean Kortge, "The Central American Policy of Lord Palmerston," his Ph.D. dissertation (University of Kansas, 1973), points out that Walker's escapades contributed to the British belief that the United States had territorial designs on Central America and therefore contributed to its hardened position regarding adjustments to the Clayton-Bulwer Treaty.

Central America's diplomatic effort to curtail Walker's activities in the United States is explained by Carlos García Bauer, *Antonio de Irisarri, diplomático de América, su acteración en los Estados Unidos: La colonizal colonizacion negro y la invasion filibustera* (Guatemala, 1970). For a discussion of the Central American campaign against Walker, see Miguel Angel Alvarez, *Los filibusteros in Nicaragua, 1855, 1856, 1857* (Managua, 1944), and Rafael Obregón Loría, *Costa Rica y la guerra del 56 (La campaña del transito, 1856–1857)* (San José, 1976). The most comprehensive study of Lincoln's colonization plan to relocate free blacks to Central America is Thomas Schoonover, "Misconstrued Mission: Expansionism and Black Colonization in Mexico and Central America during the Civil War," *Pacific Historical Review* 49 (1980): 607–20.

Walter LaFeber's *The New Empire: An Interpretation of American Expansion, 1860–1898* (Ithaca, N.Y., 1963) provides a dynamic interpretation of the pressure on behalf of the U.S. business community to expand overseas after the Civil War. One should read at the same time Ralph Lee Woodward, Jr.'s *Positivism in Latin America, 1850–1900* (Lexington, Ky., 1971) to understand the Central American desire to import Western capital and culture in an effort to modernize. Thomas Schoonover pursues the LaFeber thesis regarding Central America in his "Imperialism in Middle America: United States Competition with Britain, Germany, and France in Middle America, 1820s–1920s," in *Eagle against Empire: American Opposition to European Imperialism*, edited by Rhodri Jeffreys-Jones (Aix-en-Provence, 1983), 41–58. Other studies that deal with American business interests in Central America in the late nineteenth century include J. Fred Rippy's "United States and Guatemala during the Administration of Justo Rufino Barrios," *Hispanic American Historical Review* 22 (1942): 595–605, and his "United States and Costa Rica during the Guardia Era," *Bulletin of the Pan American Union* 77 (1943): 61–68. The exploits of Minor C. Keith are examined by Watt Stewart, *Keith of Costa Rica: A Biographic Study of Minor Cooper Keith* (Albuquerque, N.M., 1974).

The story of the isthmian canal projects that led to the selection of the Panama Canal is the subject of many works. Among the most significant are Gerstle Mack, *A Land Divided: A History of the Panama Canal and Other Isthmian Canal Projects* (New York, 1944), and David McCullough, *Path between the Seas: Creation of the Panama Canal, 1876–1914* (New York, 1977). Ralph D. Bald, Jr.'s doctoral dissertation, "The Development of Expansionist Sentiment in the United States, 1885–1895, as Reflected in Periodical Literature" (University of Pittsburgh, 1973), illustrates that businessmen pressuring for a transisthmian canal were interested, not in Central America, but rather in the west coast of Latin America and the Far Eastern markets.

The rapprochement between Britain and the United States that resulted in the second Hay-Paunceforte Treaty, which paved the way for a U.S. canal project, is examined by Charles S. Campbell, Jr., *Anglo-American Understanding, 1898–1903* (Baltimore, 1957). Dwight C. Miner, *The Fight for the Panama Route: The Story of the Spooner Act and the Hay-Herran Treaty* (New York, 1971), discusses the events surrounding the rejection of the Nicaraguan canal site in favor of the Panama route.

The Twentieth Century to 1948

Once the United States undertook the Panama Canal project, the desire to secure Central America from both external intervention and internal disruption guided the United States' policy decisions well into the 1920s. For the most part, Washington policymakers were guided by a sense of paternalism in an effort to bring constitutional government and financial stability to Central America. The pursuance of this dual policy is the subject of many works. J. Fred Rippy's "Antecedents of the Roosevelt Corollary to the Monroe Doctrine," *Pacific Historical Review* 9 (1940): 267–79, points to the relationship between the external threat and internal disorder that led to Teddy Roosevelt's corollary. A member of the State Department's Latin American division in the early twentieth century, Dana G. Munro demonstrates the paternalistic motives that lay behind an interventionist policy in his two volumes, *Intervention and Dollar Diplomacy in the Caribbean, 1900–1921* (Princeton, N.J., 1974), and *The United States and the Caribbean Republics, 1921–1933* (Princeton, N.J., 1964). Lester D. Langley is more critical in his *Banana Wars: An Inner History of American Empire, 1900–1934* (Lexington, Ky., 1983). He points to the racism inherent in U.S. policy decisions and in those who carried them out. The frustrations of these interventions are illustrated by Whitney T. Perkins, *Constraint of Empire: The United States and Caribbean Interventions* (Westport, Conn., 1981).

The search for constitutional order is the subject of William I. Buchannan, *The Central American Peace Conference of 1907* (Washington, D.C., 1907), and Thomas M. Leonard, *U.S. Arms Policy and Arms Limitation in Central America: The Washington Conference of 1923* (Los Angeles, 1983).

Central America's resistance to the United States' dominance of its internal affairs is illustrated in three doctoral dissertations: John E. Findling, "The United States and Zelaya: A Study in the Diplomacy of Expediency" (University of Texas at Austin, 1971); David H. Dinwoodie, "Expedient Diplomacy: The United States and Guatemala, 1898–1900" (University of Colorado, 1966);

and Hugo Murillo-Jimenez, "Wilson and Tinoco: The United States and the Policy of Nonrecognition in Costa Rica, 1917–1919" (University of California at San Diego, 1978). On this subject, one should also consult George W. Baker, Jr., "Ideals and Realities in the Wilson Administration's Relations with Honduras," *The Americas* 21 (1964): 3–19.

U.S. intervention in Nicaragua has received much attention. Nicaraguan dictator José Santos Zelaya explained his own position and severely criticized the United States in his *La revolución de Nicaragua y los Estados Unidos* (Madrid, 1910). Another critical account is Walter V. Scholes, "Los Estados Unidos, Mexico, y Central America en 1909," *Historia Mexicana* 10 (1961): 613–27. The United States State Department justified its intervention in *The United States and Nicaragua* (Washington, D.C., 1932).

The most significant economic intervention came from the banana companies. Among the most important studies of this aspect are Frederick Adams, *Conquest of the Tropics* (New York, 1976), Thomas L. Karnes, *Tropical Enterprise: The Standard Fruit and Steamship Company in Latin America* (Baton Rouge, La., 1978), and Stacy May and Mario Plaza, *The United Fruit Company in Latin America* (Washington, D.C., 1958). Central American literature is extremely critical of the companies' impact upon the region—see, for example, Alfredo Suarez, *La situación bananera en los paises del Caribe* (San José, 1928), and Daniel Slutzky and Esther Alonzo, *Empresas transnacionales y agricultura: El caso del enclave bananero en Honduras* (Tegucigalpa, 1980).

There are several studies indicating that the United States was moving toward the abandonment of intervention after World War I. Among the most useful are Joseph S. Tulchin, *The Aftermath of War: World War I and U.S. Policy toward Latin America* (New York, 1971), and Alexander DeConde, *Herbert Hoover's Latin American Policy* (Stanford, Calif., 1951). Until that policy change was complete in 1933, the United States intervened on several occasions in Central America. Nicaragua received the most attention. William Kamman, in *A Search for Stability: United States Diplomacy toward Nicaragua, 1925–1933* (Notre Dame, Ind., 1968), examines the diplomatic issues involved, while Neill Macauly, in *The Sandino Affair* (Chicago, 1967), examines the military intervention. Sandino tells his side of the story in *American Policy toward Nicaragua* (New York, 1927).

Studies of other interventions include Charles Hackett, "The Background on the Revolution in Honduras," *Review of Reviews* 69 (1924): 390–96; Ternot MacRenato, "The Rise to Power of Anastasio Somoza Garcia," *New Scholar* 8 (1982): 308–23; and Kenneth J. Grieb, "American Involvement in the Rise of Jorge Ubico," *Caribbean Studies* 10 (April 1970): 5–21, and "The United States and the Rise of General Maximiliano Hernández Martínez," *Journal of Latin American Studies* 3 (1971): 151–72.

American criticisms of these interventions are found in Franklin D. Roosevelt, "Our Foreign Policy: A Democratic View," *Foreign Affairs* 6 (1928): 573–96, and Lawrence Dennis, "Revolution, Recognition, and Intervention," *Foreign Affairs* 9 (1931): 301–10. Central American perspectives on U.S. intervention include Richard V. Salisbury's *Anti-Imperialism and International Competition in Central America, 1920–1929* (Wilmington, Del., 1989), and his "United States Intervention in Nicaragua: The Costa Rican Role," *Prologue* 9 (1977): 209–17; Rafael Nogales y Méndez, *The Looting of Nicaragua* (New York, 1928); Vicente Saenz, *Rompiendo cadenas: Las del imperialismo en Centro América y en otras repúblicas del continente* (Mexico City, 1933); and Kenneth V. Finney, "The Central American Reaction to Herbert Hoover's Policy," master's thesis (Tulane University, 1969).

Considered revolutionaries for their time, Augusto C. Sandino in Nicaragua and Augustín Farabundo Martí in El Salvador are the subjects of many studies. Good starting points include Joseph O. Baylen, "Sandino: Patriot or Bandit?" *Hispanic American Historical Review* 31 (1951): 394–414, and Jorge Arias Goméz, "Augustín Farabundo Martí," *La Universidad* 4 (1971): 181–240.

For the development and implementation of the Good Neighbor policy, which resulted in a policy of nonintervention in the internal affairs of Central American nations, see Bryce Wood, *The Making of the Good Neighbor Policy* (New York, 1961), and Leonard Gellman, *Good Neighbor Diplomacy: United States Policies in Latin America* (Baltimore, 1979). The immediate impact of nonintervention came with events in El Salvador. The United States did not intervene in Martínez's brutal suppression of an internal revolt; see Thomas P. Anderson, *Matanza: El Salvador's Communist Revolt of 1932* (Lincoln, Neb., 1971). Nor did it interfere with the extension of recognition to Martínez by his Central American neighbors; see Richard V. Salisbury, "Domestic Politics and Foreign Policy: Costa Rica's Stand on Recognition," *Hispanic American Historical Review* 54 (1974): 453–78. Nor did it interfere with the dictators' illegal extension of their presidencies; see Thomas M. Leonard, *The Decline of the Recognition Policy in United States–Central American Relations, 1933–1949* (Miami, 1985).

Studies of United States–Central American relations from 1933 to 1947 are sparse. In addition to Argueta's biography of Carías, mentioned above, there are Kenneth J. Grieb's *Guatemalan Caudillo: The Regime of Jorge Ubico in Guatemala, 1931–1934* (Athens, Ohio, 1979); Carmello Francisco Esmeralda Astilla's "The Martínez Era: Salvadoran-American Relations, 1931–1944" (Ph.D. dissertation, Louisiana State University, 1976); Gilberto González y Contreras, *El ultimo caudillo* (Mexico City, 1946); and Richard Millett, *Guardians of the Dynasty* (New York, 1977), all of which provide overviews of the dictators and their relations with the United States through the end of World War II. Costa Rican political history is the subject of Carlos Araya Pochet's *Historia de los partidos políticos: Liberación nacional* (San José, 1968).

Central America is generally placed within the context of larger foci. Dick Steward, *Trade and Hemisphere: The Good Neighbor Policy and Reciprocal Trade* (Columbia, Mo., 1975), and David G. Haglund, *Latin America and the Transformation of U.S. Strategic Thought, 1936–1940* (Albuquerque, N.M., 1984), place Central America within the larger U.S. economic and defense policies during the 1930s. The same is usually true for studies of World War II. With the exception of Carlos Calvo Gamboa, *Costa Rica en la segunda guerra mundial, 1939–1945* (San José, 1985), one must rely on the political studies mentioned above or on Stetson Conn and Byron Fairchild, *Framework of Hemispheric Defense: United States Army in World War II* (Washington, D.C., 1960), and Stetson Conn, Rose C. Engleman, and Byron Fairchild, *Guarding the United States and Its Outposts: The United States Army in World War II* (Washington, D.C., 1964).

Central America played an insignificant role in the United States' formulation of its immediate post–World War II policy. See Antonio Gómez Robledo, *La seguridad colectiva en el continente americano* (Mexico City, 1960), and Louis A. Pérez, "International Dimensions of Inter-American Relations, 1944–1960," *Inter-American Economic Affairs* 27 (1973): 47–68.

The Twentieth Century after 1948

International communism became the most important issue in the early Cold War years, and the experiences of the 1948 Costa Rican civil war and the 1954 Guatemalan affair demonstrated the inability of U.S. policymakers to distinguish between communism and indigenous nationalistic movements. Thomas M. Leonard's *United States and Central America, 1944–1949: Perceptions of Political Dynamics* (Tuscaloosa, Ala., 1984) illustrates the problem. John P. Bell's *Crisis in Costa Rica: The 1948 Revolution* (Austin, Tex., 1971) shows how the elite used the Communist issue for their own purposes. The best study of José Figueres, who claims he saved his country from communism, is Charles D. Ameringer, *Don Pepe: Political Biography of José Figueres of Costa Rica* (Albuquerque, N.M., 1978).

The Eisenhower administration's obsession with international communism in Latin America is the subject of Stephen G. Rabe's *Eisenhower and Latin America: The Foreign Policy of Anticommunism* (Chapel Hill, N.C., 1988). The most complete account of the United States–sponsored invasion of Guatemala is Richard H. Immerman, *The CIA in Guatemala: The Foreign Policy of Intervention* (Austin, Tex., 1982). Both conclude that Washington failed to link international communism to the Arbenz regime. The Guatemalan position is explained by Guillermo Toriello, *La batalla de Guatemala* (Mexico, 1956).

The failure of the United States to come to grips with the demands for economic and social change by the end of the 1950s is the subject of Milton Eisenhower's *The Wine Is Bitter* (Garden City, N.Y., 1963). John D. Martz, *Central America: The Crisis and the Challenge* (Chapel Hill, N.C., 1959), argues the same case, but suggests that it opened the door to communism.

The Alliance for Progress was an effort to meet the pressure for change, according to former State Department official Lincoln Gordon in *A New Deal for Latin America: The Alliance for Progress* (Cambridge, Mass., 1963). However, subsequent assessments of the alliance are consistently critical. See Simon G. Hanson, *Dollar Diplomacy Modern Style: Chapters in the Failure of the Alliance for Progress* (Washington, D.C., 1970), and Jerome Levinson and Juan de Onis, *The Alliance That Lost Its Way: A Critical Report on the Alliance for Progress* (Chicago, 1970). Because there are to date no studies analyzing the alliance's impact upon Central America, one must rely on the annual congressional presentations of the Agency for International Development for summaries of programs and their progress in Central America.

Two important studies dealing with the counterinsurgency program carried out by Presidents John F. Kennedy and Lyndon B. Johnson are Willard C. Barber and C. Neale Ronning, *Internal Security and Military Power: Counterinsurgency and Civic Action in Latin America* (Athens, Ohio, 1966), and Douglas Blaufarb, *The Counterinsurgency Era: U.S. Doctrine and Performance, 1950 to the Present* (New York, 1977). The application of the counterinsurgency program in Guatemala is the subject of Michael McClintock, *The American Connection: State Terror and Popular Resistance in Guatemala* (London, 1985). Thomas K. Whitaker, in "Revolution in Guatemala" (master's thesis, University of Florida, 1987), concludes that the Guatemalan guerrilla movement during the 1960s owed more to local conditions than to an international conspiracy. Don L. Etchison, in *The United States and Militarism in Central America* (New York, 1975), points out that the U.S. military assistance programs reinforced the military's link to the ruling oligarchy.

The origins of the 1969 Soccer War between El Salvador and Honduras provide an explanation of one of the fundamental causes of the contemporary crisis. In his *Scarcity and Survival in Central America: Ecological Origins of the Soccer War* (Stanford, Calif., 1979), William Durham examines the pressure for land reform. The impact of the war itself is examined by Thomas P. Anderson in *The War of the Dispossessed: Honduras and El Salvador* (Lincoln, Neb., 1983). The failure of the middle class to make political progress is the subject of Stephen Webre, *José Napoleón Duarte and the Christian Democratic Party in El Salvador, 1960–1972* (Baton Rouge, La., 1974).

The old order that collapsed with the fall of Somoza and was threatened with the growing civil unrest in El Salvador presented a dilemma for the United States, as explained by Richard E. Feinberg, "Central America: No Easy Answers," *Foreign Affairs* 59 (1981). Robert S. Leiken, editor, *Central America: Anatomy of Conflict* (New York, 1984), and Kenneth M. Coleman and George C. Herring, editors, *The Central American Crisis: Sources of Conflict and the Failure of U.S. Policy* (Wilmington, Del., 1985) provide an excellent selection of readings describing the internal forces contributing to revolution in Central America and the failure of the United States to deal with it. John Booth, *The End and the Beginning* (Boulder, Colo., 1982), and Tommie Sue Montgomery, *Revolution in El Salvador* (Boulder, Colo., 1982), provide sound, yet sympathetic, analyses of the origins of the 1979 upheavals in Nicaragua and El Salvador.

The response of the Carter administration is best described by Robert Pastor, *Condemned to Repetition: The United States and Nicaragua* (Princeton, N.J., 1987). Anthony Lake, a colleague of Pastor, tells much the same story in his *Somoza Falling* (New York, 1989). The Central American crisis came to the forefront of Ronald Reagan's administration. Two volumes provide a sympathetic view of his policies: Timothy Ashby, *The Bear in the Backyard: Moscow's Caribbean Strategy* (Lexington, Ky., 1987), and William F. Hahn, editor, *Central America and the Reagan Doctrine* (Washington, D.C., 1987). Both argue that the crisis is part of a Soviet-Cuban design upon the region. In contrast, much of the literature argues that the upheavals are peculiar to the region and that Reagan's policies have served as invitations for Soviet and Cuban interventions: see Morris J. Blachman, William M. Leo Grande, and Kenneth Sharpe, editors, *Confronting Revolution: Security through Diplomacy in Central America;* Bruce M. Bagley, editor, *Contadora and the Diplomacy of Peace in Central America,* volume 1 (Boulder, Colo., 1986); and Francisco Rojas Aravena and Luis Guillermo Solís Rivera, *¿Súbditos o aliados?: La política exterior de Esta-*

dos Unidos y Centroamerica (San José, 1988). A more analytical account, but one equally critical of Reagan's determination to oust the Sandinistas, is Roy Guteman's *Banana Diplomacy: The Making of American Policy in Nicaragua, 1981–1987* (New York, 1988). Reagan's battle with Congress is the subject of Cynthia Arnson's *Cross-Roads: Congress, the Reagan Administration, and Central America* (New York, 1989).

Those wishing to go beyond these works should consult Richard Dean Burns, editor, *Guide to American Foreign Relations since 1700* (Santa Barbara, Calif., 1983). An annotated bibliography, it covers all facets of U.S. diplomatic history, and its well-organized index makes it easy to use. The series of *Historical Dictionaries* published by Scarecrow Press during the 1970s provide for each Central American country annotated bibliographies on various subjects, including foreign affairs: Thomas Creedman, *Costa Rica* (1977); Philip Flemion, *El Salvador* (1972); Harvey K. Meyer, *Honduras* (1976); Harvey K. Meyer, *Nicaragua;* and Richard E. Moore, *Guatemala* (1973). These dated works have been updated by Ralph Lee Woodward, Jr., in his historiographical essay on Central America that appeared in the *Hispanic American Historical Review* 67 (1987): 462–96.

Kenneth J. Grieb, editor of *Research Guide to Central America* (Madison, Wis., 1985), best describes the problems confronting the researcher, including the inaccessibility of archival material in Central America. Students wishing to work with the United States diplomatic record should first consult the Department of State, *Foreign Relations of the United States.* These annual volumes, beginning in 1861 and running through the late 1950s, provide a glimpse into the official record. Those wishing to go beyond these cursory materials should examine the *Catalog of National Archives Microfilm Publications* to determine the vastness of the collections. For the years after 1910, the State Department developed a decimal file system, which enables the researcher to locate materials by subject. The National Archives' *Purport Lists* will guide the researcher through these materials. Congressional debates, particularly in the various committees, are an important source often overlooked by the student of foreign relations. The *CIS Annual Index* is a well-organized guide covering materials since U.S. independence. Thomas Schoonover's "Archival Materials on U.S. Businesses in Central America before the 1930s Depression," *Society for Historians of American Foreign Relations: Newsletter* 18 (1987): 1–10, is an excellent guide to private collections and papers that deal with Central America and are located in the United States. The presidential libraries of Franklin D. Roosevelt, Harry S. Truman, Dwight D. Eisenhower, John F.

Kennedy, Lyndon B. Johnson, and Jimmy Carter all contain sources related to Central America. Each publishes an appropriate guide, but researchers should be cautioned that many materials for the period after 1960 are still closed. The Library of Congress Manuscript Division houses the papers of several persons important to the study of United States–Central American relations, including Secretaries of State John Clayton, John Hay, Elihu Root, Philander Knox, and Cordell Hull.

Index

Abrams, Elliot, 179
Acheson, Dean, 122
Acosta, Julio, 75
Act of Chapultepec (1945), 122
Adams, John Quincy, 1–2, 8
Agency for International Development, 149–151, 155, 161–162, 194–195
Alcedo Bexarano, Antonio, 3
All America Anti-imperialist League, 91
Alliance for Progress: implementation, 147–149; assessment, 161–163, 169
Alvarez Martínez, Gustavo, 183, 189
American Automobile Association, 103
American Institute for Agricultural Sciences, 117
Ames, Edward W., 77
Andrés Pérez, Carlos, 193
Araña, Francisco, 133
Arana Osorío, Carlos, 158, 169, 170
Araujo, Arturo, 93
Araujo, Miguel, 112
Arbenz, Jacobo, 133–141, 155
Arce, Manuel José, 8
Arévalo, Juan José, 130–131, 134
Argüello, Leonardo, 123
Arías, Juan Angel, 83
Arías, Oscar, 190, 192, 195
Arms Limitation Agreement (1923), 82
Aronson, Bernard, 194
Authentic Anti-Communist Revolutionary Army, 143
Aycinena, José, 9, 13
Azcona Hoyo, José, 189, 192, 193

Baker, Howard, 190
Baker, James, 194
Baker, Lorenzo, 49
Banana industry, 44–45, 49

Barahona, Paz, 84
Barrios, Justo Rufino, 35–37, 39–40, 42, 66
Barrundia, José Francisco, 8
Bayard, Thomas, 37
Beals, Carlton, 91
Bennett, William Tapley, Jr., 134
Berle, Adolf A., 103, 138
Bermudez, Enrique, 186
Bernays, Edward, 137
Bertrand, Francisco, 71–72, 78
Biddle, Charles, 9–10
Bishop, Maurice, 177
Bishop's Conference, Medellín (1968), 175
Black, Eli, 169
Blaine, James G., 39–40
Bográn, Luis, 43
Boland Amendment, 186, 190
Bolívar, Simón, 91
Bolshevism, See Communism
Bonilla, Manuel, 59, 60, 65, 71, 78
Bonilla, Policarpo, 83
Borah, William, 70
Borge, Tomás, 178
Borland, Solon, 21
Bosque, Pio Romero, 93
Boston Fruit Company, 49
Braden, Spruille, 132, 138
Briggs, Ellis O., 134
Broad Opposition Front (FAO), 172–173
Bryan, William Jennings, 68, 70–71, 76
Bryan-Chammoro Treaty (1915), 70–73
Brzezinski, Zbigniew, 168, 171, 177
Buchanan, James, 14, 21, 30
Bunau-Varilla, Philippe, 54
Bush, George, 182, 194–195
Butler, Smedley, 63

237

Cabañas, José Trinidad, 28
Cabot, John M., 116, 137, 138
Caffrey, Jefferson, 93
Calderón Guardia, Rafael, 113, 117,
    125–127
Cale, Edward, 134
Calero, Adolfo, 174, 185, 194
Calles, Plutarco, 85
Cañas, Juan José, 9, 10, 200 (n.20)
Cañaz-Jerez Treaty (1858), 73
Cannon, Lee Roy, 62
Carazo, Rodrigo, 184
Carden, Lionel, 64, 68
Carías, Tiburcio: 1923 civil war, 83–84;
    presidency, 98, 100; World War II, 106,
    113–115, 118; protests against (1944),
    120–121
Caribbean Basin Initiative (CBI), 184, 187
Caribbean Legion, 128
Carranza, Venustiano, 85
Carrera, Rafael, 12, 24, 32, 36
Carter, Jimmy: policy foundations, 167–
    168; Nicaragua, 168–175; Costa Rica
    and Guatemala, 175; El Salvador,
    175–183, 185, 195
Castillo Armas, Carlos, 139–141, 145
Castañada Castro, Salvador, 172
Castellón, Francisco, 24
Castro, Fidel, 142, 155, 177, 180, 193, 194
Castro, José María, 44
Centoz, Luigi, 128
Central America: colonial social
    structure, 2–3; independence, 6–8;
    Liberal-Conservative conflict, 7–9, 11–
    13, 23, 36, 61–63, 70–71, 83–84, 85–87,
    121, 130–131, 174, 196; Kinney's
    colony, 22; Lincoln's black colony plan,
    22; William Walker, 27–29; U.S. Civil
    War, 31–32; unionization plans, 36–37,
    39–40, 48, 80–81, 149; positivist
    philosophy, 41–43, 50–51, 55–56, 79;
    World War I, 69, 74–77, 97; Nicaraguan
    civil war (1920s), 86, 91; Augusto
    Farabundo Martí, 95; Reciprocal Trade

Agreements, 103, 105–108; World
    War II, 109–118
Central American Bank for Economic
    Integration (CABEI), 150
Central American Common Market
    (CACM), 148, 149, 155, 158–161
Central American conferences: Cortino
    (1902), 58; *USS Marblehead* (1906), 58;
    Washington (1907), 59–60, 63, 72–73,
    78; *USS Tacoma* (1922), 80; Washington
    (1923), 81–96, 210 (n.4); Guatemala
    City (1934), 96; San José (1963), 149–
    150; Tesoro Beach (1989), 192, 194; Tela
    (1989), 192–193, 194, 196
Central American Court of Justice,
    59–60, 73
Central American Defense Council
    (Consejo Defensa Centroamericano)
    (CONDECA), 152, 154, 177
Central American Plantations
    Corporation (CAPO), 117
Central American Socialist Party, 94
Central American Tribunal, 81–82
Central Intelligence Agency (CIA), 132,
    137, 140–141, 152, 154, 178, 182,
    186, 189
Cerezo, Vinicio, 189–193
Chacón, Lázaro, 92
Chammoro, Diego, 70
Chammoro, Emiliano, 63, 70–71, 85–86
Chammoro, Pedro Joaquín, 171–172
Chammoro, Violetta, 174, 185, 192,
    195–196
Chatfield, Frederick, 10–11, 13–14, 18
Chicago Honduran Mining Company, 43
Christian Base Communities (CEBs), 175
Christian Democratic Party, 170, 175,
    177, 182
Christmas, Lee, 65, 72
Clark, J. Reuben, 97
Clay, Henry, 10, 17
Clayton, John M., 17–19
Clayton-Bulwer Treaty (1850), 17–20, 31,
    38–39

Clements, John, 137
Cleveland, Grover, 40–41, 73
Clifford, Clark, 172
Cochran, William, 134
Cockburn, John, 2
Coffee industry, 42, 49, 76
Cole, Bundy, 63, 70
Cole, Byron, 24
Combs, Lewis, 58, 66–67
Committee of Relatives of Disappeared
    Persons, 170
Communism, 86, 89, 90, 93–95, 111, 116,
    121, 122, 124–144, 151, 160–161,
    164–165, 173, 176–181, 196
Communist International, 126, 142
Communist party, *See* Communism
Comte, August, 41
Constitutional Democratic party, 130–131
Contadora peace process, 188–189, 195
Contras, 186–187, 189, 190–196
Convention on Rights and Duties of
    States (1933), 98
Coolidge, Calvin, 86–87
Cordero, Jorge A., 133
Cordova Cerna, Juan, 139
Corporation of Foreign Bondholders, 66
Cortés, Leon, 126
Costa Rica and Nicaragua: Boundary
    Dispute, 20–21; Cleveland Award
    (1888), 73; 1955 war, 144
Costa Rica Mining Company, 75
Council of Foreign Relations, 138
Counterinsurgency warfare, 151–153,
    156, 165
Cristiani, Alfredo, 192–193
Crosby, Elisha O., 32
Cuadra, Joaquín, 178
Cumberland, Charles, 138
Curtis, William E., 51
Cuyamel Fruit Company, 65, 72, 84, 104

Dávilia, Miguel R., 60, 64–65
Davis, Charles E., 29
Davis, Cushman, 48

Davis, Jefferson, 27, 30
Davis, Nathaniel P., 128–129
Dawson, Thomas C., 62
De Bow, J. D. B., 27
Debray, Regis, 156
Defense Intelligence Agency (DIA), 186
Democratic Liberation Union
    (UDEL), 171
Democratic party (Guatemala), 130
Democratic party (U.S.), 26, 172
Democratic Revolutionary Front (FDR)
    (El Salvador), 176
Dennis, Lawrence, 97
Devine, Frank, 176
De Witt, Charles, 8, 11
Díaz, Adolfo, 61, 63–64, 70, 78, 86–87
Díaz, Porfirio, 37, 62
Dickson, A. B., 33
Dodds, Harry W., 85
Dodge, Percival, 67
Dollar Diplomacy, 61, 68
Donovan, Andrew, 134
Douglas, Stephen A., 30
Duarte, José Napoleón, 170, 177,
    182–183, 190
Duggan, Laurence, 108, 134
Dulles, John Foster, 74, 137, 139–140,
    142, 153

Eisenhower, Dwight D., 138–139, 141,
    145–146, 151, 155, 180
Eisenhower, Milton, 144–145, 151
Electoral Projects Commission, 81–83
Electric Bond and Share Company, 77
Empressa Electrica, 77
Enders, Thomas O., 179
Estrada, Francisco, 99
Estrada, José María, 29
Estrada, Juan B., 61, 63
Estrada Cabrera, Manuel, 58, 60, 65–68,
    72, 76–77
European Recovery Program (Marshall
    Plan), 123
Evarts, William M., 39

Export-Import Bank (EXIM), 116

Farabundo Martí National Liberation
  Front (FMLN), 181–183, 190, 193
Figueres, José, 128–129, 138, 143–145, 169
Fish, Hamilton, 36
Fisher, John, 134
Flores, José Felipe, 4, 199 (n.6)
Ford, Gerald R., 163
Frelinghuysen-Zavala Treaty (1884),
  39–40
Frente Unido de Resistancia (FUR), 156
Fuerzas Armadas Rebeldes (FAR), 156

Gage, Thomas, 2
Galindo, Juan, 9–11
Galvéz, Juan, 143
Gálvez, Mariano, 11–12
Garrison, Cornelius K., 25–26
General Growers' Association, 135
General Treaty of Peace and Amity
  (1923), 81–83
Generation of Rising Expectations,
  118–119, 146
González Flores, Alfredo, 73, 74
Good Neighbor Policy: formulation of,
  97–98; politically applied in 1930s,
  98–101, 108, 118
Gorbachev, Mikhail, 193
Grant, Ulysses S., 38
Great Britain: and Belize, 6, 10–11, 13, 21,
  31; Mosquito Kingdom, 16, 31, 45–47;
  Clayton-Bulwer Treaty, 18–19, 52;
  Central American Investments, 50–51
Grew, Joseph, 116
Groce, Leonard, 62
Guardiola, Santos, 32
Guatemalan Democratic League, 131
Guervara, Ernesto, 156
Gutiérrez, Daniel, 73
Gutiérrez, López, 83

H. C. Emery Company, 43

Hague Court of Permanent
  Arbitration, 57
Haig, Alexander, 179
Hale, John, 5
Hall, George, 26
Hall, Henry C., 37
Harding, Warren G., 80
Hatfield, C. D., 90
Hay, John, 52–53
Hay-Bunau-Varilla Treaty, 54
Hayes, Rutherford B., 39
Hay-Herran Treaty (1903), 53–54
Hay-Pauncefote Treaty (1900), 52
Hepburn bill, 52–53
Hernández Martínez, Maximiliano:
  presidency (1930s), 93, 95–96, 98, 100,
  107; (World War II), 112, 114–115,
  118–119, 121
Herrera, Carlos, 80
Hill, Robert, 137
Hise, Elijah, 16–17
Hitler, Adolf, 109, 111
Holland, Henry, 145
Honduran Civil War (1923–1924), 83–84
Honduran Democratic Front, 121
Hoover, Herbert, 91, 97
Houston, Sam, 27
Hughes, Charles Evans, 81–82, 97
Hull, Cordell, 79, 96, 103
Humboldt, Alexander von, 2
Hundelhausen, Wilhelm von, 111–112

Igesis, Rafael, 92
Innes, Mitchell, 67
Institute for Urban Housing, 145
Inter-American Commission on Human
  Rights, 160
Inter-American Conferences: Washington
  (1889), 40; Havana (1928), 91;
  Montevideo (1933), 98, 100, 104;
  Buenos Aires (1936), 98, 108; Havana
  (1940), 108; Panama (1939), 108; Mexico
  City (1945), 122; Bogotá (1948), 122–
  123; Caracas (1954), 139–140; Rio de

Janeiro (1947), 140, 147; Punte del Este (1963), 147
Inter-American Defense Board, 122
Inter-American Development Bank (IADB), 150, 185
Inter-American Peace Committee, 141
International Chamber of Commerce, 103
International Coffee Agreement, 116
International Railway of Central America (IRCA), 104
Interoceanic Canal Commission, 38
Irisarri, A. J., 32
Irisarri, Juan Batista, 199 (n.6)
Iturbide, Agustín, 7

Jackson, C. D., 138
Jarquin, Brenes, 100
Jefferson, Thomas, 2, 5
Jiménez, Ricardo, 86, 96
Johnson, Lyndon B., 150, 153–155, 157, 163

Kasson, John A., 35
Keith, Minor C., 44, 49, 67, 71, 73–75, 78, 93
Kellogg, Frank B., 86
Kennedy, Edward M., 150
Kennedy, John F., 146–147, 149–153, 163, 166
Kinney, Henry L., 22–23
Kirkpatrick, Jeanne, 179, 180, 185
Kissinger, Henry, 163, 197
Knox, Philander C., 60–65
Knox-Castrillo Convention (1911), 62–63
Knox-Paredes Convention (1911), 64–65
Kyle, Edwin M., 132, 134

Labor Code, Costa Rica (1944), 125–126
Lael, Pablo, 143
Lane, Arthur Bliss, 99–100
Lansing, Robert, 72
Laugerud Garcia, Kjell Eugenio, 169–170
League of Nations, 78, 97
Lehman, Kurt, 76

Lemus, José, 145
Lend-Lease, 109, 116
Lesseps, Ferdinand de, 39, 52
Liendo y Goicoechea, José Antonio, 199 (n.6)
Lincoln, Abraham, 31–34
Linowitz Commission, 167
Livingston Codes, 9, 11
Lodge, Henry Cabot, Jr., 141
Lodge, Henry Cabot, Sr., 48
Logan, Cornelius A., 39
Long, Boaz, 71, 100, 130
López Arellano, Oswaldo, 150–151, 153–154, 169
López Lavare, Mario, 170
López Reyes, Walter, 189
Lozano, Julio, 145
Lucas García, Fernando Romero, 175
Lussan, Raveneau de, 2

McCarthy, Joseph, 137
McClintock, John, 138
McCloy, John, 137
McCormack, John, 137
MacDonald, Alexander, 13
McKinley, William, 47, 51
Madriz, José, 46, 62, 69
Magaña, Miguel A., 138
Mahan, Alfred T., 48
Manley, Michael, 177
Mann, Thomas C., 137, 144, 153
Mann, Thomas N., 1
MANO BLANCO, 157
Marcy, William L., 22–23, 26–27
Maritime Canal Company, 41
Marshall, George C., 122
Martí, Farabundo Augustín, 79, 94–95, 101
Martínez, Modesto, 75
Marxism-Leninism, *See* Communism
Matanza (1932 El Salvador uprising), 94–95
Mein, John G., 158
Mejía Victores, Oscar Humberto, 184

Melgar Castro, Juan Alberto, 169
Mena, Luis, 63
Mendez, Joaquim, 77
Méndez Montenegro, Mario, 154, 157
Menocal, A. G., 41
Merry, William L., 52–53
Mexican-American War, 15–16
Mexican Revolution, 68
Middle sector, 119–122, 124, 127, 130–
   131, 157–158, 170–171, 175, 180,
   185, 196
Miller, Edward G., 122
Moffatt, Thomas, 61
Molina, Arturo Armando, 170
Molina, Luis, 33
Moncada, José Maria, 87, 89
Monge, Luis Alberto, 184, 188, 189
Monroe Doctrine: pronounced, 10–11;
   applied to Central America, 35, 38–39,
   45–46, 61; Roosevelt Corollary, 57, 67–
   69, 78; Clark memorandum, 97, 118,
   140, 147
Mora, Juan Rafael, 28–29
Mora, Manuel, 125–129, 145
Morales, Franklin T., 84
Morazán, Francisco, 8, 11–12, 36
Morgan, Charles, 25–26
Morgan, J. P., 64–65
Morgan, John Tyler, 52–53
Morgan, Stokeley W., 83, 97
Mosquito Kingdom, 13–14, 16, 31, 44–47
Motley, Langhorne H., 187
Movimiento Revolucionario 13 de
   Noviembre (MR–13), 156
Mullins, Charles L., 113
Munro, Dana G., 78, 97
Munro, Ernest, 158
Murphy, William S., 14
Mussolini, Benito, 109, 111

Napoleon Bonaparte, Louis, 202 (n.3)
National Action party, 130
National Association of Honduran
   Peasants (ANACH), 159

National Democratic Front, 130
National Democratic Union, 170
National Federation of Farmers and
   Ranchers, 159
National Government of Reconciliation
   (GRN), 173–174
National Guard, Nicaragua, 89, 95,
   99–100, 112–113, 171, 173–174
National Opposition Union (FAO), 170
National Reform party, 130
National Republican Alliance, 182
National Republican party, 126–128
National Security Council, 144, 186,
   189, 194
National Vanguard party, 130
National Workers party, 130
Naval Disarmament Conference,
   Washington (1922), 82
Negropronte, John, 189
Newbegin, Robert, 134
Nicaraguan–Costa Rican boundary
   dispute, 20–21, 73
Nixon, Richard, 144, 151, 161, 163
North, Oliver, 189–190

Oakley, Raymond, 134
Oaksmith, Appleton, 26
O'Connell, Thomas, 63
Olds, Robert, 87
ORDEN, 176
Orellana, José Maria, 92
Organization of American States, 160,
   167, 173–174, 177, 193, 195
Organization of Central American States
   (ODECA), 149
Organization of Petroleum Exporting
   Countries (OPEC), 175
Ortega, Daniel, 177, 186, 192, 195
Ortega, Humberto, 178
Osorio, Oscar, 145
O'Sullivan, John, 15

Paine, Tom, 4
Panama, independence, 54

Panama Canal: selection of site, 52–54; and Central American instability, 57, 68, 70, 74, 82, 86; World War II, 110, 111, 113, 114, 116; post–World War II defense, 123, 151, 152, 180; counterinsurgency training, 164–165; 1977 treaties, 167–168, 180
Pan-Americanism, 68, 72, 76, 112, 140
Partido Gautemalteco del Trabajo, 156
Partridge, Thomas, 33
Pasos, Carlos, 120
Pastor, Robert, 220 (n.8)
Pastora, Edén, 173, 184, 185
Pate, Joseph, 111
Patterson, Richard C., 133–134
Paz Barnica, Edgardo, 189
Pearl Harbor, 114, 115
Pendleton, Joseph H., 63
Peralta Azurdia, Enrique, 157
Pérez, Carlos Andrés, 172
Philadelphia Centennial Exposition of Independence, 49
Phillipe, Luis, 202 (n.3)
Phillips, W. R., 111
Picado, Teodoro, 121, 126–128, 143
Pickering, Thomas, 182
Pierce, Franklin, 27
Point Four Program, 123
Polk, James K., 16
Popham, John, 75
Popular Liberation Front, 130
Popular Revolutionary Bloc (BRP), 176
Popular Vanguard party, 126–128, 142
Porterfield, L. B., 75
Positivist philosophy, 41–43, 50–51
Pradt, Abbé, 3–4
Preston, Andrew, 49
Proclaimed List of Blocked Neutrals, 117

Quetglas, José, 119
Quitman, John A., 27

Rama Road, 112–113
Reagan, Ronald: framework of policy, 178–181; El Salvador, 181–183; Costa Rica, 183–184; Nicaragua, 188; Honduras, 189; Central American peace process, 188–191, 194–195
Reciprocal Trade Agreements Act (1934), 103, 105–108
Reconstruction Finance Corporation, 116
Regional Federation of Salvadoran Workers, 94
Regional Office of Central America and Panama (ROCAP), 149
Reina Andrade, José Maria, 92
Revolutionary National Movement, 170
Reyes, Victor Manuel Ramón, 123
Reynal, Abbé, 3
Rhodes, John, 2
Rios Montt, Efrain, 184
Riotte, Charles N., 33, 36
Rivas, Patricio, 24–25, 29–30
Rivera y Damas, Arturo, 183
Roach, John, 2
Rockefeller, Nelson, 161
Rodríguez, Juan Manuel, 8
Romero, Arturo, 119
Romero, Oscar, 176
Roosevelt, Franklin D., 97, 98, 102, 112, 114, 118, 120, 132, 176
Roosevelt, Theodore, 48, 53, 55; Central American policy, 57–60
Root, Elihu, 71
Rosario Mining Company, 43
Rossell Arellano, Mariano, 131, 135

Sacasa, Juan B., 85–86, 89, 91–92, 96, 99, 107
Salazar, Carlos, 110
Sanabria, Victor, 126–127
Sandinista National Liberation Front (FSLN): ouster of Somoza, 170–174; relations with Carter, 177–178; relations with Reagan, 183–186; contra war, 186–191; and Central American peace process, 190–196

Sandino, Augusto C., 79, 88–92, 95, 99–101
San Martín, José de, 91
Savage, Charles, 7
Savage, Henry, 7, 14
Schlesinger, Arthur M., Jr., 150
School of the Americas, 165
Seligman, J. & W., 67
Seward, William H., 36
Shultz, George P., 188
Sigatoka disease, 104
Siracusa, Ernest, 133
Skinner-Klee, Alfredo, 96
Smith, Walter Bedell, 137
Smoot-Hawley Tariff, 103
Soccer War, 155, 159, 160, 169, 177
Social Democratic party, 130, 131
Solaun, Mauricio, 172
Solórzano, Carlos, 85
Somoza de Bayle, Anastasio, 154, 168; ouster from power, 171–174, 179, 184
Somoza Garcia, Anastasio: path to presidency, 99–100; World War II, 118, 120; post war protests against, 122–123; Costa Rican civil war, 128; assassination, 143–145, 170
Sorenson, Theodore, 146
Soto, Marco Aureillo, 43
Soulé, Pierre, 27
Southerland, W. H. H., 63
Southern Command (SOUTHCOM), 152, 164–165
Spanish-American war, 48
Spencer, Herbert, 41
Spiritual socialism, 131, 133
Squier, Ephraim George, 18
Stabler, G. Herbert, 74
Stahl, Adolfo, 66
Stalin, Josef, 132
Standard Fruit Company, 88, 90, 104, 143
Stark, Harold R., 109
Steins, Kennedon, 134
Stephens, John L., 13
Stettinius, Edward R., 118

Stimson, Henry L., 87, 89, 90, 92, 95, 97
Stone, Richard, 187
Suazo Córdova, Roberto, 189
Sullivan and Cromwell, 137

Taft, William Howard, 55; Central American policy, 60–68
Tannenbaum, Frank, 138
Thompson, Ambrose W., 32
Thurston, Walter, 119
Tinoco, Frederico, 73–74
Toriello, Guillermo, 140
Torrijos, Omar, 172
Transisthmian Canal: Central American interest, 4; U.S. policy before 1850, 9–11, 15–16, 17–19; Treaty of Amity and Commerce (1825), 10; Nicaragua, 16, 69–72; U.S. policy after 1850, 36–40, 48, 51–54; Maritime Canal Company, 41; San Juan River project (1939), 112
Treaty of Managua (1860), 31, 45, 47
Trejos, José Joaquin, 154
Trueblood, Edward G., 126
Truman, Harry S., 121–122
Turcos Lima, Augusto, 156, 219 (n.19)
Twenty-eighth of February Popular League (LP-28), 176

Ubico, Jorge: becomes president, 92–93, 98; 1934 Central American conference, 96; reciprocal trade agreement, 105–106; World War II, 109–110, 114–119; overthrow, 120–121, 130, 134; and communism, 132
Ulate, Otilio, 126–129
Umanzar, Juan Pablo, 99
Ungo, Guillermo Manuel, 170, 183
United Fruit Company: founded, 49; dollar diplomacy, 65–68; in Honduras, 72, 84, 159, 169, 192; in Costa Rica, 73–74, 117; in Guatemala, 93–94, 136–138, 141–143; Zemurray takes control of, 104; becomes United Brands, 169

United National Opposition (UNO), 192, 195–196

United Nations, 118, 141, 183, 193

United Popular Action Front (FAPU), 176

United Provinces of Central America, 7–14

United States: early perceptions of Central America, 5, 8; transisthmian canal policy, 9, 11, 15–17, 38–40, 48, 51–54; William Walker, 27–28; Civil War policy, 31–32; black colonization scheme, 33; intervention in Nicaragua, 61–62, 84–91; World War I, 75–78; 1923 treaty system, 81–96; Good Neighbor policy, 98–100, 103, 105–108, 122–123; World War II, 103, 108–114; military assistance programs, 122, 143, 151, 153–154, 156–158, 163, 165–166; human rights policy, 167, 170–172, 175, 178, 182, 184, 186, 189, 191

United States Information Agency (USIA), 152

University of San Carlos, 199 (n.6)

Vaccaro Brothers Fruit Company, 72, 84, 88

Valentine, Washington S., 43, 64, 78

Valle, José Celicio del, 199 (n.6)

Vanderbilt, Cornelius, 20, 25–26

Vesco, Robert, 169

Villeda Morales, Ramón, 145, 150–151

Volio Jiménez, Fernando, 185

Walker commission, 52–53

Walker, William, 22–30, 203 (n.24 and n.27)

Wallace, Henry A., 103

Wallerstein, Edward, 28

Wands, Ernst H., 62

War Trade Board, 77

Webber, John, 158

Weeks, Sinclair, 137

Weitzel, George T., 63, 70

Welles, Sumner, 84

Wells, Milton, 134

Wheeler, John H., 27

Whelan, Thomas, 144

White, David L., 17

White, Francis G., 97

Whitehouse, Sheldon, 92

Whitman, Ann, 137

Wiley, Alexander, 137

Williams, George A., 36

Williams, John, 7

Wilson, Edwin C., 97

Wilson, Robert, 134

Wilson, Woodrow, 55; policy foundation, 66–67; Nicaragua, 69–71; Honduras, 71–72; Bryan-Chammoro Treaty, 72–73; Costa Rica, 72–75

Windsor Trust Company, 67

Winsor, Curtain, 183

Wise, Murray, 134

Woodward, Robert, 134

Workers and Peasant's Bloc, 125

World Bank, 185

World War I, 69, 74–76, 97

World War II, 102, 108–114

Wright, Jim, 190

Wycke, Charles, 31

Ydígoras Fuentes, Miguel, 133, 139, 145, 155, 157

Yon Sosa, Marco Aurelio, 156–157

Yuseman Mining Company, 43

Zamora, Rubén, 183

Zavala, Joaquín, 39

Zelaya, José Santos, 45, 52, 54, 58–62, 185

Zemurray, Samuel, 65, 71, 78, 93, 104–105